DUTIES AND BLESSINGS OF THE PRIESTHOOD

Basic Manual for Priesthood Holders, Part B

Published by
The Church of Jesus Christ of Latter-day Saints
Salt Lake City, Utah
Revised 2000

Comments and Suggestions

Your comments and suggestions about this manual would be appreciated. Please submit them to:

Curriculum Planning
50 East North Temple Street, Floor 24
Salt Lake City, UT 84150-3200
USA
E-mail: cur-development@ldschurch.org

Please list your name, address, ward, and stake. Be sure to give the title of the manual. Then offer your comments and suggestions about the manual's strengths and areas of potential improvement.

CONTENTS

Gospel Principles and Doctrines

INTRODUCTION

Using This Manual

This manual provides 35 lessons related to basic gospel principles and the responsibilities of Aaronic Priesthood and Melchizedek Priesthood bearers. As prompted by the Spirit, leaders and teachers should plan and teach lessons that address the spiritual, emotional, and temporal needs of the members in their branch or ward.

This manual should be used as the instruction manual for both the Melchizedek Priesthood and Aaronic Priesthood in units of the Church where *Teachings of Presidents of the Church* and Aaronic Priesthood manuals are not yet published in the needed language. In such units, copies of this manual should be made available to all holders of the Melchizedek Priesthood and to Aaronic Priesthood leaders and instructors. Local leaders should consult *Information for Priesthood and Auxiliary Leaders on Curriculum* for the schedule showing which years part A and part B of *Duties and Blessings of the Priesthood* are to be used.

In units of the Church where *Teachings of Presidents of the Church* and Aaronic Priesthood manuals are available, this manual should be used (1) as a resource for Melchizedek Priesthood instruction on first and fourth Sundays; (2) as a supplementary resource for Aaronic Priesthood instruction; and (3) as designated, for Relief Society "Teachings for Our Time" lessons on fourth Sundays. In such units, copies of the manual should be made available to the leaders and instructors in the Relief Society, Melchizedek Priesthood, and Aaronic Priesthood. In addition, leaders may encourage Melchizedek Priesthood holders to purchase a copy of this manual for personal study and for family teaching in the home.

Preparing to Teach

Teaching helps provided in this manual include a "Teacher Preparation" section, questions teachers could ask, suggestions for class participation, and directions for using pictures and charts. In addition to the discussion questions and methods suggested, teachers may choose to use other methods or lesson approaches they find effective to involve their class members and stimulate participation and learning. Almost every lesson suggests the use of a chalkboard, so if possible teachers should arrange to have a chalkboard and chalk available for each lesson. Many of the visual aids suggested for use as posters could be drawn or written on the chalkboard. Other suggestions for teaching can be found in the *Teaching Guidebook* (34595) and in *Teaching, No Greater Call* (36123).

Class members should be encouraged to prepare for class discussion by studying the assigned lesson during the week. They should also be encouraged to bring their scriptures.

Involving Members with Disabilities

During His mortal ministry, Jesus went up into the mountain near the Sea of Galilee.

"And great multitudes came unto him, having with them those that were lame, blind, dumb, maimed, and many others, and cast them down at Jesus' feet; and he healed them:

"Insomuch that the multitude wondered, when they saw the dumb to speak, the maimed to be whole, the lame to walk, and the blind to see: and they glorified the God of Israel" (Matthew 15:30–31).

The Savior set the example for us in feeling compassion for those with disabilities. When He visited the Nephites after His Resurrection, He said:

"Behold, my bowels are filled with compassion towards you.

"Have ye any that are sick among you? Bring them hither. Have ye any that are lame, or blind, or halt, or maimed, or leprous, or that are withered, or that are deaf, or that are afflicted in any manner? Bring them hither and I will heal them, for I have compassion upon you; my bowels are filled with mercy" (3 Nephi 17:6–7).

As a teacher in a Church classroom, you are in an excellent position to show compassion. Although not usually trained to give professional assistance to class members with disabilities, teachers should desire to understand and include these members in the learning activities of the class. Class members with mental, physical, emotional, and other disabilities may need special attention. The following guidelines should help you reach every member:

- Strive to understand the needs and abilities of each class member.

- Check in advance with a class member before calling on him to read, pray, or otherwise participate. Ask such questions as "How do you feel about reading in class?" or "Would you feel comfortable praying in class?" If appropriate, check with priesthood leaders, parents, and family members to determine the member's special needs.

- Try to increase and improve the involvement and learning of the member with a disability.

- Ensure that each class member treats every other class member with respect.

- Be natural, friendly, and warm. Every son of God needs love and understanding.

As a teacher in the Church, remember that each member, regardless of physical, mental, emotional, or social capacity, has the potential for growth toward exaltation. You have an obligation to help each individual learn gospel principles in your class. Remember the words of the Savior: "Inasmuch as ye have done it unto one of the least of these my brethren, ye have done it unto me" (Matthew 25:40).

THE LIVING CHRIST

THE TESTIMONY OF THE APOSTLES

THE CHURCH OF JESUS CHRIST OF LATTER-DAY SAINTS

As we commemorate the birth of Jesus Christ two millennia ago, we offer our testimony of the reality of His matchless life and the infinite virtue of His great atoning sacrifice. None other has had so profound an influence upon all who have lived and will yet live upon the earth.

He was the Great Jehovah of the Old Testament, the Messiah of the New. Under the direction of His Father, He was the creator of the earth. "All things were made by him; and without him was not any thing made that was made" (John 1:3). Though sinless, He was baptized to fulfill all righteousness. He "went about doing good" (Acts 10:38), yet was despised for it. His gospel was a message of peace and goodwill. He entreated all to follow His example. He walked the roads of Palestine, healing the sick, causing the blind to see, and raising the dead. He taught the truths of eternity, the reality of our premortal existence, the purpose of our life on earth, and the potential for the sons and daughters of God in the life to come.

He instituted the sacrament as a reminder of His great atoning sacrifice. He was arrested and condemned on spurious charges, convicted to satisfy a mob, and sentenced to die on Calvary's cross. He gave His life to atone for the sins of all mankind. His was a great vicarious gift in behalf of all who would ever live upon the earth.

We solemnly testify that His life, which is central to all human history, neither began in Bethlehem nor concluded on Calvary. He was the Firstborn of the Father, the Only Begotten Son in the flesh, the Redeemer of the world.

He rose from the grave to "become the firstfruits of them that slept" (1 Corinthians 15:20). As Risen Lord, He visited among those He had loved in life. He also ministered among His "other sheep" (John 10:16) in ancient America. In the modern world, He and His Father appeared to the boy Joseph Smith, ushering in the long-promised "dispensation of the fulness of times" (Ephesians 1:10).

Of the Living Christ, the Prophet Joseph wrote: "His eyes were as a flame of fire; the hair of his head was white like the pure snow; his countenance shone above the brightness of the sun; and his voice was as the sound of the rushing of great waters, even the voice of Jehovah, saying:

"I am the first and the last; I am he who liveth, I am he who was slain; I am your advocate with the Father" (D&C 110:3–4).

Of Him the Prophet also declared: "And now, after the many testimonies which have been given of him, this is the testimony, last of all, which we give of him: That he lives!

"For we saw him, even on the right hand of God; and we heard the voice bearing record that he is the Only Begotten of the Father—

"That by him, and through him, and of him, the worlds are and were created, and the inhabitants thereof are begotten sons and daughters unto God" (D&C 76:22–24).

We declare in words of solemnity that His priesthood and His Church have been restored upon the earth—"built upon the foundation of . . . apostles and prophets, Jesus Christ himself being the chief corner stone" (Ephesians 2:20).

We testify that He will someday return to earth. "And the glory of the Lord shall be revealed, and all flesh shall see it together" (Isaiah 40:5). He will rule as King of Kings and reign as Lord of Lords, and every knee shall bend and every tongue shall speak in worship before Him. Each of us will stand to be judged of Him according to our works and the desires of our hearts.

We bear testimony, as His duly ordained Apostles— that Jesus is the Living Christ, the immortal Son of God. He is the great King Immanuel, who stands today on the right hand of His Father. He is the light, the life, and the hope of the world. His way is the path that leads to happiness in this life and eternal life in the world to come. God be thanked for the matchless gift of His divine Son.

THE FIRST PRESIDENCY

[signatures]

January 1, 2000

THE QUORUM OF THE TWELVE

[signatures]

THE FAMILY

A PROCLAMATION TO THE WORLD

The First Presidency and Council of the Twelve Apostles
of The Church of Jesus Christ of Latter-day Saints

WE, THE FIRST PRESIDENCY and the Council of the Twelve Apostles of The Church of Jesus Christ of Latter-day Saints, solemnly proclaim that marriage between a man and a woman is ordained of God and that the family is central to the Creator's plan for the eternal destiny of His children.

ALL HUMAN BEINGS—male and female—are created in the image of God. Each is a beloved spirit son or daughter of heavenly parents, and, as such, each has a divine nature and destiny. Gender is an essential characteristic of individual premortal, mortal, and eternal identity and purpose.

IN THE PREMORTAL REALM, spirit sons and daughters knew and worshiped God as their Eternal Father and accepted His plan by which His children could obtain a physical body and gain earthly experience to progress toward perfection and ultimately realize his or her divine destiny as an heir of eternal life. The divine plan of happiness enables family relationships to be perpetuated beyond the grave. Sacred ordinances and covenants available in holy temples make it possible for individuals to return to the presence of God and for families to be united eternally.

THE FIRST COMMANDMENT that God gave to Adam and Eve pertained to their potential for parenthood as husband and wife. We declare that God's commandment for His children to multiply and replenish the earth remains in force. We further declare that God has commanded that the sacred powers of procreation are to be employed only between man and woman, lawfully wedded as husband and wife.

WE DECLARE the means by which mortal life is created to be divinely appointed. We affirm the sanctity of life and of its importance in God's eternal plan.

HUSBAND AND WIFE have a solemn responsibility to love and care for each other and for their children. "Children are an heritage of the Lord" (Psalms 127:3). Parents have a sacred duty to rear their children in love and righteousness, to provide for their physical and spiritual needs, to teach them to love and serve one another, to observe the commandments of God and to be law-abiding citizens wherever they live. Husbands and wives—mothers and fathers—will be held accountable before God for the discharge of these obligations.

THE FAMILY is ordained of God. Marriage between man and woman is essential to His eternal plan. Children are entitled to birth within the bonds of matrimony, and to be reared by a father and a mother who honor marital vows with complete fidelity. Happiness in family life is most likely to be achieved when founded upon the teachings of the Lord Jesus Christ. Successful marriages and families are established and maintained on principles of faith, prayer, repentance, forgiveness, respect, love, compassion, work, and wholesome recreational activities. By divine design, fathers are to preside over their families in love and righteousness and are responsible to provide the necessities of life and protection for their families. Mothers are primarily responsible for the nurture of their children. In these sacred responsibilities, fathers and mothers are obligated to help one another as equal partners. Disability, death, or other circumstances may necessitate individual adaptation. Extended families should lend support when needed.

WE WARN that individuals who violate covenants of chastity, who abuse spouse or offspring, or who fail to fulfill family responsibilities will one day stand accountable before God. Further, we warn that the disintegration of the family will bring upon individuals, communities, and nations the calamities foretold by ancient and modern prophets.

WE CALL UPON responsible citizens and officers of government everywhere to promote those measures designed to maintain and strengthen the family as the fundamental unit of society.

PRIESTHOOD AND CHURCH GOVERNMENT

THE OATH AND COVENANT OF THE PRIESTHOOD

Lesson 1

The purpose of this lesson is to help us understand the oath and covenant of the priesthood and how to magnify our callings.

Introduction

Elder Reed Smoot was a member of the Quorum of the Twelve Apostles from 1900 until his death in 1941. During much of this time he was also an outstanding member of the United States Senate. Many people encouraged him to run for president of the United States. But they told him he would have to give up his religion because people at that time would not elect a Mormon for president. He said, "If I had to take my choice of being a deacon in The Church of Jesus Christ of Latter-day Saints, or being President of the United States, I would be a deacon" (quoted in Bryant S. Hinckley, *The Faith of Our Pioneer Fathers* [1956], 202).

▪ Why do you think Elder Smoot placed such value on the priesthood?

Elder Smoot had to meet certain requirements to be a United States senator. Likewise, in order for us to receive the priesthood we must meet certain requirements. We must be interviewed by our priesthood leaders, who ask us certain questions to determine our worthiness to receive the priesthood and our willingness to accept sacred priesthood responsibilities.

▪ What are some of the questions that our priesthood leaders might ask?

After Elder Smoot was elected as a senator, he took the oath of office and promised to fulfill his duties in the government. In the same way, when we receive the priesthood we promise to fulfill our duties to the Lord.

The Oath and Covenant of the Priesthood

We receive the holy priesthood by an "oath and covenant." This means that Heavenly Father gives us His oath (guarantee) that we can have the power and blessings of the priesthood if we covenant (promise)

2

with Him to do certain things. "Therefore, all those who receive the priesthood, receive this oath and covenant of [the] Father, which he cannot break, neither can it be moved" (D&C 84:40).

President Marion G. Romney explained the meaning of a covenant: "A covenant is a contract, and a contract is an agreement between two or more [people]. If I should enter into a covenant with you, I would promise you something in consideration for you promising me something. If I entered into agreement with you to pay you a certain sum of money for an automobile, and you promised to give me the automobile for that sum of money, that would be a covenant. Now, in a covenant of the priesthood, we promise the Lord, and he promises us something in return for what we do give him" (in Conference Report, Korea Area Conference 1975, 36).

The oath and covenant of the priesthood is explained in Doctrine and Covenants 84. This section clearly describes the promises we make and the promises the Lord makes when we receive the priesthood.

- Write on the chalkboard *Our Promises* and *Lord's Promises.* List under these headings the promises we make and those promises the Lord makes as they are discussed.

Our Promises to the Lord

- Read Doctrine and Covenants 84:33.

In the first half of verse 33 the Lord identifies our part of the covenant: "For whoso is faithful unto the obtaining these two priesthoods of which I have spoken, and the magnifying their calling . . ."

- According to this verse, what is our part of the covenant? (We promise to magnify our callings.)

To magnify our callings is to do our best in accepting and carrying out all our priesthood duties so we can enlarge the Lord's kingdom on earth. When we receive the priesthood we also promise to be faithful and keep all the commandments.

The Lord's Promises to Us

- Read Doctrine and Covenants 84:33–38. Pause after each part of the Lord's promise, write it on the chalkboard, and then discuss it.

The Lord promises that if we keep our part of the covenant, we will be "sanctified by the Spirit unto the renewing of [our] bodies" (D&C 84:33). We can expect to be strengthened in body and spirit as we fulfill our callings.

We may also "become the sons of Moses and of Aaron" (D&C 84:34). The sons of Moses and Aaron administered the ordinances of salvation to the children of Israel. We have the same privilege of administering these sacred ordinances through the priesthood today.

The Lord promises that we will become "the seed of Abraham" (D&C 84:34). In other words, we may receive the blessings promised to Abraham and his seed.

- Ask a class member to read Abraham 2:8–11.

God covenanted with Abraham and his seed that through them all the nations of the earth would be blessed with the gospel. It is through the power and authority exercised by faithful priesthood bearers that these blessings are given to the world.

The Lord also promises that faithful priesthood holders will "become . . . the elect of God" (D&C 84:34). This means that we priesthood bearers who magnify our callings and enter into all of the sacred saving ordinances of the priesthood will be given the fulness of the Father's kingdom.

Then the Lord says, "All that my Father hath shall be given unto [them]" (D&C 84:38).

President Spencer W. Kimball explained: "Have you ever stopped to [count] the blessings, the powers that the Lord has? All power, all influence, all strength will be yours, and this is according to the oath and covenant of the holy priesthood which you bear" (in Conference Report, Buenos Aires Area Conference 1975, 51).

There is no doubt that the Lord will fulfill His promises to the faithful and obedient. The responsibility, therefore, is ours. Failure to keep our promises to the Lord will prevent Him from giving us all that He is prepared to give us.

Magnifying Our Priesthood Callings

We have promised, in covenant with our Father in Heaven, to magnify our callings.

- In what ways can we magnify our priesthood callings?

When the Aaronic Priesthood is conferred upon us, we are ordained to an office in that priesthood: deacon, teacher, or priest. Each of these offices is a calling with certain duties and responsibilities. Offices in the Melchizedek Priesthood are elder, high priest, patriarch, Seventy, and Apostle. (See *Gospel Principles* chapter 14, pages 85–93, for an explanation of these callings.)

"God gives priesthood authority to worthy male members of the Church so they can act in His name for the salvation of the human family. . . .

"A man receives the Aaronic or Melchizedek Priesthood when an authorized priesthood holder confers it on him and ordains him to an office in that priesthood (see Articles of Faith 1:5; D&C 42:11). No man can take this honor unto himself (see Hebrews 5:4)" (*Church Handbook of Instructions, Book 2: Priesthood and Auxiliary Leaders* [1998], 161).

President Spencer W. Kimball said:

"This priesthood is not a plaything. It isn't something just to hold and forget about. It is about the most important thing in all the world, and we receive it with an oath and covenant. . . .

". . . The Lord knew that we were weak humans and might be tempted, and he said that that is why he asked us to pray night and morning and all the time. That is why he gave us home evening so that we could remind ourselves frequently. That is why he gave us priesthood meetings, where we would go and mingle with our brethren and keep ourselves reminded" (in Conference Report, Korea Area Conference 1975, 40–41).

Before anyone can magnify his priesthood calling he must know what is expected of him. He must first "learn his duty, and [then] act in the office in which he is appointed, in all diligence" (D&C 107:99).

The following story shows that President Kimball understood his duties and magnified his calling as a deacon:

"I remember when I was a deacon. . . . I thought it was a great honor to be a deacon. My father was always considerate of my responsibilities and always permitted me to take the buggy and horse to gather fast offerings. My responsibility included that part of the town in which I lived, but it was quite a long walk to the homes, and a sack of flour or a bottle of fruit or vegetables or bread became quite heavy as it accumulated. So the buggy was very comfortable and functional. . . . It was a very great honor to do this service for my Heavenly Father; and . . . it is still a great honor to perform this service.

"I am a deacon. I am always proud that I am a deacon. When I see the apostles march up to the stand in a solemn assembly to bless the sacrament, and others of the General Authorities step up to the sacrament tables to get the bread and the water and humbly pass it to all the people in the assembly and then return their emptied receptacles, I am proud that I am a deacon, and a teacher, and a priest" (in Conference Report, Apr. 1975, 117; or *Ensign*, May 1975, 79).

- What was President Kimball's attitude about his priesthood calling? How can the way we magnify our callings influence others?

Receiving Help in Magnifying Our Callings

President Marion G. Romney said: "In order to magnify our callings in the priesthood, three things at least are necessary: One is that we have a *motivating desire* to do so. Another is that we *search and ponder the words of eternal life.* And a third is that we *pray*" (in Conference Report, Apr. 1973, 116; or *Ensign,* July 1973, 89; italics added).

- What three things did President Romney say are necessary for us to magnify our callings? (List the responses on the chalkboard. Responses should include having a desire, studying the scriptures and the words of the living prophets, and praying.)

If we do these things and keep the commandments, Heavenly Father will help us magnify our callings.

Elder Orson Pratt, one of the great missionaries of the Church, believed this with all his heart. When he was called on a mission to Scotland, there were only 80 members of the Church in that country. The previous missionaries to Scotland had been forced to leave the area amid a shower of stones, rubbish, and abuse. When he arrived in early 1840, "he traveled . . . to Edinburgh, the capital. On the day after his arrival there, he climbed a rugged, rocky hill that rises in the middle of a natural park, commanding a magnificent view of the ancient city. Locally it was called Arthur's Seat, but it is affectionately known by the Saints as Pratt's Hill. There Orson Pratt pleaded with the Lord to give him two hundred souls to convert. The Lord heard and answered that prayer" (Muriel Cuthbert, "Strong Saints in Scotland," *Ensign,* Oct. 1978, 36).

Elder Pratt magnified his calling, and because of this, others were blessed. By 1853, just 13 years after Elder Pratt climbed the hill and pleaded with the Lord for help, there were 3,291 members of the Church in Scotland.

Conclusion

"The blessings of the Lord are offered to the Saints and to the world through the ministrations of those who hold his holy priesthood. . . . Holding the priesthood is not a light or small thing. We are dealing with the Lord's power and authority, which he has given to us by the opening of the heavens in this day so that every blessing might again be available to us" (Joseph Fielding Smith, "Blessings of the Priesthood," *Ensign,* Dec. 1971, 98).

The Savior has promised by oath and covenant that when we magnify our priesthood callings, we will receive all that our Father has. The greatest gift He has for us is eternal life (see D&C 14:7), and we have the promise that it can be ours and that we can help others obtain it. We should think often about the great blessings the Lord has promised us if we are faithful. As we do so, our desire to keep our covenants will increase and lead us toward eternal life.

Challenge

Decide today that you will magnify your callings. Study the scriptures to receive inspiration; then pray earnestly for help. Keep in mind the oath and covenant of the priesthood, remembering that our Heavenly Father wants to give you all that He has. Be generous with your service to others, using your offices and callings in the priesthood to bless their lives.

Additional Scriptures

- Jacob 1:17–19 (magnify callings)

- Mosiah 2:20–24 (our indebtedness to God)

- Doctrine and Covenants 58:26–29 (be anxiously engaged in a good cause)

- Doctrine and Covenants 121:34–36 (priesthood governed by principles of righteousness)

Teacher Preparation

Before presenting this lesson:

1. Read Doctrine and Covenants 84:1–48. Become especially familiar with verses 33 to 44.

2. Assign class members to present any stories, scriptures, or quotations you wish.

THE KEYS OF THE PRIESTHOOD

Lesson 2

The purpose of this lesson is to improve our understanding of the meaning and use of the priesthood keys.

Introduction

A key unlocks the door to a house. We cannot appropriately enter a house unless we receive the key or the owner's permission. Likewise, except for the right that husbands and fathers have to bless their families, a man who holds the priesthood can use it only when he receives proper permission. A priest, for example, has the authority to ordain another to an office in the Aaronic Priesthood, but he cannot do it without receiving permission to do so from his bishop or branch president. This power to give permission is called the keys of the priesthood.

"It is necessary that every act performed under this authority shall be done at the proper time and place, in the proper way, and after the proper order. The power of directing these labors constitutes the *keys* of the Priesthood" (Joseph F. Smith, *Gospel Doctrine,* 5th ed. [1939], 136).

President Joseph Fielding Smith explained: "These keys are the right of presidency; they are the power and authority to govern and direct all of the Lord's affairs on earth. Those who hold them have power to govern and control the manner in which all others may serve in the priesthood. All of us may hold the priesthood, but we can only use it as authorized and directed so to do by those who hold the keys" (in Conference Report, Apr. 1972, 98; or *Ensign,* July 1972, 87).

- What is the difference between the priesthood and the keys of the priesthood? (The priesthood is the power or authority of God. The keys are the right to use this power or authority in specific ways.)

Who Holds the Keys of the Priesthood?

Jesus Christ has always held all of the keys of the priesthood. When He first called His twelve Apostles, Jesus gave all of them the priesthood (see John 15:16).

- Show visual 2-a, "Christ ordained His Apostles and gave them the keys of the priesthood."

Before He was crucified, Christ gave the keys of the priesthood to Peter, James, and John. This was done on the Mount of Transfiguration. (See *Teachings of the Prophet Joseph Smith,* sel. Joseph Fielding Smith [1976], 158; Matthew 17:1–9.) However, in the centuries that followed the death of the Apostles, these keys were lost; and before men could exercise the priesthood again, these keys had to be restored. For this reason the Lord sent Peter, James, and John to the Prophet Joseph Smith to restore the Melchizedek Priesthood and the keys of that priesthood (see D&C 27:12–13).

These sacred keys have been given to all the Apostles and prophets of the Church and are held by the prophet and Apostles of the Church today.

- Show visual 2-b, "President Gordon B. Hinckley."

Although each Apostle holds all the keys of the priesthood, it is the Lord's plan that only one man at a time exercise these keys on behalf of the Church. For this reason the senior living Apostle (by date of ordination, not by age) is ordained President of the Church by the Quorum of the Twelve and given the right to exercise all the keys of the priesthood. When he dies, the remaining Apostles ordain the next senior living Apostle (the President of the Quorum of the Twelve) to use his apostolic keys in their fulness as President of the Church.

The President of the Church, therefore, is the only man on earth who has the power to exercise all of the keys of the priesthood (see D&C 132:7). However, he delegates certain keys to the leaders who preside in the Church. These men include mission presidents, branch presidents, temple presidents, stake presidents, bishops, and Melchizedek Priesthood quorum presidents. They in turn delegate a portion of their authority (but not their keys) to men and women in their units by setting them apart to different offices and callings.

President Joseph F. Smith explained: "In their fulness, the keys are held by only one person at a time, the prophet and president of the Church. He may delegate any portion of this power to another, in which case that person holds the keys of that particular labor. Thus, the president of a temple, the president of a stake, the bishop of a ward, the president of a mission, the president of a quorum, each holds the keys of the labors performed in that particular body or locality. His Priesthood is not increased by this special appointment" (*Gospel Doctrine,* 136).

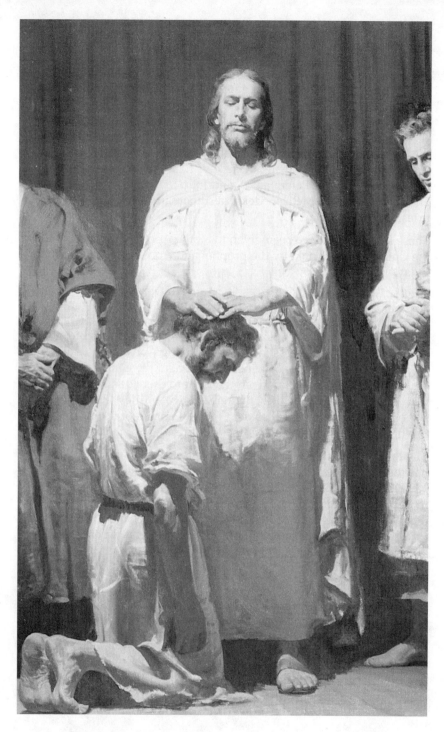

2-a, Christ ordained His Apostles and gave them the keys of the priesthood.

Some rights are given to a man automatically when he is given the Aaronic or Melchizedek Priesthood. For instance, when a man receives the Melchizedek Priesthood, he is given the authority to give father's blessings, to give blessings of comfort, and to administer to the sick. He will hold these rights as long as he bears that priesthood. Even death cannot take this authority from him.

However, there are certain rights that one can be given that are only temporary. A branch president, for example, holds the keys of his branch only for the time he remains branch president. When he is released from that position, he no longer holds these keys.

Importance of Priesthood Keys

When a person is called to a temporary Church assignment as an officer or teacher, he is set apart to that calling. The Church officer holding the keys to that calling gives the individual the right to act in that calling in the setting-apart blessing. Thereafter, no one else can act in his calling—just as he cannot assume the duties of someone else's job. The individual retains this right until he is released from the position. This release is given by the presiding officer; afterward the individual no longer holds the right to act in that position. Church members may be set apart to serve in positions of Church service for a period of weeks, months, or years. The length of service is according to need, individual performance, and the Lord's guidance to the presiding officer.

Although both men and women can be set apart to callings, only priesthood bearers are ordained to priesthood offices. These offices include deacon, teacher, priest, elder, high priest, bishop, patriarch, Seventy, and Apostle. Ordination to any of these offices enables a person to serve the Church in specific ways—but only, as discussed earlier, when given permission to do so by those who hold the keys of the priesthood.

The following story shows how the proper use of priesthood keys keeps order in the Church:

In the early days of the Church, Hiram Page assumed he had the authority to reveal the word of the Lord to the Church. He began telling others about his revelations, and many members of the Church believed everything he taught. The Prophet Joseph Smith prayed and asked the Lord what to do. The Lord answered him, saying, "No one shall be appointed to receive commandments and revelations in this church excepting my servant Joseph Smith, Jun." (D&C 28:2). The Lord also said that Joseph should tell Hiram Page that the things Hiram had been teaching and writing were from the devil. The Lord explained that Hiram was not the one to receive revelations for the Church:

2-b, President Gordon B. Hinckley

"These things have not been appointed unto him. . . . For all things must be done in order" (see D&C 28:11–13).

The Prophet Joseph did as the Lord instructed. He met with Hiram Page and told him what the Lord had said. Humbled in spirit, Brother Page expressed his sorrow and promised to stop what he had been doing. Seeing his repentance, Joseph asked him to go on a mission. Later, at a conference, the Prophet told the members of the Church what the Lord had revealed and asked them to forget what Hiram Page had taught them. They all agreed and voted to accept Joseph as their only prophet, seer, and revelator. (See *History of the Church,* 1:109–15.)

- Why is it important that only one man exercise all the keys to the priesthood?

The Lord's Church Is a "House of Order"

Because the priesthood is sacred, we are told to use it with care. The priesthood is therefore governed in an orderly way to avoid confusion and prevent its misuse. "Behold, mine house is a house of order, saith the Lord God, and not a house of confusion" (D&C 132:8).

Such order has always been a part of the Lord's kingdom on earth. Moses, for example, learned the necessity of order soon after he was called to lead the Israelites. The Israelites needed leadership to keep them united, but Moses found it impossible to guide all the people by himself. He therefore chose "able men, such as fear God, men of truth" and called them to be rulers. He set apart some to be rulers of hundreds, some to be rulers of fifties, and others to be rulers of tens. He then taught them how to preside over their groups. (See Exodus 18:17–22.)

Today our priesthood leaders—bishops and stake, district, mission, branch, and quorum presidents—are given the keys of the priesthood so we can be led in an orderly way and receive the necessary ordinances of the gospel. Church leaders have many responsibilities because they hold keys of the priesthood. These responsibilities include:

Interviewing those who are to receive ordinances.

Explaining the importance of the ordinances.

Determining whether members are ready to receive the ordinances.

Keeping necessary records.

Determining the worthiness of those who are to perform the ordinances.

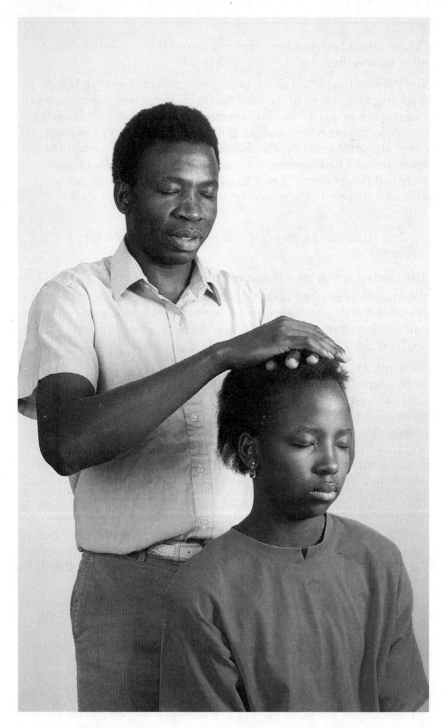

2-c, Priesthood blessings are available to all family members.

Asking someone to conduct the services of the Church.

Asking for a sustaining vote from the members of the Church.

A Father Has Keys to Bless His Family

By appointment of the Lord, a father is head of his home. To be effective as the spiritual head of his family, he must bear his priesthood honorably. If he does so, he will have the power to guide and bless his family in love and harmony.

- What keys do we hold as heads of our families? What do these keys allow us to do for our family members?

The priesthood can bring many wonderful blessings into our lives. Bishop H. Burke Peterson listed some of these: "If we live [in a way that will prepare us to receive it], ours can be a power given us from our Heavenly Father that will bring peace to a troubled household. Ours can be a power that will bless and comfort little children, that will bring sleep to tear-stained eyes in the [early] hours of the morning. Ours can be the power that will . . . calm the unsettled nerves of a tired wife. Ours can be the power that will give direction to a confused and vulnerable teenager. Ours, the power to bless a daughter before she goes on her first date or before her temple marriage, or to bless a son before his departure for a mission or college. . . . Ours can be the power to heal the sick and comfort the lonely" (in Conference Report, Apr. 1976, 50–51; or *Ensign,* May 1976, 33).

- How do you feel about a worthy father having the power and authority to bless his wife and children? How would you feel if a member of your family asked you for such a blessing?

Sister Kyuln Lee of Korea received the comfort of a priesthood blessing in her home. She told the following story:

"It happened about seven years ago, when my first baby was only ten months old. My husband, a member of the Korea District presidency, had to travel long distances almost every weekend to carry out his assignments for the Church, leaving me alone with our daughter, Po Hee. On this particular weekend, he had traveled 270 miles to Pusan on Saturday (a seven-hour train ride each way) and then returned to Seoul that night to attend conference in the Seoul East Branch on Sunday. It was tiring, and I felt sorry for him.

"Po Hee was in normal health Saturday and Sunday, and, though she was a bit noisy at sacrament meeting, after we returned home she drank her bottle and went to sleep. About 9:30 P.M. she began to cry.

She was crying louder than usual, and when I picked her up, I discovered she had a high fever. I didn't know what to do. I found out that the only hospital near our home had closed for the day. Her cries continued for some time, and when my husband finally walked in the door, I started crying, too.

"My husband embraced the baby and me together and asked what was wrong. Po Hee looked miserable. When I told him what had happened, he put down his coat and briefcase and took out his consecrated oil. Then he administered to our daughter. I don't remember all the words but after saying the formal words of administration he went on: 'Heavenly Father, I'm grateful for life, for my wife and baby. I'm grateful for this restored gospel and the opportunity to serve. You sent me down to Pusan and Seoul East Branch to handle some Church affairs. I have fulfilled my given responsibility yesterday and today, and now I find my baby very ill. You have helped me all the time. Please help me tonight.'

"Before he concluded the prayer, the baby was asleep, and when I looked up, my husband stood there with tears in his eyes.

"Our little girl is now in the second grade and is healthy and happy, but I can still remember very clearly the part of my husband's prayer where he told the Lord, 'I have fulfilled my given responsibility yesterday and today.' I hope I will continue to support him so that he can always tell the Lord he has been obedient. What a blessing to have a husband who honors the priesthood!" ("Our Baby, My Husband, and the Priesthood," *Ensign*, Aug. 1975, 65).

- Show visual 2-c, "Priesthood blessings are available to all family members."

Special priesthood blessings are available to all family members. A child with a problem or a wife in need of comfort or guidance can request a special blessing and thereby receive the help she or he needs from the Lord. In receiving such blessings, we need to remember that many trials are for our experience. We should work them out as best we can ourselves. But when we find that we need extra help, we can turn to a priesthood holder in our family, our home teachers, or another priesthood leader and ask for a special priesthood blessing.

- Invite a few class members to share briefly some of the blessings their families have received through the priesthood.

"The father must hunger and thirst and yearn to bless his family, go to the Lord, ponder the words of God, and live by the Spirit to know the mind and will of the Lord and what he must do to lead his family" (Ezra Taft Benson, *God, Family, Country: Our Three Great Loyalties* [1974], 185).

"[In addition to providing this kind of leadership,] a worthy father who holds the Melchizedek Priesthood should be encouraged to name and bless his children. He should administer to the sick in his home. . . . He may give a father's blessing.

"As the Patriarch of his home, a father is also a revelator to his family . . . and . . . in this sense stands in line to receive the revelations from the Lord for the good and blessing of that family (see *Doctrines of Salvation,* 3:172)" (A. Theodore Tuttle, in Conference Report, Oct. 1973, 86; or *Ensign,* Jan. 1974, 66–67). Worthy fathers should also baptize their children, confirm upon them the gift of the Holy Ghost, and ordain them to the priesthood. However, unlike the rights associated with his fatherhood, a father can perform these ordinances only after receiving permission from the priesthood leaders who hold the keys in his Church unit.

Conclusion

Although we have the authority to perform certain ordinances as priesthood holders, we cannot perform some of them until we have received permission from our Church leaders to do so. The power to give this permission is called the keys of the priesthood. The prophet is the only man on earth who holds all the priesthood keys, but he has given some of these keys to the leaders who preside over the units of the Church; they in turn grant us permission to use our priesthood to bless Heavenly Father's children.

Also, when we are ordained to the Melchizedek Priesthood, we receive certain keys for use as fathers. With these keys we can use the priesthood to bless our families.

Challenge

Prayerfully consider how you can use your priesthood to bless your family members.

Additional Scriptures

- Doctrine and Covenants 65:1–6 (the keys of the kingdom of God committed to man)

- Doctrine and Covenants 110:11–16 (the keys of this and other dispensations committed to man)

Teacher Preparation

Before presenting this lesson:

1. Study 1 Corinthians 12:12–28.

2. Assign class members to present any stories, scriptures, or quotations you wish.

HONORING THE PRIESTHOOD

L e s s o n   3

The purpose of this lesson is to help us understand the sacred power of the priesthood and increase our desire to honor it.

Introduction

- Sing "High on the Mountain Top" (*Hymns*, no. 5; or *Gospel Principles*, 338).

"Two missionaries laboring in Hong Kong had been invited to dinner at the apartment of Brother and Sister Wong. The table was set with an assortment of tin bowls and plates. Sister Wong smiled politely at the two missionaries from the corner of the room where she labored over the smoking burner. Presently she set bowls and platters of food on the table. The elders were surprised at the dinner. There were bowls of rice, but there were also platters of shrimp and other oriental delicacies, all far beyond the means of this humble refugee family. Brother Wong pronounced a blessing and the meal commenced; but Brother and Sister Wong held back, taking only token portions for themselves, but urging the food on the two elders. The elders could sense that the gesture was sincere, and while they recognized that they were eating up finer food than the Wongs could ever afford for regular meals—food that cost the Wongs probably the equivalent of a whole month's salary—still the elders did not want to offend or hurt or refuse, where such evident sacrifice was involved.

"It was a difficult meal to eat; wanting to accept the gift so obviously given from the heart, yet realizing that hardship and hungry days—sacrifice—made the gift possible. Brother and Sister Wong and their sons merely sampled the dinner. But when it was completed, they expressed their own satisfaction and were anxious to know if the elders had had enough. As everyone stood to allow Sister Wong to clear away the dishes, one of the elders took Brother Wong by the hand and with deep emotion said: 'Why have you honored us in this way, at such great expense to yourselves?' With quiet gentleness that could only come from leaving his home and country and accepting the truth

3-a, The earth was created through the power of the priesthood.

in a foreign land, Brother Wong said: 'We did this for you because you hold the priesthood, and God has sent you here to teach us' " (*Life and Teachings of Jesus, New Testament Volume 1* [Church Educational System manual, 1974], 134).

- How did Brother and Sister Wong show honor to those bearing the priesthood of God? Why is it important that we honor the priesthood we hold?

Priesthood—The Greatest Power on Earth

The priesthood is the greatest power on earth. It is not only the power of God given to men on the earth to do His work, but it is the same power by which our Heavenly Father and Jesus Christ perform Their work. In fact, it was through the power of the priesthood that the Savior created the earth.

- Show visual 3-a, "The earth was created through the power of the priesthood."

It is a great privilege for us to be given this priesthood and its power.

- Have the class members read Doctrine and Covenants 107:1–4. What is the official name of the Melchizedek Priesthood? ("The Holy Priesthood, after the Order of the Son of God")

We call the higher priesthood the Melchizedek Priesthood to avoid using the name "the Son of God" too often, but the priesthood is actually the Savior's priesthood.

Many of us do not understand how powerful the priesthood is. At the time of Enoch, God made a promise "that every one being ordained after this order and calling should have power, by faith, to break mountains, to divide the seas, to dry up waters, to turn them out of their course, to put at defiance the armies of nations, to divide the earth, to break every band, to stand in the presence of God; *to do all things according to his will,* according to his command" (Joseph Smith Translation, Genesis 14:30–31; see also John Taylor, *The Mediation and Atonement* [1882], 85; italics added).

Those who hold the priesthood represent Christ. Therefore, we must do what He would have us do if we are to have His power. We must obey His commandments and try, whenever we exercise the priesthood, to act how He would have us act.

Elder H. Burke Peterson explained: "I understand that there is a difference between priesthood authority and priesthood power. . . . All of us who hold the priesthood have the authority to act for the Lord, but the effectiveness of our authority—or if you please, the power that comes through that authority—depends on the pattern of our lives; it depends on our righteousness" (in Conference Report, Apr. 1976, 50; or *Ensign,* May 1976, 33).

If worthy, we have power to bless our families, receive revelation for our priesthood callings, perform miracles, and overcome Satan. The priesthood is the power by which ordinances are performed, temple work is done, and the gospel is preached. We could not receive any of these ordinances and blessings without the power of the priesthood.

- Invite a few class members to share how they have seen the power of the priesthood in their life.

Personal experience helped one young missionary understand the power of the priesthood:

This missionary and his companion went up into one of the poorer districts of a city to give a discussion. The young couple who were investigating the Church were extremely poor. Of most worth to them was their infant daughter, who at the time was extremely ill. Her little face looked blue and black. She kept closing her eyes as if she were falling asleep. The father and mother were mourning and crying. They realized their precious little daughter was about to die. The thought came strongly to this young missionary, "Use your priesthood!" And so he asked the father to take his little daughter in his arms. The missionary and his companion then placed their hands on the tiny head of the baby and proceeded to exercise their faith and give her a blessing. The voice of the Spirit told them to bless her that she would gain her health and grow up to be a fine young woman. That blessing was fulfilled. The child was restored to good health.

The young missionary rejoiced in the Lord for the opportunity of being His servant. His experience was thrilling and yet sobering. It taught him something of God's mighty power, to which His servants have access through the priesthood.

- Why is our faith important in exercising priesthood power?

Honoring the Priesthood

President Harold B. Lee related the following: "I remember a story told by one of our servicemen once. He was invited to an officers club where a drinking party was going on, and the men were conducting themselves in a rather riotous manner. He noticed one apart from the rest who seemingly wasn't interested in what was going on, and so he sidled off to this man who, like himself, was not partaking, and said, 'You don't seem to be very much interested in this kind of party.' This young man straightened himself to his fullest height and said, 'No, sir, I don't engage in this kind of a party because, you see, I am a member of the Royal House of England.' And our Latter-day Saint officer said, just as proudly, 'Neither do I, because I am a member of the Royal House of God' " (*Ye Are the Light of the World* [1974], 22; see also 1 Peter 2:9).

Because this is the Savior's priesthood, we should honor it as Christ would have us honor it. Elder James E. Talmage wrote about his ordination to the priesthood and the feelings he had as he tried to honor it:

"As soon as I had been ordained, a feeling came to me such as I have never been able to fully describe. It seemed scarcely possible that I, a little boy, could be so honored of God as to be called to the priesthood. . . . I forgot that I was but an eleven-year-old lad; I felt strong in the thought that I belonged to the Lord, and that he would assist me in whatever was required of me. . . .

"The effect of my ordination [as a deacon] entered into all the affairs of my boyish life. I am afraid that sometimes I forgot what I was, but I have ever been thankful that oft-times I did remember, and the recollection always served to make me better. When at play on the school grounds, and perhaps tempted to take unfair advantage in the game, when in the midst of a dispute with a playmate, I would remember, and the thought would be effective as though spoken aloud—'I am a deacon; and it is not right that a deacon should act in this way.' On examination days, when it seemed easy for me to copy some other boy's work, . . . I would say in my mind, 'It would be more wicked for me to do that than it is for them, because I am a deacon.'

" . . . The sense of the great honor of my ordination made all service welcome. . . .

"The impression made upon my mind when I was made a deacon has never faded. The feeling that I was called to the special service of the Lord, as a bearer of the priesthood, has been a source of strength to me through all the years. When later I was ordained to higher offices in the Church, the same assurance has come to me, on every occasion,— that I was in truth endowed with power from heaven, and that the Lord demanded of me that I honor his authority. I have been ordained in turn a teacher, an elder, a high priest, and lastly an Apostle of the Lord Jesus Christ, and with every ordination there has come to me a new and soul-thrilling feeling which I first knew when I was called to be a deacon in the service of the Lord" (*Incidents from the Lives of Our Church Leaders* [deacon's instruction manual, 1914], 135–36).

- How did Elder Talmage honor the priesthood?

President Harold B. Lee counseled: "We must say, 'Because I am a holder of the priesthood of the living God, I am a representative of our Heavenly Father and hold the priesthood by which He can work through me; I can't stoop to do some of the things that I might have done otherwise because of my fellowship with the priesthood of God. . . .'

"And that is what the holders of the priesthood must say to themselves: 'We can't be holders of the priesthood and be like other men. We must be different' " (in Conference Report, Oct. 1973, 115; or *Ensign,* Jan. 1974, 97).

Church leaders have given much instruction on how members should honor the priesthood. President Brigham Young said that "men who [hold] the holy Priesthood, who are charged with words of eternal life to the world, should strive continually in their words and actions . . . to do honor to the great dignity of their calling and office as ministers and representatives of the Most High" (*Discourses of Brigham Young,* sel. John A. Widtsoe [1954], 130).

President David O. McKay said: "God bless you men of the priesthood. May you hold it with dignity and righteousness that comes from within, not from without. To hold the priesthood of God by divine authority is one of the greatest gifts that can come to a man. He is greatly blessed who feels the responsibility of representing Deity. He should feel it to such an extent that he is conscious of his actions and words under all conditions" (in Conference Report, Oct. 1967, 152–53; or *Improvement Era,* Dec. 1967, 109).

- According to Presidents Young and McKay, how should priesthood holders honor the priesthood?

Elder Robert L. Simpson explained:

"To bear the priesthood of God with dignity means . . . that we move about with a quiet dignity, not only at the sacrament table but also at work, at school, and even as Dad walks along the roadway on his way to work; we are priesthood holders; we are different, not particularly better than anyone else, but we're different. A representative of God dresses properly; he's always modest. . . . And most certainly, our bodies, as well as our clothing, should be very, very clean. . . .

". . . Sometimes a priesthood holder has need to improve his speech. There is no dignity in the extreme use of slang. Profanity is an insult to God. . . .

". . . We rob God if we fail to observe the law of tithing. (See Malachi 3:8.) No priesthood holder stands with greater dignity than when his financial account with the Lord is up to date and paid in full.

"No priesthood holder stands with less dignity than when his body is not maintained and regarded as a temple of God. . . . Brethren, we are indeed without dignity when we violate Heavenly Father's law of health [by using alcohol, drugs, or tobacco]" (in Conference Report, Melbourne Area Conference 1976, 38).

- What did Elder Simpson suggest that could help us bear the priesthood with dignity? (List the responses on the chalkboard. The responses might include having humility, dressing properly, being modest, being clean, using proper speech, paying tithing, and obeying the Word of Wisdom.) What else should we do to honor the priesthood?

- Have class members ponder what they can do to better honor the priesthood they now hold or will hold someday.

Conclusion

The priesthood is the power of God. As such, it is the greatest power on earth. We can honor the priesthood by remembering that we hold the authority of God and that the Lord requires that we honor that authority. We bear the priesthood with dignity when we obey the commandments and do all we can to be righteous.

Challenge

Ponder these questions: Is there anything I am doing that is not right for a priesthood holder to do? Am I taking my priesthood seriously enough that it influences all my actions? Pray diligently to get the inner feeling that Elder Talmage described. Try harder to bear the priesthood with dignity by improving your life.

Additional Scriptures

- 1 Peter 2:9 (a chosen generation)

- Doctrine and Covenants 121:39–43 (guidelines for priesthood bearers)

Teacher Preparation

Before presenting this lesson:

1. Read *Duties and Blessings of the Priesthood, Part A,* lesson 2, "The Priesthood from Adam to the Restoration."

2. Prepare to have the class sing "High on the Mountain Top" as an opening song (*Hymns*, no. 5; or *Gospel Principles*, 338).

3. Assign class members to present any stories, scriptures, or quotations you wish.

THE PURPOSE OF PRIESTHOOD ORDINANCES

Lesson 4

The purpose of this lesson is to increase our understanding of priesthood ordinances and their importance in our lives.

Introduction

"We believe that through the Atonement of Christ, all mankind may be saved, by obedience to the laws and ordinances of the Gospel" (Articles of Faith 1:3).

In the Church the word *ordinances* usually refers to rites and ceremonies that the Lord has given us for our salvation, guidance, and comfort (see Bruce R. McConkie, *Mormon Doctrine*, 2nd ed. [1966], 548–49). These ordinances are physical actions that symbolize spiritual experiences. By taking part in them we receive the spiritual power we need to change our lives. For example, baptism represents, among other things, a washing away of sins following true repentance.

Heavenly Father requires that the ordinances of the gospel be performed by men who hold the proper priesthood authority. Only when an ordinance is performed by this authority will our Father in Heaven approve it.

There are two types of priesthood ordinances: those necessary for exaltation and those performed for our comfort and guidance.

Ordinances Necessary for Exaltation

President Wilford Woodruff said, "No [one] will receive of the celestial glory except it be through the ordinances of the House of God" (in *Journal of Discourses*, 19:361; see also D&C 84:20–22). Ordinances that are necessary for us to return to Heavenly Father include baptism, confirmation, the sacrament, conferral of the Melchizedek Priesthood (for brethren), the temple endowment, and temple marriage.

- Display a poster of the following list, or refer to the information on the chalkboard:

4-a, Baptism is the first ordinance of the gospel.

Ordinances Necessary for Exaltation

1. Baptism
2. Confirmation
3. The sacrament
4. Conferral of the Melchizedek Priesthood (for men)
5. The temple endowment
6. Temple marriage

Baptism

- Show visual 4-a, "Baptism is the first ordinance of the gospel."

- Read John 3:3–5. What ordinance is mentioned in this scripture? (Baptism of the water and of the Spirit, or the Holy Ghost)

Baptism is the first ordinance we must receive if we are to return to live with our Heavenly Father. To live with Him we must be spiritually clean and worthy. Through repentance and baptism we are forgiven of our sins and become pure enough to live in the Lord's presence. (See *Duties and Blessings of the Priesthood, Part A,* lesson 29, "Baptism, a Continuing Covenant.")

Being baptized is like beginning a new life. When we are baptized we are placed under the water. The scriptures compare this to burying, or leaving behind, our old self (see Romans 6:4; Mosiah 18:14; D&C 76:51).

When we come out of the water we are washed clean of sin. With our past sins washed away, we receive greater spiritual power to change our lives and become more like Heavenly Father.

- Invite a few class members to share how baptism has affected their lives.

Confirmation

After we are baptized we receive the ordinance of confirmation. In this ordinance, men who hold the Melchizedek Priesthood lay their hands on our heads and (1) confirm us members of The Church of Jesus Christ of Latter-day Saints and (2) bestow on us the gift of the Holy Ghost, also called the "baptism of fire" (2 Nephi 31:13).

- Show visual 4-b, "Bestowing the gift of the Holy Ghost is a Melchizedek Priesthood ordinance."

4-b, Bestowing the gift of the Holy Ghost is a Melchizedek Priesthood ordinance.

Joseph Smith said: "The baptism of water, without the baptism of fire and the Holy Ghost attending it, is of no use; they are necessarily and inseparably connected. An individual must be born of water and the Spirit in order to get into the kingdom of God" (*Teachings of the Prophet Joseph Smith*, sel. Joseph Fielding Smith [1976], 360).

- What advantages are we given with the gift of the Holy Ghost?

The gift of the Holy Ghost gives us the right, through our faith, to have the Holy Ghost as our guide. The Holy Ghost helps us obey the laws, principles, and ordinances of the gospel. He bears witness of the Father and the Son (see 3 Nephi 28:11), shows things to come (see John 16:13), brings things to our remembrance (see John 14:26), and teaches us the truth of all things (see Moroni 10:5). (See *Duties and Blessings of the Priesthood, Part A*, lesson 30, "The Gift of the Holy Ghost.")

- Invite a few class members to share how the Holy Ghost has influenced their lives.

The Sacrament

The ordinance of the sacrament reminds us of the promises we made when we were baptized. We renew our baptismal covenant by partaking of the sacrament. As we partake of the bread and water, we remember our Savior's life and His sacrifice. We remember our promise to follow Him. When taken worthily, the sacrament is a source of spiritual strength. It helps us develop greater power to keep the commandments. With sincere repentance it helps cleanse us of the sins we commit after baptism.

- How can we make the sacrament more meaningful in our lives?

Conferral of the Melchizedek Priesthood

- Show visual 4-c, "To become exalted, men must receive the Melchizedek Priesthood."

Worthy adult male members of the Church should have the Melchizedek Priesthood conferred on them and be ordained to an office in that priesthood. This priesthood allows a man to receive the power and authority of God. It becomes a source of knowledge for him, helping him understand spiritual things. With it he can be authorized to perform the ordinances of salvation for other people, both living and dead.

A woman can receive the blessings of the Melchizedek Priesthood by receiving the ordinances of the gospel and by being married to a righteous priesthood holder. The blessings that come into a home when a man magnifies his priesthood affect his wife as much as they affect him. Perhaps the most important way a woman participates in the blessings

4-c, To become exalted, men must receive the Melchizedek Priesthood.

of the priesthood is by receiving her endowment and being married in the temple.

The Temple Endowment

▪ Show visual 4-d, "Exaltation comes through temple ordinances."

The endowment is a sacred ordinance performed only in the temple. President Brigham Young said, "Your *endowment* is, to receive all those ordinances in the House of the Lord, which are necessary for you, after you have departed this life, to enable you to walk back to the presence of the Father, passing the angels who stand as sentinels, being enabled to give them the key words, the signs and tokens, pertaining to the Holy Priesthood, and gain your eternal exaltation" (in *Journal of Discourses*, 2:31).

The temple endowment teaches us many things that we must know and do in order to return to our Father in Heaven. During the endowment we also promise the Lord to obey the laws of sacrifice and chastity and to be willing to give everything we have to help in His work. Because these promises are so sacred, we receive the endowment only after we have shown diligence in keeping Heavenly Father's commandments. To remind us of these promises, we are given a sacred garment to wear.

▪ How does receiving this ordinance help us return to Heavenly Father?

Temple Marriage

The ordinance of temple marriage is also necessary for us to become like our Father in Heaven. Temple marriage makes it possible for us to have eternal families. When we receive this ordinance worthily and keep the covenants we make, our families will be blessed to live together throughout eternity. Parents should teach children reverence for the temple and prepare them for temple marriage.

Recounting his return to full activity in the Church, one brother explained the importance of a temple marriage to his family:

"One of our lessons [in our branch's institute class] was on temple marriage and vicarious work for the dead. One night soon after, I dreamed that I saw my uncle, who had died nineteen years before, and my stepfather, who had also passed away. They seemed to want something from me. I felt something whisper to me that I must go to the temple, that temple marriage is a commandment of God.

"When I awoke, I knelt down and asked Heavenly Father to permit us to go. Then, wanting to strengthen my resolve, I took out a piece of paper and wrote down the prayer I had just offered. 'Heavenly Father,'

4-d, Exaltation comes through temple ordinances.
(Portland Oregon Temple)

I wrote, 'if it is thy will, I ask thee to let me go to the temple with my wife, Ceci, and my children, Diego and Adrianita.' I awoke my wife and told her what I had done. She cried and hugged me. She knew how hard this goal would be to reach.

"Since we lived in Ambato, Ecuador, the nearest temple was across national boundaries in Lima, Peru. A trip there would involve a lot of paperwork, a thirty-six-hour bus ride, and real economic sacrifice. It would be hard on our children, who had never traveled and were very active. But we were strengthened in our resolve when we received our patriarchal blessings.

"On 20 May 1987, my wife, my daughter, my son, and I finally saw the temple. There was the figure of the angel Moroni, facing heaven from one of the towers. What joy we felt as my wife and I received our endowments and were sealed to our children for eternity! Then we did vicarious ordinance work for our loved ones" (Vicente Muñoz Ulloa, "Our Return to Full Activity," *Tambuli*, Sept. 1994, 22).

- Have a class member read Doctrine and Covenants 131:1–4. According to this scripture, why is it essential to be married in the temple?

- How does knowing that your marriage can be eternal make a difference in your marriage and your other family relationships?

Ordinances for Comfort and Guidance

The Lord has given many priesthood ordinances that we may receive or perform for guidance and comfort. These include the naming and blessing of children, administering to the sick, patriarchal blessings, father's blessings, blessings of guidance and comfort, and dedications of graves.

- Display a poster of the following list, or refer to the information on the chalkboard:

Ordinances for Comfort and Guidance

1. Naming and blessing of children
2. Administering to the sick
3. Patriarchal blessings
4. Father's blessings
5. Blessings of guidance and comfort
6. Dedications of graves

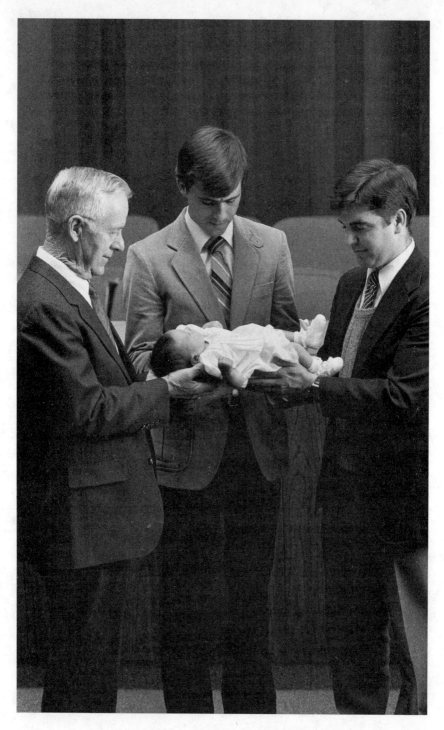

4-e, Infants are usually named and blessed in testimony meeting.

Naming and Blessing of Children

- Show visual 4-e, "Infants are usually named and blessed in testimony meeting."

Children are usually given a name and blessing in a fast and testimony meeting. This ordinance is performed by someone who holds the Melchizedek Priesthood, preferably the father (see D&C 20:70).

After blessing his baby son, a new father spoke about this experience in his testimony. He said: "I am very touched this afternoon. When I stood to bless Mark I wasn't sure what I was going to say, though I did have a few things in mind. But when I actually held him in my hands and began the prayer, impressions began crowding in on my mind. I wasn't left on my own to give my son a blessing: the Lord inspired me through the power of the Holy Ghost to know what to say" (Jay A. Parry, "Miracles Today?" *Ensign*, Jan. 1978, 53).

- Invite a few class members who have performed this ordinance to share their feelings about it.

Administering to the Sick

- Show visual 4-f, "Faithful elders have the power to give the sick a blessing of health."

Just as Jesus blessed the sick, faithful Melchizedek Priesthood holders have the power to bless and heal the sick. Brethren who administer to the sick should seek to know and express the will of the Lord in the blessing (see D&C 42:43–48).

- Invite a few class members to share briefly their experiences with administering to the sick.

Patriarchal Blessings

Patriarchal blessings are inspired blessings given to worthy Church members by ordained patriarchs. These blessings give a person direction and counsel from the Lord. They also reveal the person's lineage in the royal house of Israel. The Church records and preserves patriarchal blessings given by ordained patriarchs. These blessings are personal and sacred and should not be made public.

Father's Blessings

A father who holds the Melchizedek Priesthood may give father's blessings to his children. These blessings may be especially helpful when a child goes to school, goes on a mission, gets married, enters military service, or faces special challenges. A family may record a father's blessing for family records, but it is not preserved in Church records.

Blessings of Guidance and Comfort

A blessing of guidance and comfort may be given by a husband, bishop, branch president, home teacher, or other Melchizedek Priesthood holder. These blessings are similar to father's blessings. They help individuals prepare for special times or overcome problems that require special help from our Heavenly Father.

- Invite a few class members to share briefly their experiences with giving father's blessings and other blessings of guidance and comfort.

Dedications of Graves

The dedication of graves is performed by a Melchizedek Priesthood holder. The dedicatory prayer usually consecrates the burial plot as the resting place of the deceased, prays that the place will be hallowed and protected until the Resurrection (where appropriate), includes words of comfort for the family of the deceased, and includes other thoughts as the Spirit directs.

Conclusion

Heavenly Father has given priesthood ordinances to bless us. These ordinances are accompanied by great spiritual power that helps us become more like Heavenly Father and prepare to return to Him.

To be accepted by God, these ordinances must be performed by the proper priesthood authority. President Lorenzo Snow said: "There is but one way by which exaltation and glory can be secured. We have to be baptized for the remission of sins and have hands laid upon us for the reception of the Holy Ghost. These and other ordinances are absolutely necessary for exaltation and glory" (*Millennial Star*, 27 June 1895, 405).

We should remember that the promised blessings associated with any ordinance are realized only through righteous living.

Challenge

Make specific plans to receive all the ordinances necessary for exaltation. Live worthy to administer priesthood ordinances for others. Plan to make a special, sacred occasion of each ordinance performed for members of your family.

Additional Scriptures

- James 5:14–15 (elders have the power to bless the sick)

- 3 Nephi 11:32–40 (necessity for baptism and the gift of the Holy Ghost)

- Mormon 9:24 (laying on of hands to bless the sick)

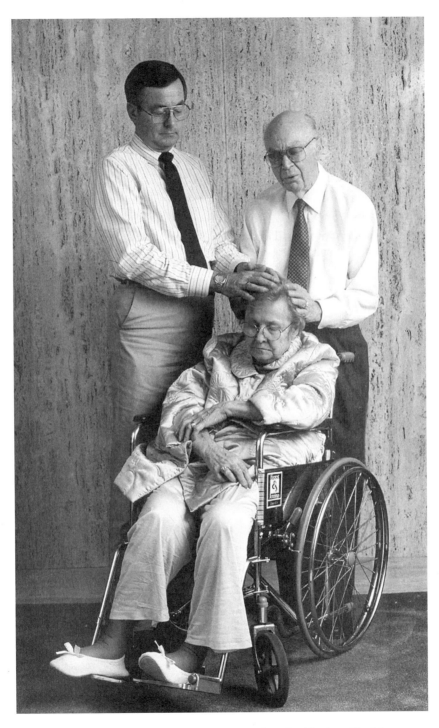

4-f, Faithful elders have the power to give the sick a blessing of health.

- Doctrine and Covenants 20:41 (receiving the gift of the Holy Ghost)

- Doctrine and Covenants 105:33 (endowment to be given)

Teacher Preparation

Before presenting this lesson:

1. Prepare the posters suggested in the lesson, or write the information on the chalkboard.

2. Assign class members to present any stories, scriptures, or quotations you wish.

Note: Do not go into detail about how to perform the ordinances. This information is given in lesson 5.

PERFORMING PRIESTHOOD ORDINANCES

Lesson 5

The purpose of this lesson is to teach us how to perform priesthood ordinances.

Introduction

The Lord has told us, "Wherefore, now let every man learn his duty, and to act in the office in which he is appointed, in all diligence" (D&C 107:99). Priesthood holders should know how to perform priesthood ordinances and be worthy to have the guidance of the Holy Ghost in performing them.

Our ability to bless the lives of others through priesthood ordinances is determined by our faithfulness and obedience. Joseph Fielding Smith stated, "I am sure . . . that we would see more manifestations of the Spirit of God, for instance in the healing of the sick, if we would live just a little nearer to these fundamental truths [of exercising faith in God by performing our duties as members of the Church]" (*Doctrines of Salvation*, comp. Bruce R. McConkie, 3 vols. [1954–56], 2:311–12).

Our effectiveness as priesthood holders can also be enhanced by prayer. Before we perform priesthood ordinances we should seek the Lord in prayer. Even fasting may sometimes be necessary in special circumstances. (See *Duties and Blessings of the Priesthood, Part A,* lesson 31, "Prayer and Fasting.") If we approach the Lord in the spirit of prayer and fasting and live His teachings to the best of our ability, the Spirit will direct us in our priesthood work.

What Ordinances Can We Perform?

- What ordinances can we perform through the priesthood offices we hold? (Use the following information to direct the discussion.)

Deacons

Deacons participate in the sacrament ordinance by passing the bread and water to members of the Church.

Teachers

Teachers participate in the sacrament ordinance by preparing the sacrament. They may also pass the sacrament in the absence of deacons.

Priests

Priests participate in the sacrament ordinance by blessing the bread and water. They may help prepare and pass the sacrament when needed. If authorized by the bishop or branch president, priests can perform the ordinance of baptism, confer the Aaronic Priesthood, and ordain others to offices in the Aaronic Priesthood.

Melchizedek Priesthood Holders

Melchizedek Priesthood holders may perform all the ordinances of the Aaronic Priesthood. In addition, they may bless and name children, confirm members of the Church and bestow the gift of the Holy Ghost, consecrate oil, administer to the sick, dedicate graves, give father's blessings to their children, give blessings of guidance and comfort, and confer the Melchizedek Priesthood when authorized by the stake or mission president. Elders may ordain others to the office of elder, and high priests may ordain others to the office of high priest or elder.

- For more complete information about the ordinances performed by the priesthood, see *Duties and Blessings of the Priesthood, Part A,* lessons 5, 6, 7, and 9.

How to Perform Ordinances

Brethren who perform priesthood ordinances should prepare themselves to be guided by the Holy Spirit. They should perform each ordinance in a dignified manner, making sure it meets the following requirements:

1. All ordinances must be performed in the name of Jesus Christ. When a person performs priesthood ordinances, he should realize that he is acting on behalf of the Savior.

2. All ordinances must be performed by the authority of the priesthood. Only brethren who hold the necessary priesthood and are worthy should perform or stand in the circle for an ordinance.

3. The following ordinances must be authorized by the presiding authority who holds the proper keys (normally the bishop or stake president): naming and blessing children, baptizing, confirming, administering the sacrament, conferring the priesthood and ordaining to an office, and dedicating graves. Consecrating oil, administering to the sick, and giving father's blessings do not need to be authorized by the presiding authority. A man is authorized to perform these ordinances if he holds the Melchizedek Priesthood and is worthy.

4. All ordinances must be performed with their necessary procedures such as using specified words or laying on hands.

"Priesthood leaders teach brethren how to perform ordinances and blessings. Leaders also help fathers be prepared and worthy to perform ordinances and blessings for family members" (*Church Handbook of Instructions, Book 2: Priesthood and Auxiliary Leaders* [1998], 171).

■ The following information concerns the basic ordinances of the gospel administered by the priesthood. Under the direction of priesthood leaders, select some of the following ordinances to review with class members.

Naming and Blessing of Children

Under the direction of the presiding authority, only brethren who hold the Melchizedek Priesthood may participate in the ordinance of naming and blessing children (see D&C 20:70). Worthy fathers who hold the Melchizedek Priesthood should be encouraged to bless their own children.

When blessing a baby, brethren gather in a circle and place their hands under the baby. When blessing an older child, brethren place their hands lightly on the child's head. The person who gives the blessing:

1. Addresses Heavenly Father.

2. States that the blessing is performed by the authority of the Melchizedek Priesthood.

3. Gives the child a name.

4. Gives a priesthood blessing as the Spirit directs.

5. Closes in the name of Jesus Christ.

Baptism

The ordinance of baptism is performed only by a worthy priest or Melchizedek Priesthood holder under the direction of the presiding authority. The priesthood holder:

1. Stands in the water with the person to be baptized.

2. (For convenience and safety) holds the person's right wrist with his left hand; the person being baptized holds the priesthood holder's left wrist with his or her left hand.

3. Raises his right arm to the square.

4. States the person's full name and says, "Having been commissioned of Jesus Christ, I baptize you in the name of the Father, and of the Son, and of the Holy Ghost. Amen" (D&C 20:73).

5. Has the person hold his or her nose with the right hand (for convenience); then the priesthood holder places his right hand high on the person's back and immerses the person completely, including the person's clothing.

6. Helps the person come up out of the water.

Each baptism must be witnessed by two priests or Melchizedek Priesthood holders, who make sure it is performed properly. The baptism must be repeated if the prayer was not stated accurately or if part of the body or clothing of the person being baptized was not immersed completely.

Confirmation

A person receives the ordinance of confirmation after he or she has been baptized (see D&C 20:41). Under the direction of the bishopric or branch presidency, one or more Melchizedek Priesthood holders may participate in this ordinance. They place their hands lightly on the person's head. Then the person who performs the ordinance:

1. States the person's full name.

2. States that the ordinance is performed by the authority of the Melchizedek Priesthood.

3. Confirms the person a member of The Church of Jesus Christ of Latter-day Saints.

4. Bestows the gift of the Holy Ghost by saying, "Receive the Holy Ghost."

5. Gives a priesthood blessing as the Spirit directs.

6. Closes in the name of Jesus Christ.

The Sacrament

The sacrament is a very sacred ordinance and is administered under the direction of the bishopric or branch presidency. Aaronic Priesthood holders usually perform these duties. However, Melchizedek Priesthood holders may bless and pass the sacrament when there are not enough Aaronic Priesthood brethren or if the bishop or branch president occasionally invites them to do so.

Every priesthood holder who participates in this ordinance should understand that he is acting on behalf of the Lord. The personal appearance and attitude of all who participate should reflect the sacred nature of the ordinance. Priesthood holders should wash their hands before preparing, blessing, or passing the sacrament.

Worthy teachers, priests, and Melchizedek Priesthood holders may prepare the sacrament. Before the meeting begins, those who prepare the sacrament should make sure that clean bread trays with unbroken bread, clean water trays with cups filled with fresh water, and clean white tablecloths are in place.

Worthy priests and Melchizedek Priesthood holders may bless the sacrament. Worthy deacons, teachers, priests, and Melchizedek Priesthood holders may pass the sacrament.

During the sacrament hymn, the priesthood holders who will bless the sacrament should break the bread into bite-sized pieces. Following the hymn, the person who blesses the bread kneels and offers the sacrament prayer for the bread (see D&C 20:77). The sacrament prayers were revealed by the Lord. The bishop or branch president makes sure that they are spoken clearly, accurately, and with dignity. If the bishop or branch president must correct an error, he should be careful to avoid causing embarrassment or distracting from the sacred nature of the ordinance.

After the prayer, deacons or other priesthood holders pass the bread to the congregation in a reverent and orderly manner. The presiding officer receives the sacrament first. When brethren finish passing the bread, they return the trays to the sacrament table. Those officiating at the sacrament table replace the cloth over the bread trays and uncover the water trays. The person who blesses the water kneels and offers the sacrament prayer for the water (see D&C 20:79), substituting the word *water* for *wine*. After the prayer, deacons or other priesthood holders pass the water to the congregation. When they finish, they return the trays to the sacrament table, wait for the officiators to cover the trays, then reverently take their seats.

Conferral of the Priesthood and Ordination to a Priesthood Office

Ordination to an office in the Aaronic Priesthood is done by or under the direction of the bishop or branch president. Ordination to an office in the Melchizedek Priesthood is done by or under the direction of the stake or mission president. To perform a priesthood ordination, one or more authorized priesthood holders place their hands lightly on the person's head. The priesthood bearer who performs the ordination:

1. Calls the person by his full name.

2. States the authority by which the ordination is performed (Aaronic or Melchizedek Priesthood).

3. Confers the Aaronic or Melchizedek Priesthood unless it has already been conferred.

4. Ordains the person to an office in the Aaronic or Melchizedek Priesthood and bestows the rights, powers, and authority of that office.

5. Gives a priesthood blessing as the Spirit directs.

6. Closes in the name of Jesus Christ.

Consecration of Oil

One or more Melchizedek Priesthood holders must consecrate olive oil before it is used to anoint the sick or afflicted. No other oil may be used. To do this, a priesthood holder:

1. Holds an open container of olive oil.

2. Addresses Heavenly Father.

3. States that he is acting by the authority of the Melchizedek Priesthood.

4. Consecrates the oil (not the container) and sets it apart for anointing and blessing the sick and afflicted.

5. Closes in the name of Jesus Christ.

▪ Have each Melchizedek Priesthood holder consecrate some olive oil for himself and for others in the class who may need some in their home.

Administering to the Sick

Only Melchizedek Priesthood holders may administer to the sick or afflicted. Administering to the sick has two parts: (1) anointing with oil and (2) sealing the anointing.

The anointing is done by one Melchizedek Priesthood holder. He:

1. Puts a small amount of consecrated oil on the person's head.

2. Places his hands lightly on the person's head and calls the person by his or her full name.

3. States that he is acting by the authority of the Melchizedek Priesthood.

4. States that he is anointing with consecrated oil.

5. Closes in the name of Jesus Christ.

Normally, two or more Melchizedek Priesthood holders place their hands lightly on the person's head. The one who seals the anointing:

1. Calls the person by his or her full name.

2. States that he is acting by the authority of the Melchizedek Priesthood.

3. Seals the anointing.

4. Gives a priesthood blessing as the Spirit directs.

5. Closes in the name of Jesus Christ.

If a person requests more than one blessing for the same illness, the priesthood holder usually does not need to anoint with oil after the first blessing. Instead, he gives a blessing by the laying on of hands and the authority of the priesthood.

Dedication of Graves

Graves should be dedicated by a Melchizedek Priesthood holder, as authorized by the priesthood officer who conducts the service. To dedicate a grave, he:

1. Addresses Heavenly Father.
2. States that he is acting by the authority of the Melchizedek Priesthood.
3. Dedicates and consecrates the burial plot as the resting place for the body of the deceased.
4. (Where appropriate) prays that the place may be hallowed and protected until the Resurrection.
5. Asks the Lord to comfort the family and expresses thoughts as the Spirit directs.
6. Closes in the name of Jesus Christ.

Father's Blessings and Blessings of Comfort and Counsel

Fathers and others who hold the Melchizedek Priesthood may give blessings of comfort and counsel. Fathers may give their children blessings on special occasions such as when the children enter military service or leave home to go to school or on missions. A family may record a father's blessing in family records, but it is not preserved in Church records.

To give a father's blessing or other blessings of comfort and counsel, one or more worthy Melchizedek Priesthood holders place their hands lightly on the person's head. Then the priesthood leader who gives the blessing:

1. Calls the person by his or her full name.
2. States that the blessing is performed by the authority of the Melchizedek Priesthood.
3. Blesses the person as the Spirit directs.
4. Closes in the name of Jesus Christ.

Conclusion

As priesthood holders, we should prepare ourselves for times when we need to perform ordinances. Being ready to perform priesthood ordinances means that we are living the commandments to the best of our ability and that we understand how to perform the ordinances. Such preparation will bless ourselves and others.

Challenge

Study the procedures for performing ordinances. Set a goal to study one each week. Think of one area in your life in which you can improve your worthiness to perform priesthood ordinances. Resolve to improve your life in that area.

Additional Scriptures

- Matthew 3:13–17 (baptism of Jesus)

- Mark 6:13 (sick anointed with oil)

- Mark 16:17–18 (laying hands on the sick)

- James 5:14–16 (elders of the Church to anoint the sick)

- 3 Nephi 11:22–26 (method of baptism)

- Moroni 2:2 (Holy Ghost bestowed by the laying on of hands)

- Doctrine and Covenants 42:11 (men to be ordained by those in authority)

Teacher Preparation

Before presenting this lesson:

1. Read *Duties and Blessings of the Priesthood, Part A,* lessons 4, "The Priesthood Quorum," and 31, "Prayer and Fasting."

2. Obtain several small bottles of pure olive oil—one for each family represented in the class. This will enable every home to have a bottle of consecrated oil to be used by Melchizedek Priesthood bearers when giving blessings.

3. Plan to move rapidly through the first section of the lesson in order to spend most of the class time discussing the ordinances.

4. Assign class members to present any stories, scriptures, or quotations you wish.

HOME TEACHING

Lesson 6

The purpose of this lesson is to help us understand and fulfill our responsibilities as home teachers.

Introduction

As teachers, priests, or Melchizedek Priesthood holders, we may be assigned to be home teachers. This assignment gives us an opportunity to magnify the priesthood by teaching, visiting, watching over, and assisting Church members.

Elder Boyd K. Packer said, "I have heard men say in response to a question about their Church assignment, 'I am only a home teacher.' " He then explained that home teaching is one of the most important priesthood assignments in the Church. Home teachers are guardians of a flock. They are appointed where the ministry matters most. They are servants of the Lord. (In Conference Report, Oct. 1972, 104; or *Ensign,* Jan. 1973, 90.)

■ Show visual 6-a, "Home teachers are assigned by their quorum leader."

Melchizedek Priesthood quorum leaders give home teaching assignments to quorum members after consulting with the bishop or branch president. A member of the bishopric or branch presidency assigns teachers and priests of the Aaronic Priesthood to be home teachers. Priesthood leaders usually assign two brethren to be home teaching companions, with Aaronic Priesthood brethren serving as junior companions.

Home Teachers—Servants of the Lord

The following story shows the importance of home teaching:

As home teachers, Brother Earl Stowell and his companion were assigned to visit some less-active families. Brother Stowell related: "We arrived at this particular door. Being short, I usually tip my head back to look someone in the face. But this time I had to drop my head as the door opened, and the doorway framed a little man no more than five feet tall.

6-a, Home teachers are assigned by their quorum leader.

- Show visual 6-b, "Little Ben."

"He was thin [and old], but his erect stature and energetic movements let us know every year had to fight to sit on his unbowed shoulders. His tiny piercing eyes were set wide apart. His mouth was a straight gash, set low in his face, and running from ear to ear, or so it seemed. His skin was as grained leather.

"We said we were neighbors and members of the Church, that we had come by to get acquainted. He seemed uncomfortable as he invited us into a tiny living room, well-furnished with ash trays. . . . He said he drove a truck. I imagined a pickup; it turned out to be a big dump truck. I was amazed.

" 'Drivers are usually pretty hefty. How do you—'

"He cut me off. 'I got a twelve-inch crescent wrench on the seat by me. The other guys know it. That makes us equal.' . . .

"As the months slipped by, we began looking forward to our visits with Ben. [One evening when we visited him, he was tired from working on his truck] so we stayed only a few minutes. As we approached the door, little Ben looked up and asked, 'When yuh goin' to start tellin' me what I ought to be doin'—stop smokin', start comin' to priesthood and church, and all that?'

" 'Ben,' I told him, 'both of us would be more happy if you were doing those things, but that is for you to decide. We'd just be insulting you if we tried to tell you what to do when you already know. We come to see you because—well, because our family isn't complete without you.' He hung onto my hand. . . .

"A phone call later that week asked, 'What time is priesthood meeting?' I told him and offered to pick him up just for company.

" 'No, I know the way and no one has to drive me where I ought to be.'

"I found him standing outside the church. 'Maybe I hadn't better go in until I quit smoking,' he said. I told him it would be easier to do with the Lord's help. He said, 'I smoked since I was eight, and I'm not sure I can quit.' I told him I thought he could.

"He was soon dubbed Little Ben, behind his back, and in spite of his almost total lack of formal education, his size, and his age, he soon made firm friends and was in the thick of any project undertaken by the elders quorum.

"Then one evening I got a phone call. 'I got to talk to you.' His voice sounded as if he were on the edge of hysteria. 'They want me to be a [home] teacher. I can't do that. I smoke and I don't know nuthin'. How can I teach people what I don't know? . . . What am I goin' to do?'

6-b, "Little Ben"

"I too was shaken. Little Ben was special to us, and we didn't want him to get lost again. Inwardly I began to pray as hard as I could. Then I took a deep breath and began, 'Ben, did we ever try to tell you what to do?'

" 'No, you just showed I was important to you, made me feel important. Maybe that was why I started going to church myself.'

" 'When we met you, we discovered someone worth any effort we could make. Now can you call on these people and remember how important they are? Can you just tell them they are important enough that you want to sit with them now and then and tell them about something you found that is so valuable to you, you'd like to share it with them?'

"There were several moments of silence, and then, 'By Golly, I'll do her!'

"At day's end I frequently drove down the street where several of Ben's families lived. All were confirmed inactives, mostly with non-member husbands or wives, and strangers to the Church for many years. One evening I saw Little Ben toting the largest watermelon I had seen that season. His fingers were interlaced under it and every step was an effort. He was three blocks from the market. As I drove by, he turned into one of the houses.

"When next I saw him, I mentioned it. He hung his head, 'Well, on my way home I passed the market. I got to thinkin' about those kids. Their daddy is out of work. Watermelon is scarce and high this year. I knew the kids hadn't had any. And to make sure every kid would get all they wanted, I bought the biggest melon in the store.'

"Later I saw him walking briskly in the evening heat holding a big birthday card in his hand. He explained later, 'This one little girl has all brothers. They get all the attention. So I figgerd if I carried the card to her instead of mailing it, that would let her know she was important. Just like a few weeks ago at another place, some kids had pulled the arm off a doll. No one but the little girl seemed to care. I took her doll home, got an old button-hook out of the bureau, and fished out the spring that held the arm on. I got her fixed all right. Took the whole evening, but it was worth it when I took it back. Now when I go there, she gets her doll, sits on the floor in front of me, and leans her head against me.' I thought I detected a catch in his voice.

"Shortly after that, I got an excited phone call. 'A little girl I [home] teach is getting baptized!' It was a tangible result [of his home teaching]. I too was excited. . . .

"In the previous five years, those families had had no Church contact other than [home] teachers and an occasional call from a visiting

6-c, Home teachers are assigned to visit families.

teacher. But eight times in the next three years Little Ben called, always excited, to tell me of a blessing to be done, an upcoming baptism, or a priesthood advancement for a young boy. I asked how he was able to touch their lives so. 'I just did what you told me. I let them know I wasn't better than they were and hadn't come to tell them what they should be doin'. I was there because the good Lord had set a spiritual table for his family, and when they didn't share it with us, it left an empty place at the table, the family wasn't complete' " ("Little Ben," *Ensign*, Mar. 1977, 66–68).

■ Why were Little Ben's home teachers successful? What can we learn from them and from Little Ben to help us as home teachers?

Responsibilities of Home Teachers

■ Show visual 6-c, "Home teachers are assigned to visit families."

The responsibility of home teachers to visit the homes of members and encourage them to pray and attend to their family duties was given by the Lord. He has called them to be "watchmen" to care for and watch after His children (see Jeremiah 31:6; Ezekiel 33:1–9).

President Harold B. Lee said home teachers should understand that their mission is to watch over, strengthen, and help members do their duty. He asked priesthood leaders to change the emphasis from being home *teachers* teaching lessons to being home *guardians* watching over the Church. When we understand this idea, we will do home teaching that will get results. (See regional representatives' seminar, Apr. 1972, 8.)

■ What does it mean to be a guardian over the Church? Why is it important that the families we home teach know we care about them before we try to teach them? (Refer to the story of Little Ben.)

As home teachers we represent the bishop or branch president to the people we serve. In regular interviews with priesthood leaders we report on our home teaching visits and on the needs of these members. If members become seriously ill or have other problems that might require the attention of priesthood leaders, we should report them immediately.

Meeting the Needs of Members

As home teachers we should prayerfully determine the individual and family needs of the members we serve. Then we should plan and work to help meet those needs, providing support and encouragement. Merely offering to help is not enough.

One need that everyone has is the presence and influence of the Spirit. President David O. McKay said, "It is our duty as Home Teachers to carry the divine spirit into every home and heart" (quoted by Marion G. Romney, "The Responsibilities of Home Teachers," *Ensign*, Mar.

1973, 15). To help families obtain the Spirit, we should encourage them to hold family home evening, have family and individual prayer, and participate actively in the Church (see D&C 20:51, 53–55).

People also need help during times of sickness. The Lord has counseled that in such times we should "call for the elders of the church" (James 5:14; see also verse 15). As home teachers we should know when members of our assigned families are sick, and we should be worthy and ready to administer to them if they request it.

Home teachers should also provide help when an individual or family faces special challenges or becomes discouraged.

- What needs do most families have? (List the responses on the chalkboard. Add other needs to this list as they are suggested later in the lesson.)

- How did Little Ben meet the needs of his home teaching families?

The following story illustrates how a good home teacher helped a family:

"Brother and Sister Robertson . . . were a young and active couple in the Church who failed to hold family prayer or family home evening 'because there are just the two of us.' We had presented lessons on these subjects and encouraged them, but to no avail. . . .

"During the next two weeks my companion and I met several times to discuss the possible needs of our families. We pinpointed those things that we felt needed our special attention. And then on our next visit we tried our new approach. To Brother and Sister Robertson it wasn't, 'What can we do to help?', but rather, 'Won't you meet with us next Thursday at my home and join us in a special family home evening?' . . . [They replied,] 'Why yes, thank you!' . . .

"After a recent sacrament meeting, Brother and Sister Robertson came up to me and shared their sincere testimonies, telling me how the happiness in their home has increased since they have begun holding family prayer and family home evening" (Don B. Center, "The Day We Really Started Home Teaching," *Ensign*, June 1977, 18–19).

Helping the Head of the Family

- Show visual 6-d, "Home teachers are to assist the head of the household in leading the family."

The head of the family—the father, unless no father is present—has the primary responsibility for leading the family toward exaltation. As home teachers we will be most effective as we help the head of the family achieve this.

6-d, Home teachers are to assist the head of the household in leading the family.

One of the best ways of finding out how we can help is first to have a private, personal visit with the head of the family. At this time, we can ask about the needs of the family and what we can do to help meet those needs.

The following account shows how two home teachers worked through the head of a family:

"Samuel Bowen was [not a member] of the Church. His wife and children were members and because of this, many auxiliary and home teaching visits were made to the Bowen family. These visits were usually directed specifically to the members of the Church in the home. As a result, Brother Bowen would excuse himself or not present himself at the time of a visit. . . .

"Within the last two years, a new home teacher, Brother Walker, was assigned to the Bowen family. After he met with them and had discussed the situation with the priesthood leader, Brother Walker felt strongly impressed to concentrate his attention on . . . Brother Bowen. In the ensuing months, he did this in a deliberate, well-thought-out manner. For example, he [made appointments] through Brother Bowen. . . . On these visits he would discuss how he might be helpful to each member of his family. At first, Brother Bowen was taken back by this deference to him since it was not according to the accustomed pattern, but he soon grew to appreciate Brother Walker. Many cordial visits were made to the home, but seldom was a direct gospel message delivered to the family.

"One evening Brother Walker was visiting privately with Brother Bowen in his living room. He asked, 'Sam, how is it that with such a wonderful family in the Church and all their activity, that you have never contemplated membership in the Church?' Brother Walker was startled by the reply: 'I guess no one ever asked me if I was interested. Actually, I have read much of your Church literature and believe as you do.'

"A month later, Samuel Bowen was baptized into the Church, and today his family has been sealed . . . in the temple" (*When Thou Art Converted, Strengthen Thy Brethren* [Melchizedek Priesthood manual, 1974], 217–18).

- Ask the assigned home teacher to bear his testimony about home teaching. Then ask the assigned father to bear his testimony about how home teaching has blessed his family.

Conclusion

As home teachers we are given responsibility to watch over Church members. We are to visit them regularly, teach them the gospel, and encourage them to live righteously. We should develop love for each person we serve. We should also work prayerfully with the head of each family in identifying and helping meet the family's needs.

Challenge

Prayerfully determine ways you can improve your performance as a home teacher, help your companion be a better home teacher, work with the head of each assigned family, and meet the needs of individual family members.

Discuss with your own family how you can help your home teachers.

Additional Scriptures

- John 21:15–17 (commanded to teach others)

- 2 Timothy 2:2 (the faithful to teach others)

- 1 Peter 5:1–4 (responsibility and potential glory of elders)

- Doctrine and Covenants 46:27 (gift of discernment given to home teachers)

- Doctrine and Covenants 84:106 (the strong to edify the weak)

Teacher Preparation

Before presenting this lesson:

1. Study Doctrine and Covenants 20:46–47, 53–55.

2. Ask a home teacher to prepare to bear his testimony about home teaching at the conclusion of the lesson.

3. Ask a father to prepare to bear his testimony about the effect home teaching has had on his family at the conclusion of the lesson.

4. Assign class members to present any stories, scriptures, or quotations you wish.

SELF-RELIANCE

Lesson 7

The purpose of this lesson is to help us be self-reliant.

Introduction

On 9 February 1971 an earthquake shook California's San Fernando Valley. Sister Ina Easton described some of the conditions following the earthquake:

"From early Tuesday morning, February 9—shortly after the earthquake hit—to late Friday afternoon, February 12, we had in our home 17 [to] 22 guests to care for. We had no electricity for a day and a night and no gas for heating and cooking or sufficient water for the time they were here.

". . . It was a real challenge to care for so many with limited space and facilities. We were able to manage well under the circumstances, thanks to our wonderful guests and the Church food and water storage plan. . . . All of the stores were down that were near us. Roads were broken. We could not go to the grocery store. We were thankful and grateful for the food and water that we had stored. . . .

"We learned many things. Among them were good storage items: soap and detergents that dissolve in cold water; old towels . . . ; toilet tissue and paper towels; toothbrushes and toothpaste. . . . What about extra clothing—one change for each member of the family? First-aid materials are a must. We had cut feet and injuries everywhere. Some of them were not serious, but they became so because there were not supplies to bandage and care for them. Many children cried because they were hungry and uncomfortable. Babies were especially unhappy. Baby food, bottles, blankets, formula, and disposable diapers would have made the difference. . . . Some things people forgot in their hurry were heart pills and diabetic medicine. In some cases, it was really tragic.

"We found that a portable gas stove is a valuable thing to have. Its fuel is safe and easy to store. A gas lantern gives wonderful light when the electricity is gone. . . .

"There is much more that could be said, but the important thing for all of us to remember is that the Lord has told us to store food, water, clothing, and money, because someday we will need them. My testimony is that we did need them. By obeying the commandments given to us by our leaders, we had plenty and enough to share with our wonderful friends and ward members that were forced to leave their homes" (*Relief Society Courses of Study 1977–78*, 78–79).

The Lord's Plan

The Lord's plan for Church members to be self-reliant is simple. It is that we do our best to provide for our personal and family needs by developing good work habits; being thrifty; gathering a home supply of items necessary to sustain us for at least one year; planning for our future needs; and maintaining physical, spiritual, emotional, and social health. Self-reliance begins at home, with the individual and the family.

- Who is responsible to care for our needs and the needs of our loved ones?

If we cannot provide for our own needs, we should first seek help from relatives. For example, a person who is disabled may require more help than the immediate family can provide. In this case, other relatives should be asked to assist. Finally, if we cannot meet our basic needs through our own best efforts and the efforts of relatives, we can seek temporary help from the Church.

Being well prepared not only helps us care for ourselves, but it also helps us assist others in times of need. We grow spiritually as we give unselfishly of our means, time, and talents to help others.

- Why do you think Heavenly Father wants us to provide for ourselves and our families?

- How are we blessed when we help others in need?

Preparing Our Families

- Display a poster of the Self-Reliance Chart (visual 7-a), or refer to the information on the chalkboard.

Members of the Church should become self-reliant in the six basic areas that follow.

Home Storage

Where legal and when possible, each person and family should have enough food to take care of basic needs for a minimum of one year. This means that we should grow and preserve food and then use and replace that food to avoid spoilage (see lesson 16 in this manual for a discussion on home gardening). We should also know how to make clothing and, if possible, store fuel and medical supplies. Production and storage help us care for ourselves, our own families, and others in times of need. (See *Duties and Blessings of the Priesthood, Part A,* lesson 22, "Home Production and Storage.")

- How can we increase our self-reliance in home production and storage?

Physical Health

Our physical bodies are sacred, and it is important that we keep them clean, strong, and healthy. As revealed in the Word of Wisdom, we should eat nutritious foods and not consume alcohol, tobacco, and other harmful substances (see D&C 89). To avoid disease we should keep our homes and yards clean and receive the immunizations recommended for our area. We should exercise regularly, keep ourselves clean, and follow other practices of good health. As we keep our bodies healthy we are better able to care for our own needs and serve others.

- How can we improve our physical health?

Spiritual, Emotional, and Social Strength

We should strengthen ourselves and our families spiritually, emotionally, and socially. As we do so we will be better prepared to work through problems and sorrows. Elder Boyd K. Packer said:

"It was meant to be that life would be a challenge. To suffer some anxiety, some depression, some disappointment, even some failure is normal.

"Teach our members that if they have a . . . miserable day once in a while, or several in a row, to stand steady and face them. Things will straighten out.

"There is great purpose in our struggle in life" (in Conference Report, Apr. 1978, 140; or *Ensign,* May 1978, 93).

When challenges come, we should love, support, and encourage one another. By helping each other, we develop the strength to overcome our problems. Elder Marvin J. Ashton told of a family that developed this kind of strength:

The youngest daughter suffered severe brain damage at birth and was never able to grow or develop normally. She died when she was 17 years old, but the family grew stronger during that time. Elder Ashton observed: "Constant care from a loving mother, patience and warmth from a kind father, and understanding from three noble brothers and a thoughtful sister made her presence special in the family. . . . [Her father] said, 'Nothing that money could buy could have ever brought

Self-Reliance Chart

7-a, The six areas of self-reliance

us together in love, patience, and humility like just taking care of her did.' Here was a tragedy . . . turned into an opportunity for blessings" ("Family Home Storage," in *1977 Devotional Speeches of the Year*, 69).

As this story illustrates, a kind, prayerful, loving family relationship can be a great blessing in the life of every family member. Such a relationship should be the goal of every family. Elder Marvin J. Ashton explained:

"Often the greatest [helps] we receive come from within the ranks of our families. Sometimes the hands needed most are those closest to us. . . . God has decreed family members are to help family members. . . .

"We must take family members by the hand and show our love is real and continuing" (in Conference Report, Oct. 1973, 131; or *Ensign*, Jan. 1974, 104).

- How can we develop and give emotional support in our families?

- Why is helping, understanding, and loving others important to our peace and happiness? How can this help us prepare for the future?

Education

In the Doctrine and Covenants the Lord tells us that "the glory of God is intelligence, or, in other words, light and truth" and commands us "to bring up [our] children in light and truth" (D&C 93:36, 40). Each of us should learn to read, write, and do basic mathematics and then teach these skills to our children. We should study the scriptures regularly, as well as other good books, and read them with our children. We should take advantage of public and other educational opportunities.

- Why should we and our families learn to read, write, and do basic mathematics? Why is education important?

Employment

When possible, we should obtain jobs that will enable us to provide adequately for our families and that will provide us personal satisfaction. Our employment should also be in harmony with Church teachings and allow us to fulfill our Church duties. In addition to obtaining such employment for ourselves, we should counsel our children and other youth in selecting an appropriate career.

Elder Marvin J. Ashton advised: "Make education a continuing process. Complete as much formal, full-time education as possible. This includes the trade schools. This is money well invested. Use night school and correspondence classes to further prepare. Acquire some special skill or ability that could be used to avoid prolonged unemployment" ("One for the Money," *Ensign*, July 1975, 73).

- Discuss the resources that are available to help class members develop their employment skills. Resources may include correspondence courses offered by universities, community courses for adults, internships, and on-the-job training. Find out from your bishop or branch president if your ward or branch has a welfare specialist who is responsible for employment. If so, explain that the specialist can help members find employment.

- How can young men prepare themselves for a career?

Resource Management

To be prepared financially, we should learn how to live within our income. This requires setting up and managing a budget. A working budget includes making practical financial goals, paying tithes and offerings, and avoiding debt. In addition to a budget, wise management of our income includes buying food and other essential items when they are least expensive, avoiding waste, and, if possible, developing a savings fund to provide for emergency financial needs.

One family offered the following suggestion for managing family finances: "One thing that never works . . . is the attitude, 'This is *my* money, so I'll spend it the way I like.' No matter whether the husband or the wife is bringing in the money, all the money should belong equally to both. Neither the husband nor the wife has the right to go spending 'because it belongs to me' " (Orson Scott Card, "Family Finances," *Ensign,* June 1978, 13).

- How does wise use of money bring peace to the home?

- Have class members ponder how well prepared they and their families are in each of the six basic areas of self-reliance.

Being Prepared to Help as a Church

The Lord has asked us to help one another in addition to caring for our own individual and family needs (see D&C 52:40). Sometimes our efforts to help others can be on our own initiative. Other times the efforts and resources of Church members are combined and used as directed by priesthood leaders.

Elder Joseph B. Wirthlin explained:

"The Church does not limit its relief efforts to its members but follows the admonition of the Prophet Joseph Smith when he said, 'A man filled with the love of God, is not content with blessing his family alone, but ranges through the whole world, anxious to bless the whole human race.' He instructed members 'to feed the hungry, to clothe the naked, to provide for the widow, to dry up the tear of the orphan, to comfort the afflicted.'

"In a little over a decade, the Church has shipped more than 27,000 tons of clothing, 16,000 tons of food, and 3,000 tons of medical and education supplies and equipment to relieve the suffering of millions of God's children in 146 countries in many parts of the world. We do not ask, 'Are you members of our church?' We ask only, 'Do you suffer?' " (in Conference Report, Apr. 1999, 100; or *Ensign,* May 1999, 77).

The following are examples of disasters that required help from the Church to aid local efforts:

"In the devastating floods in Rapid City, South Dakota [USA], the Saints in that area responded immediately to assist the victims of the rampaging water. Clothing, bedding, and warm food were furnished through the efforts of the local Church organization. . . . Only one truckload of items, such as baby food, diapers, and blankets, [needed to be] shipped in" (Junior Wright Child, "Welfare Is the Church," *Ensign,* Sept. 1973, 71).

Following the December 1972 earthquake in Managua, Nicaragua, in Central America, "the only thing sent to these Saints from [the United States] was typhoid serum. . . . All other assistance was acquired locally; the Saints in Costa Rica, arranging the relief supplies and working through government officials, administered the program" (*Ensign,* Sept. 1973, 71).

Elder Russell M. Nelson explained that "such cooperative efforts to help neighbors in distress transcend any barriers posed by religion, race, or culture. Those good deeds are latter-day love in action!" (in Conference Report, Apr. 1994, 91; or *Ensign,* May 1994, 70).

We need to prepare as a Church, as individuals, and as families to survive in emergencies. When the Church is fully organized in our area, we can work together to prepare food, clothing, and household items to be used in emergencies. This way, those who are in need and whose families have done all they can will receive this help. If we help each other in every way we can, we will be worthy to receive help if we need it.

Conclusion

As we actively work toward becoming self-reliant, our love for our families and others will increase and our testimony of the need for self-reliance will grow. With that testimony we will want to help others help themselves.

The Lord said, "All things unto me are spiritual, and not at any time have I given unto you a law which was temporal" (D&C 29:34). The foundation of helping ourselves and others is love and charity. The Savior said, "Inasmuch as ye have done it unto one of the least of these my brethren, ye have done it unto me" (Matthew 25:40).

Challenge

In your next family home evening, evaluate your self-reliance. Identify any weak areas, and make plans for improvement. As a home teacher, be aware of the needs of the families under your care. Encourage them to prepare themselves to meet their needs.

Additional Scriptures

- 1 Timothy 5:8 (we must provide for our families)

- 1 John 3:17 (the importance of helping others)

- Alma 34:28 (our obligation to help others)

- Doctrine and Covenants 56:16–18 (admonitions to the rich and the poor)

- Doctrine and Covenants 68:30–32 (idlers chastised)

Teacher Preparation

Before presenting this lesson:

1. Study *Gospel Principles* chapters 27, "Work and Personal Responsibility," and 37, "Family Responsibilities."

2. Prepare the poster suggested in the lesson, or write the information on the chalkboard.

3. Assign class members to present any stories, scriptures, or quotations you wish.

OUR TEMPLE AND FAMILY HISTORY RESPONSIBILITIES

Lesson 8

The purpose of this lesson is to help us understand our temple and family history responsibilities.

Ordinances Are Necessary for Salvation

In order to return to the presence of our Heavenly Father, each of us must receive the ordinances necessary for salvation. Elder Boyd K. Packer said:

"Ordinances and covenants become our credentials for admission into His presence. To worthily receive them is the quest of a lifetime; to keep them thereafter is the challenge of mortality.

"Once we have received them for ourselves and for our families, we are obligated to provide these ordinances vicariously for our kindred dead, indeed for the whole human family" (in Conference Report, Apr. 1987, 27; or *Ensign,* May 1987, 24).

Receiving Our Own Temple Ordinances and Helping Family Members Receive Theirs

Baptism and confirmation, the first ordinances of the gospel, are the gate by which we enter the narrow path that leads to eternal life (see 2 Nephi 31:17–18). To continue on this path after baptism, we must also receive the sacred ordinances of the temple—the endowment and the sealing ordinances. We must remain faithful to the covenants we make. These ordinances are essential to our exaltation.

President Howard W. Hunter explained the importance of temple ordinances: "All of our efforts in proclaiming the gospel, perfecting the Saints, and redeeming the dead lead to the holy temple. This is because the temple ordinances are absolutely crucial; we cannot return to God's presence without them. I encourage everyone to worthily attend the temple or to work toward the day when you can enter that holy house to receive your ordinances and covenants" (in Conference Report, Oct. 1994, 118; or *Ensign,* Nov. 1994, 88).

Adult members who have not yet been to the temple should talk to their bishop or branch president to find out how to prepare to receive temple blessings. We should also instill in our children and other family members a desire to prepare for baptism and temple ordinances.

- How can we teach our children and other family members the importance of the temple? (Write the responses on the chalkboard. These could include setting a good example by attending the temple regularly or actively working toward going, holding a temple recommend, expressing gratitude in our family prayers for the temple and its ordinances, and taking children 12 years of age and older to the temple to be baptized for the dead.)

Holding a Current Recommend and Going to the Temple Regularly

- Display visual 8-a, "A house of the Lord."

Regarding temples, President Gordon B. Hinckley said: "These unique and wonderful buildings, and the ordinances administered therein, represent the ultimate in our worship. These ordinances become the most profound expressions of our theology. I urge our people everywhere, with all of the persuasiveness of which I am capable, to live worthy to hold a temple recommend, to secure one and regard it as a precious asset, and to make a greater effort to go to the house of the Lord and partake of the spirit and the blessings to be had therein. I am satisfied that every man or woman who goes to the temple in a spirit of sincerity and faith leaves the house of the Lord a better man or woman. There is need for constant improvement in all of our lives. There is need occasionally to leave the noise and the tumult of the world and step within the walls of a sacred house of God, there to feel His spirit in an environment of holiness and peace" (in Conference Report, Oct. 1995, 72; or *Ensign*, Nov. 1995, 53).

Even if our circumstances do not allow us to attend regularly, we should hold a temple recommend. President Howard W. Hunter said: "It would please the Lord if every adult member would be worthy of—and carry—a current temple recommend. The things that we must do and not do to be worthy of a temple recommend are the very things that ensure we will be happy as individuals and as families" (in Conference Report, Oct. 1994, 8; or *Ensign*, Nov. 1994, 8).

- What blessings are we promised if we hold a temple recommend and attend the temple regularly?

To obtain a temple recommend, we must have yearly private interviews with our priesthood leaders. We may also be invited to attend special preparation and orientation classes. (For more information on

8-a, A house of the Lord
(Guatemala City Guatemala Temple)

preparing to attend the temple, see *Duties and Blessings of the Priesthood, Part A,* lesson 35, "The Eternal Family.")

Providing Ordinances for Deceased Ancestors

The Lord desires that all who have lived upon the earth past their eighth birthday have the privilege of receiving the baptism, endowment, and sealing ordinances. He sent the prophet Elijah to Joseph Smith to restore the priesthood keys of salvation for the dead, which keys make it possible for the living to perform ordinances in behalf of those who have died. As members of the Church, we have the responsibility to provide the saving ordinances of the gospel for our ancestors who died without them.

- Read Doctrine and Covenants 128:15. Why is it important for us to provide ordinances for our deceased ancestors? (They cannot be fully saved without us, and we cannot be fully saved without them.)

As we turn our hearts to our ancestors, learn more about them, and perform priesthood ordinances for them, we can share the joy our ancestors feel as they receive the opportunity to attain eternal life. Further, as we serve our brothers and sisters, we come to better understand and appreciate the meaning of the Savior's Atonement in our own lives. The Prophet Joseph Smith explained our role in temple and family history work:

"The keys are to be delivered, the spirit of Elijah is to come, . . . and the Saints to come up as saviors on Mount Zion.

"But how are they to become saviors on Mount Zion? By building their temples . . . and receiving all the ordinances . . . in behalf of all their progenitors who are dead, and redeem them that they may come forth in the first resurrection and be exalted to thrones of glory with them; and herein is the chain that binds the hearts of the fathers to the children, and the children to the fathers, which fulfills the mission of Elijah" (*Teachings of the Prophet Joseph Smith,* sel. Joseph Fielding Smith [1976], 330).

- What blessings can come from doing ordinance work for our deceased ancestors?

Remembering Our Ancestors

To begin fulfilling our family history responsibilities we can each make a list of our deceased relatives whom we knew or remember. No special research aids or resources are needed. This list can help us identify relatives who died without receiving their saving temple ordinances. Even if our ancestors were early Church members or if others in our families have worked on family history, we can often identify deceased relatives whose temple work has not yet been done.

8-b, Family history consultants can help prepare information.

- Pass out pencils and paper to the class. Have the class members make a list of deceased relatives whom they remember, and then have them identify those who died without temple ordinances.

When we identify relatives whose temple work is not yet done, we should make sure that it is done. President Gordon B. Hinckley emphasized the temple's importance in family history work: "All of our vast family history endeavor is directed to temple work. There is no other purpose for it. The temple ordinances become the crowning blessings the Church has to offer" (in Conference Report, Apr. 1998, 115–16; or *Ensign*, May 1998, 88).

- Display visual 8-b, "Family history consultants can help prepare information."

Family history consultants in our ward, branch, stake, or mission can help us prepare the information that the temple will need before ordinances may be done. Church family history publications, local priesthood leaders, and temples should also have these instructions.

- Discuss with class members the process and requirements for preparing names for temple work. If possible, introduce the family history consultant, and have him or her lead this discussion.

In addition to performing temple ordinances for the ancestors whom we remember, we should consider other ancestors. We can talk to our parents, grandparents, aunts, uncles, cousins, and other family members who may remember people we may not have known. We can make sure that temple work is done for these ancestors as well.

Recording Your Information

As we learn about our ancestors, we will probably need to record the information we find. Church family history forms and computer programs can help us do this. However, you may use any method that helps you remember what you learn. It is also very helpful to record the dates when ordinances were performed so that you know which ones still need to be done.

Some Guidelines

As we submit names for temple work, we should remember these guidelines:

1. Our foremost obligation is for our own ancestors. We should not submit the names of people who are not related to us, including names we may obtain from personal extraction projects.

2. A person whose name is submitted must have been deceased for at least one full year.

8-c, Writing personal and family histories is important.

3. If the person was born in the past 95 years, permission should be obtained from a close living relative before the name is submitted.

4. No ordinances are necessary for children who are stillborn. However, if there is any possibility that a child lived after birth, he or she should be sealed to the parents, unless the child was born in the covenant (meaning that the child's parents were sealed before he or she was born).

5. Children who died before age eight and were not born in the covenant need only to be sealed to their parents. They do not need any other ordinances.

Other Ways to Participate in Family History

- Display visual 8-c, "Writing personal and family histories is important."

Other important ways we can participate in family history include:

Gathering information about ancestors who lived before those whom we and our family remember and having their temple work done.

Teaching our children about their ancestors and encouraging them to fulfill their own family history responsibilities.

Writing personal and family histories.

Keeping important personal and family documents and records.

Keeping a journal.

Participating in the Church's family history programs such as submitting family names to Ancestral File and participating in family record extractions.

- If you have time, display visual 8-d, "Pedigree Chart." Then help class members fill out a current family history form (obtained from your family history consultant or local priesthood leaders) for their own families.

Conclusion

We need to receive the ordinances of the gospel to be able to return to our Heavenly Father. To receive all of the blessings associated with these ordinances, we should:

1. Receive our own ordinances and help our immediate family members receive theirs.

Pedigree Chart

No. 1 on this chart is the same as no. _____ on chart no. _____.

Mark boxes when ordinances are completed.

- B Baptized
- E Endowed
- SP Sealed to parents
- SS Sealed to spouse
- F Family Group Record exists for this couple
- C Children's ordinances completed

8

(Father of no. 4) B E SP SS F C   Cont. on chart no. ____
When born
Where
When married
When died
Where

4

(Father of no. 2) B E SP SS F C
When born
Where

9

(Mother of no. 4) B E SP SS   Cont. on chart no. ____
When born
Where
When died
Where

When married
Where

2

(Father) B E SP SS F C
When born
Where

When married
Where

When died
Where

When died
Where

10

(Father of no. 5) B E SP SS F C   Cont. on chart no. ____
When born
Where
When married
When died
Where

5

(Mother of no. 2) B E SP SS
When born
Where

11

(Mother of no. 5) B E SP SS   Cont. on chart no. ____
When born
Where
When died
Where

When died
Where

1

(Name) B E SP SS F C
When born
Where

When married
Where

When died
Where

12

(Father of no. 6) B E SP SS F C   Cont. on chart no. ____
When born
Where
When married
When died
Where

(Spouse) B E SP SS

6

(Father of no. 3) B E SP SS F C
When born
Where

When married
Where

13

(Mother of no. 6) B E SP SS   Cont. on chart no. ____
When born
Where
When died
Where

3

(Mother) B E SP SS
When born
Where

When died
Where

When died
Where

14

(Father of no. 7) B E SP SS F C   Cont. on chart no. ____
When born
Where
When married
When died
Where

Your name and address

7

(Mother of no. 3) B E SP SS
When born
Where

Telephone number | Date prepared

When died
Where

15

(Mother of no. 7) B E SP SS   Cont. on chart no. ____
When born
Where
When died
Where

Published by The Church of Jesus Christ of Latter-day Saints. 3/96. Printed in USA. 31826

8-d, Pedigree Chart

2. Hold a current temple recommend and attend the temple as often as we can. Even if we do not live where we can go to the temple, we should hold a temple recommend.

3. Identify our ancestors who died without receiving the ordinances and make sure that ordinances are performed in their behalf.

As we faithfully fulfill our priesthood responsibility for temple and family history work, Heavenly Father will help us through the inspiration of His Spirit.

Challenge

If you have not yet received your own temple ordinances, arrange for an interview with your bishop or branch president to find out what you can do to prepare.

Teach your family about the importance of baptism and the temple ordinances.

Identify at least one ancestor who died without receiving all of the saving ordinances of the gospel, and have his or her ordinances done.

If you do not have a temple recommend, prepare to obtain one.

Additional Scriptures

- Malachi 4:5–6 (turning the hearts of fathers and children to one another)

- 1 Corinthians 15:29 (baptism for the dead)

- 1 Peter 3:18–19; 4:6 (gospel preached to the dead)

- Moroni 8:5–23 (baptism for little children is not needed)

- Doctrine and Covenants 124:26–39 (house to be built to the Lord, wherein work for the dead may be done)

- Doctrine and Covenants 128 (directions on accurate record keeping and baptism for the dead)

- Joseph Smith—History 1:38–39 (mission of Elijah)

Teacher Preparation

Before presenting this lesson:

1. Read *Gospel Principles* chapter 40, "Temple Work and Family History."

2. For more information on record keeping and personal and family histories, see *The Latter-day Saint Woman, Part B,* lesson 19, "Family and Personal Histories."

3. Obtain paper and a pencil for each class member.

4. Obtain copies of current Church family history forms for recording temple and family information for each class member.

5. If your ward, branch, stake, or mission has a family history consultant, ask him or her for the procedures used to submit names for temple work. If possible, arrange for the consultant to teach a portion of the class. If a family history consultant is not available, you may also find out what these procedures are from a local Family History Center, your local priesthood leaders, current Family History publications, or your nearest temple.

6. Assign class members to present any stories, scriptures, or quotations you wish.

SHARING THE GOSPEL

Lesson 9

The purpose of this lesson is to motivate us to share the gospel more effectively.

Introduction

In the following story a convert told how she and her family were introduced to the Church:

"Shortly after we moved to a new neighborhood, I was out working in my garden when one of my neighbors offered me a huge armful of tomatoes she had just picked. That was just the beginning of what was to be a forever friendship.

"In the months that followed, [our neighbors] proved to be the best friends . . . we had ever met. They were not afraid to be too friendly and took our family in just as though we were their own family. We enjoyed the hot homemade bread sent over almost every week; the complete dinner brought in one evening when I was too sick to make our own; the beautiful pageant one summer evening in Independence, with ice cream on the way home. . . .

"We were always invited to Church activities but never pressured to go. When we did decide to go, our neighbors' sweet, dependable daughter came over to babysit for us—and sometimes even refused to be paid for it.

"After I had had a hard day at home, my friend would ask me to come to Relief Society with her. I was generally eager just to get out of the house at that point. But in going I found much more than a [rest] from household chores. The warm welcome the sisters gave me made me into a regular attender for almost a year before our baptisms. . . .

"After a while, though, we knew in our hearts that we wanted a more complete life like theirs. We were then invited out to church on Sundays and began to go to the investigators class each week.

"In March 1976 we entered the waters of baptism.

"Not long after that we heard a special talk in sacrament meeting about a person who had been too hesitant to share the gospel for fear he might seem too forward—and the family had to wait ten years before the opportunity came again. Ten years, I thought. Where would we be in ten years if we didn't have the Church now? My heart swelled and I could hardly wait to find our neighbors outside after church.

" 'Thanks for sharing the gospel with us' was all I could get out. I wanted to say so much more, but I really didn't need to. Tears came to their eyes, too, as we all exchanged loving words and hugs, just as I know we always will, for time and all eternity" (Doris E. Heydon, quoted by Jay A. Parry, "Converts Tell . . . What Brought Me In," *Ensign*, Feb. 1978, 43).

- What did this family do to prepare its neighbors to receive the gospel?

- Have the class members ponder for a moment with whom they could share the gospel today.

Sharing the Gospel—Our Call from the Lord

- Show visual 9-a, "Every member should be a missionary."

Through His prophets the Lord has commanded every member of the Church to be involved in missionary work. Some of us may think that missionary work is only for full-time missionaries. But all of us who have been baptized are responsible for inviting others to accept the blessings of the gospel. The Lord said:

"Again, I say unto you, I give unto you a commandment, that every man, both elder, priest, teacher, and also member, go to with his might, with the labor of his hands, to prepare and accomplish the things which I have commanded.

"And let your preaching be the warning voice, every man to his neighbor, in mildness and in meekness" (D&C 38:40–41).

- Why does Heavenly Father want us to share the gospel? (He depends on us to share the gospel with those who have not heard it so that all His children can enjoy its blessings.)

- What blessings of the gospel do we enjoy and want others to have also? (One blessing is the knowledge that we are children of a loving Heavenly Father, to whom we can pray for help and guidance. The gospel helps us be happy in this life and live worthy to be with our Heavenly Father in the next life. The gospel also enables us to have our families forever.)

9-a, Every member should be a missionary.

Some of our friends and relatives may never have the blessings of the gospel unless we care enough about them to be effective missionaries. They may never ask to be taught the gospel unless we talk to them about it. It is true that being a good example of what we believe is part of being a missionary, but we should also find ways to tell people about our beliefs. The Lord has said: "For there are many yet on the earth among all sects, parties, and denominations, who are blinded by the subtle craftiness of men, whereby they lie in wait to deceive, and who are only kept from the truth because they know not where to find it" (D&C 123:12).

Sharing the Gospel Effectively

President Spencer W. Kimball gave us some advice to help us share the gospel effectively: "Father, you are to take the lead. By working together as families, much great work can be accomplished. With your family, prayerfully select one or two families to friendship. Decide whom of your relatives or friends you will introduce to the Church. Perhaps you could plan a family home evening with them . . . or participate together in any number of ways. Then, when these families show interest, arrange through your ward or branch mission leader to invite them and the missionaries into your home to share the message of the Restoration. If you will follow this simple procedure, you will bring a number of fine families into the Church" (*Sharing the Gospel through Priesthood Missionary Service* [filmstrip, 1975]).

Most of us want to share the gospel with others because of our love and concern for them. But some of us do not know how to share the gospel, and others are afraid to do so. The following plan can help us share the gospel more effectively.

- Display a poster of the following list, or refer to the information on the chalkboard:

How to Share the Gospel Effectively

1. Prayerfully select a family or individual.
2. Friendship the family or individual.
3. Introduce the family or individual to the Church.
4. Invite the family or individual to meet with the missionaries.

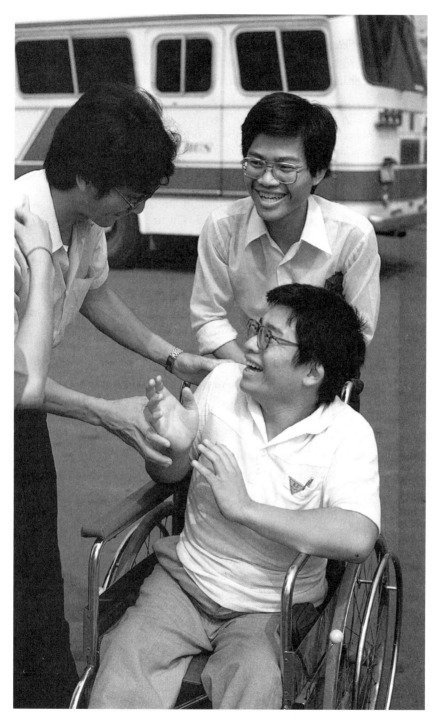

9-b, Being a good missionary means being a good friend.

Prayerfully Select a Family or Individual

First, prayerfully select a family or individual to introduce to the Church. People in the following circumstances are usually most receptive:

1. People who are experiencing a significant change in their lives (those who are new to a neighborhood or are experiencing a new birth, new marriage, or recent death in the family).

2. People who have recently attended a Church meeting or activity; visited a temple open house, a visitors' center, a Church historical site, or another Church facility; seen a Latter-day Saint television program; or listened to the Tabernacle Choir.

3. People who are friends of Church members.

4. People who are related to Church members (part-member families or relatives of those who have recently joined the Church).

5. People who are interested in or curious about the Church (those who ask questions about the Church, talk positively about Church members, express interest in Church beliefs or principles, or are seeking a new religion).

President Gordon B. Hinckley said: "The gospel is nothing to be ashamed of. It is something to be proud of. 'Be not thou therefore ashamed of the testimony of our Lord,' wrote Paul to Timothy (2 Tim. 1:8). Opportunities for sharing the gospel are everywhere" ("Find the Lambs, Feed the Sheep," *Ensign,* May 1999, 105–6).

Friendship the Family or Individual

▪ Show visual 9-b, "Being a good missionary means being a good friend."

The head of the household should be an example to his or her family members in friendshipping nonmembers.

▪ How can we befriend nonmember families or individuals? (Answers could include being cheerful, being a good listener, remembering their names, doing kind deeds for them, discussing their interests with them, visiting their home, inviting them to our home, going out for entertainment together, and doing other things that let them know we love them.)

In the following account a man explained how friendship led to his interest in the Church:

"Through work [a coworker and I] got to know each other very well. I really came to respect him. As we grew closer in our friendship,

9-c, Sharing the gospel is a rewarding experience.

we would talk about our families and our activities, which led to the Church. I could tell that it was the Church that made him and his family different—in a very positive way—from most people. Soon we were talking about some of the doctrines of the Church, but never did he pressure me or preach to me. . . . One day at afternoon break he asked me if I would like to know more. . . . [Our family took the missionary lessons] at his home.

"If it were not for the real concern and the interest that the Brookses have shown to our family, I really think that we would not be members of the one true church and have the light and knowledge of our Father in heaven and his plans for us" (Keith Knoblich, quoted by Jay A. Parry, *Ensign*, Feb. 1978, 39).

Another convert said, "We have to make friends before we can make converts."

Introduce the Family or Individual to the Church

▪ Display visual 9-c, "Sharing the gospel is a rewarding experience."

▪ How can we introduce people to the Church?

Some ways we can introduce people to the Church are to talk with them about the gospel; give them a Book of Mormon or Church magazine; bear our testimony; take them to Church meetings, activities, firesides, and open houses; invite them to family home evenings and to neighborhood parties; invite them to participate in a Church service project; and invite them to visit a Family History Center. We could also invite people to baptismal services, view Church videocassettes with them, visit people who are new to the neighborhood, and give community service.

Another important way to introduce others to the Church is to set a good example. If we do this, people will often become interested because our lives are different.

Above all, we should show our love and concern for nonmembers as we strive to create opportunities to teach the gospel. The feeling we share with them matters more than the approach we use.

Invite the Family or Individual to Meet with the Missionaries

When we feel that someone is prepared to hear the missionary discussions, we should "extend a direct, simple, and clear invitation to hear the missionary discussions by using the words 'will you.' Friendships often become more positive after invitations are extended, even if the person chooses not to meet with the missionaries" (*Church Handbook of Instructions, Book 2: Priesthood and Auxiliary Leaders* [1998], 251).

When inviting people to meet with the missionaries we should not be afraid that they will be offended, nor should we be discouraged if they do not respond positively. Inviting them to learn about the gospel will not hurt our friendship, and the Spirit will help us recognize when it is time to ask again.

President Gordon B. Hinckley declared: "Great is our work, tremendous is our responsibility in helping to find those to teach. The Lord has laid upon us a mandate to teach the gospel to every creature. This will take the very best efforts of every [member]" (*Ensign*, May 1999, 107).

- Read Doctrine and Covenants 84:85. How does this scripture apply to missionary work?

In all aspects of missionary work we must have faith in the Lord and prayerfully seek His Spirit. When we do so, the Spirit will guide us and help us as we do the Lord's work (see D&C 100:5–8).

Conclusion

The Lord said, "It becometh every man who hath been warned to warn his neighbor" (D&C 88:81). If we do as the Lord has instructed, using the steps outlined in this lesson, we will help many people find the truth.

Challenge

Be a good friend and example to nonmember friends and family members. Prayerfully select a nonmember family or individual to introduce to the Church. Friendship the family members or individual, and introduce them to the Church. Invite them to meet with the missionaries.

Teacher Preparation

Before presenting this lesson:

Assign class members to present any stories, scriptures, or quotations you wish.

FELLOWSHIPPING: A PRIESTHOOD RESPONSIBILITY

Lesson 10

The purpose of this lesson is to motivate us to strengthen Church members through fellowshipping.

Introduction

- Read Doctrine and Covenants 18:10. Why is each individual important to Heavenly Father?

Regardless of who we are, where we live, what language we speak, or to what race we belong, Heavenly Father's work and glory is to bring to pass our immortality and eternal life (see Moses 1:39). To help Him in this work, the Lord has restored the priesthood to earth and given us the responsibility of loving one another as He loves us. It is our responsibility and privilege to help our brothers and sisters receive the blessings prepared by Heavenly Father for those who are faithful.

Missionary work is important, but helping our brothers and sisters does not stop with baptism. President Gordon B. Hinckley said: "There is absolutely no point in doing missionary work unless we hold on to the fruits of that effort. The two must be inseparable. These converts are precious. Every convert is a son or daughter of God. Every convert is a great and serious responsibility. It is an absolute imperative that we look after those who have become a part of us" ("Find the Lambs, Feed the Sheep," *Ensign*, May 1999, 108).

- Read Luke 22:32. How can we as priesthood holders strengthen others?

We are here to help each other progress. We need to take care of one another as children of the Lord. President Hinckley said, "I am convinced that we will lose but very, very few of those who come into the Church if we take better care of them" (*Ensign*, May 1999, 109).

Fellowshipping in the Church

Fellowshipping means encouraging and helping each other to enjoy the full blessings of the gospel. It is showing courtesy and kindness, sharing experiences, and extending service and love. We fellowship by being a good friend and neighbor.

When we share our time, talents, and possessions with others, we develop a spirit of unity. Paul described this unity when he said that the new members of the Church were no longer to be strangers "but fellowcitizens with the saints" (Ephesians 2:19).

Although we should be friendly and neighborly and try to show our love to all people, giving help and friendship to new and less-active members is a basic priesthood responsibility. The Church helps us do this in many ways. It provides programs such as home teaching that encourage us to serve our brothers and sisters. It provides meetings where we can associate with each other. And it provides instruction in the correct expression of our love and concern.

We should also be concerned with those families among us who have a father, mother, son, or daughter who is not a member. These families need us. By fellowshipping them and sharing with them our understanding and love, we may help these part-member families become united in the gospel.

- Write on the chalkboard a list of those who need our fellowshipping.

Ways to Fellowship

How we fellowship a person depends on the circumstances and our relationship to him or her. The members of one family explained how they fellowshipped a stranger at church: "The stranger beside us was uneasy. He looked straight ahead and scarcely breathed. He didn't even smile at our two young children, who always made friends for us. After church, my husband asked the solemn fellow home with us for dessert. A smile relaxed his long face. 'I was just baptized last week, and then moved into your ward,' he explained. He dropped in on us several times a week thereafter, excited about his [growing knowledge of the gospel], eager to discuss the scriptures, anxious over his personal affairs. Ours was the great joy of watching our brother grow. He was no longer a stranger" (Susan Spencer Zmolek, "The Strangers within Our Gates," *Ensign,* Mar. 1976, 49).

Home teaching also provides opportunities for fellowshipping. One woman told how her home teachers included her and her son in their activities: "I wanted to make a fresh start after a painful divorce, so I took my young son and moved south to finish a college degree. Supposing that the climate would be hot, we left our sweaters and blankets in storage. Oh, we were cold in our drafty summer cottage that winter, but were too afraid to light the space heaters or ask to borrow blankets. I didn't know anyone. I felt I didn't fit in with the people at church because I was divorced, and I certainly didn't want anyone to think I was a [burden]. I was so glad when home teachers came!

They really wanted to make us welcome and they came regularly, even though we didn't have a telephone and weren't always home. They often included us in their families' activities. Eventually I didn't mind asking to borrow blankets from them" (as quoted by Susan Spencer Zmolek, *Ensign*, Mar. 1976, 47–48).

- List on the chalkboard the different ways to fellowship that were demonstrated in the above experiences.

When we feel genuine love for others, our fellowshipping activities extend beyond Sunday meetings to other times and activities throughout the week. Such activities include inviting them to our homes, social activities, and community and Church events. Fellowshipping is a sign of a true Saint, to whom Jesus referred when He said, "I was a stranger and ye took me in" (Matthew 25:34–36).

The following story shows how two brethren demonstrated genuine fellowship:

A young man was lonely and unhappy. His church attendance was irregular, and he found difficulty being dependable in Church assignments. Two men, both widowers, invited the young man to join them for family home evenings.

Before long, Monday evening became the most important time in his week. There he engaged in many gospel discussions and gained a desire to begin praying more diligently. It was not long before his testimony changed from a passive knowledge to a burning witness of the truth.

The two brethren accepted him and extended their friendship in the most total way they knew. They sat with him at Church meetings, invited him into their homes for dinner, and helped him fix up his home.

Before long he was reaching out to others, and he became responsible in his Church assignments. One day as he discussed with an acquaintance the happiness in his life, the other asked, "What do you think caused it to happen?"

"The kindness of two friends has been the most important part," he said. "I have come to trust and feel secure in their love, which has helped me do things I never even thought were possible" (adapted from *Relief Society Courses of Study, 1977–78*, 130).

- Add to the list on the chalkboard the ways these two brethren fellowshipped the lonely member.

FELLOWSHIPPING ACTIVITIES

Activities in Your Home

Have a dinner.

Have a recreational event.

View a good television program.

Show family slides or pictures.

Have a picnic.

Hold an informal party.

Work on a project together.

Activities in Their Home

Deliver a treat.

Plan a party together.

Help them move in, plant a garden, or repair something.

Visit them.

Tend their children.

Activities in the Community

Go to a special movie or program.

Pick them up on the way to a school function
(have refreshments in your home afterward).

Go on a picnic.

Attend a common activity of the children,
such as a ball game.

10-a, Fellowshipping activities

One brother told the following story about fellowshipping:

"Susan Munson [was] an active member of the Church who [had] waited patiently for her nonmember husband to show some interest in the Church. He [had] always said, 'Oh, that's fine for you and the kids, honey, but I'm just not interested.'

"That's partly true. But Jack [was] also shy. . . . Susan [finally] asked Brother Caldwell, the ward mission leader, if there wasn't something that could be done. He promised to take the matter up in his weekly missionary meeting.

"The group . . . decided a 'block party' might be the best way to begin. They asked three member families in the area to plan a backyard party for the Munsons and the Nobles, an investigating family. . . . All three joined in the fellowshipping.

"Jack, initially reluctant to come, was surprised and delighted with the easy, natural friendliness of the group. By the evening's end, he enthusiastically supported the idea of a second party, a picnic in two weeks. No one said anything about going to church, but Allen Westover, who had discussed Jack's house-painting project at the party, showed up on Saturday with his own ladder—and came back evenings after work. Steve Caldwell and Glen Rivers also helped several times.

"Later that month when the elders quorum had a project, Jack was anxious to help *them*. . . . As the summer progressed, Jack spent more and more time with Church members. There were chats about fishing rods and politics and raising children, about gardening, working out marital difficulties, and handling job pressures. Jack was talking as well as listening. Social evenings with different families included family home evenings and spiritual discussions. To Susan's great joy, Jack told her one evening that he was ready to take the next step of being taught by the missionaries and . . . joining the Church."

He added: "There is nothing more transparent than 'friendshipping' activities without friendship feelings. The feelings must come first." He suggested that we be good listeners, find out about the individual's likes and dislikes, family activities, and business. He stressed that those being fellowshipped need to know we care. (Ernest Eberhard, "That Part-Member Family," *Ensign*, July 1978, 38–39).

- What fellowshipping methods used in this story can we add to the list on the chalkboard?

- Display visual 10-a, "Fellowshipping activities." Mention those activities listed in the visual that have not already been discussed. Have the class members suggest other fellowshipping activities.

Conclusion

Fellowshipping is an important priesthood responsibility. It helps new converts and other Church members feel wanted and needed and motivates them to participate in the Church. As we accept the responsibility to help others become active in the Church, we will experience joy and satisfaction. The Lord promises that this joy will be eternal.

- Read Doctrine and Covenants 18:15–16. How can fellowshipping bring us joy?

- Ask the assigned class member to bear his testimony of how fellowshipping helped him.

Challenge

Identify a new convert and fellowship him. Increase your fellowshipping of your assigned home teaching families. Select a less-active family, and fellowship its members back into church activity. Be friendly with all Church members, especially those who are strangers. If there is a part-member family in your area, include the nonmembers in Church activities.

Teacher Preparation

Before presenting this lesson:

1. Ask a class member to bear his testimony about how fellowshipping helped him. He could be a recent convert, a member brought back into church activity, or someone who helped bring another into activity.

2. Assign class members to present any stories, scriptures, or quotations you wish.

HOME AND FAMILY
RELATIONS

THE FATHER AS PATRIARCH

Lesson   11

The purpose of this lesson is to strengthen our understanding of the father's role as patriarch in the home.

Introduction

▪ Show visual 11-a, "The Lord expects fathers to lead their families."

President Spencer W. Kimball said: "The Lord organized [His children] in the beginning with a father who procreates, provides, and loves and directs, and a mother who conceives and bears and nurtures and feeds and trains[, and children who] come to love, honor, and appreciate each other. The family is the great plan of life as conceived and organized by our Father in heaven" (in Conference Report, Apr. 1973, 151; or *Ensign*, July 1973, 15).

▪ What does President Kimball name as the father's responsibilities?

"The title *father* is sacred and eternal. It is significant that of all the titles of respect and honor and admiration that are given to Deity, he has asked us to address him as Father" (*Father, Consider Your Ways* [pamphlet, 1973], 2).

▪ Sing "O My Father" (*Hymns*, no. 292; or *Gospel Principles*, 350).

During the Savior's mission on earth, He spoke of His Father often and in a sacred way. The scriptures show that He knew His Father, because He talked with Him and did His will (see Mark 14:36). We should follow, and teach our children to follow, the Savior's example of respect and honor for His Father.

▪ How can we show respect for our Heavenly Father? for our earthly father?

A father who holds the priesthood should live worthy for his children to call him the sacred name of *father*. If he does so, he will be prepared for eternal fatherhood. Each of us has the power to experience joy with our family throughout eternity.

A Father Is Patriarch of His Family

▪ Read Ephesians 5:23.

Heavenly Father has designated the husband or father as the head of the household—he is the patriarch of the family. We are especially blessed as members of the Church because we have the priesthood to help us be effective patriarchs.

Each family in the Church is a kingdom or government within itself. The father is the head of that government; he is the highest authority in the home and presides over all family functions. (See Joseph F. Smith, *Gospel Doctrine,* 5th ed. [1939], 286–88.) Concerning this matter, President Joseph F. Smith wrote: "It sometimes happens that the elders are called in to administer to the members of a family. Among these elders there may be presidents of stakes, apostles, or even members of the first presidency of the Church. It is not proper under these circumstances for the father to stand back and expect the elders to direct the administration of this important ordinance. The father is there. It is his right and it is his duty to preside. He should select the one who is to administer the oil, and the one who is to be mouth in prayer, and he should . . . direct the administration of that blessing of the gospel in his home" (*Gospel Doctrine,* 287).

The Lord wants the father to bless his family members, not just rule over them. To do this a father must use his priesthood righteously to bless each of them. Eldred G. Smith, emeritus Patriarch to the Church, told about a woman who came to him seeking a special priesthood blessing. He said:

"When I asked her why she wanted a special blessing, she refused to tell me. I learned from her that her husband was a member of the Church and held the Melchizedek Priesthood, so I spent considerable time trying to teach her the principle of priesthood order, where the father in the home should bless the members of the family. [I asked her to] go home to get her blessing from her husband instead of from me.

"Sometime later she returned to my office, refreshed my memory of this experience, and said she [had] left my office very resentful. . . .

"She said the reason she refused to tell me why she wanted a blessing was that she wanted the blessing because there wasn't the proper relationship between her and her husband, and then I had sent her home to get a blessing from her husband. So naturally she was a little bit resentful.

"Then she added, 'That was one of the finest things that ever happened.' She said she went home, she prayed about it, she thought about it, and then finally she mustered enough courage to ask her husband for the blessing. Of course it shocked him, but she was patient; she let him think it over a bit, ponder about it, and pray about it; and finally he gave her a blessing. Then she added, 'There has never been such a fine relationship in our home in all our lives as we have had since he gave me that blessing' " (in Conference Report, Apr. 1965, 115; or *Improvement Era*, June 1965, 534).

The home is the place for the family to progress—both together and individually. To encourage this progression the father should always preside in the home with love, wisdom, gentleness, understanding, and patience. As the patriarch in the home, the father should be the guiding example. Faithful and obedient fathers who lead their families in righteous living on earth will help them be worthy to live together in the eternities.

As patriarchs in our families we should treat our wives and children with the utmost respect.

- Read Ephesians 5:25–28. How should we treat our wives?

- Read Ephesians 6:4. How should fathers rear their children?

President N. Eldon Tanner said, "As a man realizes that he is the earthly father of a spirit child of God, he cannot help but feel keenly his responsibility to nurture that child with all the tender loving care possible" ("Fatherhood," *Ensign*, June 1977, 2).

- Read Doctrine and Covenants 121:41–45. How can these words from the Lord help us be good patriarchs in our families?

The scriptures contain many stories of fathers who were good patriarchs. Alma the Younger gathered his sons together and gave each one his counsel and blessing (see Alma 35:16). King Benjamin taught his sons to understand the scriptures (see Mosiah 1:2). Before Adam and Lehi died, each blessed his children (see D&C 107:53; 2 Nephi 3:1–25; 4:1–11). Through the power of the priesthood these prophets fulfilled their patriarchal responsibilities to their families. Through our priesthood we too can be righteous patriarchs in our families.

Meeting Basic Family Needs

As the patriarch of his family, a father is responsible to help family members meet their needs. First, everyone has physical needs such as food, shelter, and clothing.

- What other basic needs do members of our family have? (List the following ideas on the chalkboard as they are mentioned.)

11-a, The Lord expects fathers to lead their families.

To Be Wanted and Loved

We can satisfy our family members' need for love and acceptance by showing them affection and telling them we love them. Elder Loren C. Dunn gave us an example of this need:

"I recall a stage play that recently was made into a movie. It dealt with parents whose only child, a son, returned from military service. The father and son had never been close. It was a situation in which both father and son loved each other but were unable to find ways to express themselves, and therefore hostilities arose because each thought the other did not like him. . . .

"The high point of the play came when the boy said to his father something like this:

" 'Dad, I always resented you when I was younger because you never told me that you loved me, but then I realized that I had never told you that I loved you either. Well, Dad, I'm telling you now: I love you.'

"For one electrifying moment the father and son embraced each other as the pent-up love and appreciation of years came flooding out" (in Conference Report, Apr. 1969, 22–23; or *Improvement Era*, June 1969, 52–53).

- Why should we tell family members we love them? How else can we show them they are wanted and loved?

To Have Self-Esteem

We can help our family members build self-esteem by praising their achievements. We can teach them that they are God's children and help them develop their talents. All these things help them build confidence, a positive self-image, and a feeling of worth. Parents should constantly look for ways to praise and encourage their children. Children, in turn, should regularly express thanks to their parents. One father said: "I spend my family home evening time praising my children rather than criticizing them. I'd rather tell them what I've seen them do that's right than what I've seen them do that's wrong" (quoted by George Durrant, "A Gift from Heaven," *Ensign*, Mar. 1971, 7).

To Have a Purpose in Life

Everyone needs to feel that life has meaning. We can help family members fill this need by teaching them the gospel. Everyone needs to know that earth life is to help us grow and become more like God. We must teach our children that our purpose on earth is to find peace and happiness and to prepare ourselves to return to our Father in Heaven.

To Have Self-Discipline and Be Able to Work

Brother Glenn E. Nielson, president of a large oil company, was once asked what teacher influenced his life the most. He replied: "My father

. . . taught me the joy of work well done. He taught me how to put more hay on my pitchfork and to step forward as I pitched it into the hayrack, and he would add, 'All work is easier and lighter if you step into it rather than away from it' " (*Church News,* 25 Mar. 1978, 2).

- Show visual 11-b, "Fathers need to teach their children to work."

The benefits of learning to work are illustrated in the following story: "Two elderly neighbors one day were [talking] about their lives and those of their children. John's oldest boy was just finishing college and had been on the honor roll through all of his studies. Jim's boy had just been convicted of a serious crime and sent to the state [prison]. Jim and John had lived side by side and been good neighbors during their sons' growing-up period. Their boys had played together and had gone to school together. Jim, in discussing what had happened, stated, 'The whole difference between our sons' lives was that you kept a cow, John. I recall that when the boys were playing, your boy would leave early so that he could milk and feed the cow. By keeping that cow you taught your boy to accept responsibility' " (*1967–68 Priesthood Study Course: Aaronic Priesthood—Adult,* 35).

Each of us should give our children work to do. We should also give them the freedom to work out the problems that come with work; we should not do their work for them but should help them successfully complete their tasks. (See lesson 15, "Sharing in Family Work.")

Meeting Family Members' Spiritual Needs

Fathers who hold the priesthood have the right and responsibility to bless their family members with priesthood leadership and to perform for them appropriate priesthood ordinances. Fathers can lead and bless them in the following ways:

1. Preside in the home.

2. Conduct personal interviews with their children. (President N. Eldon Tanner said that his father interviewed him when he was a young man: "He told me how important the priesthood was and what was necessary for me to do to be worthy of that priesthood. He was the best friend I had" [in Conference Report, Oct. 1978, 58; or *Ensign,* Nov. 1978, 41].)

3. Give blessings of comfort to their wives and children (Melchizedek Priesthood bearers only).

4. Administer to the sick in their families (Melchizedek Priesthood bearers only).

5. Receive revelation and inspiration for their families.

6. Hold family prayers morning and evening.

7. Call on family members to pray and bless the food.

8. Hold family home evening every Monday night.

9. Encourage family members to participate in missionary work, family history research, and temple ordinances.

10. Be a good example and keep the commandments.

11. Create a feeling of love and understanding in the home.

- Ask the assigned priesthood holder to bear his testimony of the joy of being part of a close, loving family.

Conclusion

In the Lord's plan, husbands and fathers are the heads of their homes and the patriarchs of their families. Thus a father should develop a relationship of love, trust, and cooperation with his wife and children and should be concerned about the welfare of each family member. The following questions will help him discover how he might improve:

1. Do I really take time to be concerned about my family?

2. Do I show respect for my family members' thoughts, desires, property, and so on?

3. Do I recognize that each member of my family is an important individual?

4. Do I tell my family members I love them? Do I show them my love?

President N. Eldon Tanner explained, "It is a joyous privilege and blessing, and a heavy responsibility, to be the father and the patriarchal head of a family, with the challenge to teach and prepare its members to go back into the presence of their Heavenly Father, where the family can continue to enjoy eternal life together" (*Ensign,* June 1977, 2).

Challenge

Husbands and fathers: Understand your responsibility as patriarch in your home. Discuss this with your wife during the week, and gain her support in helping you fulfill your duties. Honor your father; he remains your patriarch even after your marriage.

Young and unmarried men: Honor your priesthood. Prepare yourself to be a righteous patriarch in your home. Honor your father; he is the patriarch of your family.

Additional Scriptures

- Deuteronomy 6:1–7 (parents to teach their children to love the Lord and keep His commandments)

- Joshua 24:14–15 (choose whom you will serve)

11-b, Fathers need to teach their children to work.

- 1 Timothy 3:4–5 (fathers to rule their homes well)

- Doctrine and Covenants 75:28–29 (fathers to provide for their families)

Teacher Preparation

Before presenting this lesson:

1. Read *Duties and Blessings of the Priesthood, Part A,* lesson 12, "The Father's Responsibility for the Welfare of His Family."

2. Prepare to have the class sing at the beginning of the lesson "O My Father" (*Hymns,* no. 292; or *Gospel Principles,* 350).

3. Ask a priesthood holder who has a close, loving family to prepare to bear his testimony of the joy he feels in his family.

4. Assign class members to present any stories, scriptures, or quotations you wish.

EFFECTIVE FAMILY LEADERSHIP

Lesson 12

The purpose of this lesson is to motivate us to seek and follow the inspiration of the Holy Ghost in guiding our families.

Introduction

Elder Bruce R. McConkie told the following story about why we should listen to the Spirit:

"One of my earliest childhood recollections is of riding a horse through an apple orchard. The horse was tame and well broken, and I felt at home in the saddle.

"But one day something frightened my mount, and he bolted through the orchard. I was swept from the saddle by the overhanging limbs, and one leg slipped down through the stirrup. I desperately hung to an almost broken leather strap. . . . My weight should have broken the strap, but somehow it held for the moment. Another lunge or two of the stampeding horse would have broken the strap or wrenched it from my hands and left me to be dragged to injury or death with my foot entangled in the stirrup.

"Suddenly the horse stopped, and I became aware that someone was holding the bridle tightly and attempting to calm the quivering animal. Almost immediately I was snatched up into the arms of my father.

"What had happened? What had brought my father to my rescue in the split second before I slipped beneath the hoofs of my panic-driven horse?

"My father had been sitting in the house reading the newspaper when the Spirit whispered to him, 'Run out into the orchard!'

"Without a moment's hesitation, not waiting to learn why or for what reason, my father ran. Finding himself in the orchard without knowing why he was there, he saw the galloping horse and thought, *I must stop this horse.*

"He did so and found me. And that is how I was saved from serious injury or possible death" ("Hearken to the Spirit," *Friend*, Sept. 1972, 10).

- What prompted Elder McConkie's father to go out into the orchard? Why was it important that his father obey the Spirit immediately?

- Ask the assigned class member to share his experience of when the Holy Ghost helped him as a father.

The Holy Ghost Can Guide the Family

One of our greatest responsibilities on earth is guiding our families. President N. Eldon Tanner explained: "The father must realize always that the family is the most important thing in his life. . . . It is in the home that the most impressive teachings are taught and where the lives of our children are shaped" (*Ensign*, July 1973, 92). President David O. McKay taught that "no other success can compensate for failure in the home" (quoted from J. E. McCulloch, *Home: The Savior of Civilization* [1924], 42; in Conference Report, Apr. 1935, 116).

Parents' responsibility to teach their children has always been important, but it is becoming even more so as the world becomes more wicked.

In facing the challenges we do today as parents we may feel we are not wise enough or strong enough to always decide correctly for our families. The Lord understands this and has provided a way for us to receive the guidance we need. This guidance comes to us through the Holy Ghost.

To receive help from the Holy Ghost we must live the commandments. The Holy Ghost will not be with someone who takes the commandments lightly or fails to obey them. If we want His help we must continually repent of our sins and do what the Lord wants us to do.

In recognizing that family is their primary responsibility, parents can find comfort in knowing that they can pray and be guided by the Holy Ghost to do the right things for their families. One father, for example, "after seeking the help of the Lord, gathered his family together before deciding to accept a job in another city. He asked the family [members] their advice on the desirability of the move and gave them the opportunity to go to the Lord and receive an answer for themselves as to what they should do. After they had prayed, they felt inspired, as the father did, that they should make the move. Thus, because he gave them the opportunity to get the spiritual answer that he had also received, they were able to believe and follow his counsel" (Henry B. Eyring, "Family Followership," *Ensign*, Apr. 1973, 32).

Following the Guidance of the Holy Ghost

- Read 2 Nephi 32:5.

The Holy Ghost helps us solve our problems and answer our questions in many ways. One way He does this is to bear witness of solutions already found in the scriptures. When we have problems, we should study the scriptures for the answers. As we do so, the Holy Ghost will help direct us to the answers and will bear witness to us that the solutions are true. The Holy Ghost also helps us remember things we once learned but have forgotten (see John 14:26).

Although the Holy Ghost can and will help us solve our problems, He is only a helper. He may not solve our problems for us just because we ask for help. In the early days of the Church, Oliver Cowdery learned that often we must do more than just ask for answers.

- Read Doctrine and Covenants 9:1–9. According to this scripture, what can we do before we ask the Lord about a problem we have? (We can study it out in our minds.) How will we know if the decision we made is correct? (We ask the Lord, who will let us know if it is right.)

Other ways the Holy Ghost helps us solve problems are by revealing answers to us directly in a still, small voice (see 1 Kings 19:11–13) or indirectly through advice from a Church leader, a family member, a friend, the scriptures, or another reliable source. At other times the Holy Ghost simply prompts us as we go about our daily activities. Such a prompting may simply be a feeling that we ought to spend more time with someone in our family or do something special for him or her.

Although an answer to a prayer may come in many different ways, the Lord has provided a way for us to know that the answer is from Him. He tells us that if the decision we make is right, we will have peace in our hearts and minds (see D&C 6:14–16, 22–24; 8:2).

An answer to our prayers may not come as soon as we would like it to come. But the Lord loves us and knows what is best for us. We should not become discouraged, therefore, if we do not receive an answer immediately. We should continue to pray, live righteously, study the scriptures, and seek for the guidance of the Holy Ghost.

When we get an answer to our prayers, we must do what the answer requires us to do. We cannot expect the Holy Ghost to keep helping us if we ignore His promptings. Even if the answer is not what we want or if the effort He asks of us seems too great, we must be willing to do as He directs. Otherwise, we risk losing contact with the Holy Ghost and thus His comfort and direction.

The Lord leaves some decisions up to us. These decisions may simply be a matter of what we like rather than a matter of right and wrong. (See D&C 58:26–28; 60:5; 80:3.) In such cases we should use good judgment based on our knowledge and experience.

President Joseph Fielding Smith gave this counsel: "Now, I think that above all else in the world I, and you, and all members of the Church should seek to be guided by the Spirit of the Lord. To the extent that we gain the guidance of that Spirit we will be prophets to ourselves and in our own affairs, and we will also find ourselves in harmony with those prophets whom the Lord has placed in the First Presidency and in the Council of the Twelve" (*Joseph Fielding Smith: A Prophet Among the People*, ed. J. M. Heslop and Dell R. Van Orden [1971], 24–25).

How the Holy Ghost Can Bless Our Families

When the Holy Ghost guides us, we are greatly blessed and in turn can bless our families. For example, when Elder Bruce R. McConkie was a boy, his father's heeding the Holy Ghost saved his son from harm. This kind of protection can be ours if we are open to inspiration from the Holy Ghost and if we do what He tells us to do.

Besides keeping us safe physically, the Holy Ghost also helps us avoid temptations that could harm us spiritually. Through the Holy Ghost we may also know when something is wrong in our families. Perhaps one or more family members have a special problem they need to talk about. Or perhaps they have questions about the Church or are concerned about why they do not seem to be able to live the commandments as well as they should. With the help of the Holy Ghost we can assist and strengthen our families. We may be able to save them much pain and heartache.

When we discipline our children, we should also seek direction from the Holy Ghost. As we follow the Holy Ghost's guidance and treat our children with love and respect, they will see that we are simply trying to help them. (See D&C 121:41–44.)

The Holy Ghost can help when we give father's blessings. He can prompt us to give our families advice, even for problems of which they may not be aware. Such a blessing can be a sacred experience for our family.

▪ Show visual 12-a, "Father's blessings can strengthen family members."

President Ezra Taft Benson told of the following experience:

"A young man came to my office . . . for a blessing. He had problems . . . ; he was confused; he was concerned and worried. And so we talked for a few minutes and I said to him, 'Have you ever asked your father for a blessing?' 'Oh,' he said, 'I don't know that Dad would do a thing like

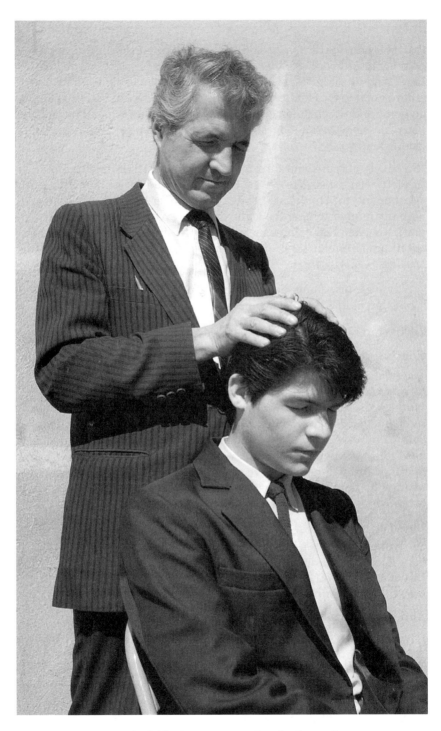

12-a, Father's blessings can strengthen family members.

that. He is not very active.' I said, 'But he's your father.' 'Yes.' 'Does he hold the priesthood?' 'Yes, he is an inactive elder.' I said, 'Do you love him?' And he said, 'Yes, I love him. He is a good man, he's good to the family, good to the children.' . . . I said, 'All right, would you be willing to go home and watch for an opportunity, and ask your father if he will give you a blessing? And if it doesn't work out, you come back, and I will be glad to help you.'

"So he left, and in about three days he came back. 'Brother Benson, this has been the sweetest thing that's happened in our home,' he said. 'Mother and the children sat there, my younger brothers and sisters, with my mother wiping the tears from her eyes. She expressed her gratitude later. Father gave me a lovely blessing.' He added, 'I could tell it came from his heart' " (*God, Family, Country: Our Three Great Loyalties* [1974], 84).

- Why was this young man's father the best person to give him a blessing at that particular time?

- How can we tell when our experiences are guided by the Holy Ghost?

Conclusion

The Lord has given us a precious gift to help us make decisions and solve problems. This gift is the companionship of the Holy Ghost. Through the Holy Ghost we can come closer to Heavenly Father and receive revelation to lead our families righteously. This revelation can help us provide some of the strength and wisdom our family members need to overcome their temptations and problems. We can feel assured that the Lord will help us if we are willing to do our best. Two important things can happen as we receive this help: our children will turn to us for comfort and guidance, and we will come closer to the Lord.

Challenge

Study the scriptures to learn the various ways the Holy Ghost can help you. Through repentance, keep yourself worthy of being guided by the Holy Ghost. Follow the promptings you receive from Him, no matter how difficult doing so may seem.

Additional Scriptures

- Luke 12:11–12 (the Holy Ghost tells us what to say)

- John 16:13 (the Spirit shows things to come)

- 3 Nephi 28:11 (the Holy Ghost bears witness of the Father and the Son)

- Moroni 10:3–5 (by the power of the Holy Ghost we may know truth)

- Doctrine and Covenants 39:6 (the Holy Ghost teaches us peaceable things)

Teacher Preparation

Before presenting this lesson:

1. Read *Duties and Blessings of the Priesthood, Part A,* lesson 30, "The Gift of the Holy Ghost."

2. Read *Gospel Principles* chapter 21, "The Gift of the Holy Ghost."

3. Ask one of the fathers in the class to prepare to tell of a time when the Holy Ghost helped him as a father.

4. Assign class members to present any stories, scriptures, or quotations you wish.

STRENGTHENING THE FAMILY THROUGH FAMILY HOME EVENING

Lesson 13

The purpose of this lesson is to teach us how to strengthen our families through family home evening.

Introduction

Every family should spend at least one evening a week gathered together to teach and strengthen each other. To encourage this, the Church has set aside Monday evening for family home evening.

- Show visuals 13-a, "Every family should hold family home evening once a week"; 13-b, "The family is the most important unit in the Church"; 13-c, "Gospel study should be part of family home evening"; and 13-d, "Children need help in developing spiritual sensitivity."

Since all families are different, so are all family home evenings. Some families have two parents with children at home, others have one parent, and others have a husband and a wife. There are also many single adults who live alone or with roommates. Whatever the size or shape of the family, home evening is for everyone. Parents and children should meet together weekly. Those living alone will be blessed by participating in family home evening alone, with other individuals, or with families.

"There is no more appropriate place for teaching the gospel than the home. Only at home can children learn the nature of family life as authored by our Heavenly Father. Monday night with the family together sets a spirit for all family experiences. Those who have this spirit in their midst find it the source of their greatest joy" (The First Presidency, *Family Home Evening* [manual, 1971], 4).

We should not be discouraged if every family home evening is not ideal; it is important just to spend time together. The Lord promises that if we patiently continue to hold family home evening, He will strengthen our families.

13-a, Every family should hold family home evening once a week.

Planning and Conducting Family Home Evening

It is good to hold a short family council or planning meeting as part of each home evening to review the activities of family members for the coming week. This is especially helpful when there are many members in the family.

One father said that for family council "we gather around the dinner table, with Daddy in charge, and we discuss family business. . . . We make any announcements of importance to the family and discuss and compliment any achievements made by the children during the week. As each child hears his own [accomplishments] retold to the family he glows with pride—and so, I might add, do his parents" (Glen W. Harper, "Participation: Our Family Home Evening Success Key," *Ensign*, Dec. 1977, 17).

Fathers are the patriarchs of their families and should preside over family home evenings. In the absence of a husband or father, the wife or mother should preside. Parents should plan in advance each family home evening and make assignments to family members.

- Show visual 13-e, "Family home evening should involve all family members."

The father either teaches the lesson or delegates the teaching to his wife or children. The teacher can make additional assignments to involve other family members.

There are many activities that are appropriate for family home evening, such as reading the scriptures, discussing the gospel, sharing testimonies, performing a service project, going on a picnic, or playing a family game. Family home evening activities should include a prayer.

Following is a sample of a family home evening plan:

1. Chorister: (name of family member to be chorister)
2. Opening song: (name of hymn or Primary song)
3. Opening prayer: (name of family member to give prayer)
4. Family business: (conducted by head of household)
5. Musical number: (name of family member to give musical number)
6. Lesson from *Gospel Principles* manual: (name of family member to present lesson)
7. Discussion and planning for coming week
8. Closing song: (name of hymn or Primary song)
9. Closing prayer: (name of family member to give prayer)
10. Enjoyable activity: (name of family member assigned)
11. Refreshments: (name of family member assigned)

13-b, The family is the most important unit in the Church.

We should not hesitate to ask even small children to help teach the family home evening lesson. One young member of the Church shared the following: " 'When Dad suggested that everyone in the family take a turn at giving the family night lesson, I thought that it would be funny to say, "Yeah, let John give the lesson next week." John is three years old. So Dad assigned John the lesson, and with Mom's help, John gave one of the best family night lessons that we have ever had, and the joy on that little guy's face was worth more than we will ever be able to give him in return' " (quoted by Lowell Durham Jr., in "What Makes a Good Family Home Evening," *New Era*, June 1972, 13).

Each family member can help make family home evening a success. Everyone can leave Monday night free for family home evening. Also, each family member can help prepare or present the home evening lesson or activity. Young children enjoy praying, leading the music, reading scriptures, holding pictures, performing, presenting simple flannel board stories, passing out refreshments, and participating in other activities. Mother or one of the older children can help them prepare these or other assignments during the week. Children participate more readily when their father and mother include them and are patient with their efforts.

One father discovered that careful planning without love and patience does not ensure a successful family home evening:

"Some years ago I felt a bit ornery one Monday evening. As we began our home evening, the children were poking at each other and acting wild. I became upset and announced in a loud voice, 'Sit up straight and knock off the fooling around or else there is going to be some big trouble around here.' The children could see by the red in my face that I was serious. They became quiet. I continued by saying, 'I don't know why you can't sit still for a few minutes and listen. Now, I don't want to hear anything out of any of you until I finish this lesson. And when I finish I'm going to ask some questions. You'd better know the answers.' . . .

"Finally I finished the lecture and began to ask the questions. They knew every answer. I had taught the ideas very well. I then asked, 'Do you children have any questions?'

"My oldest son said in a subdued tone, 'I do.' He then asked, 'Next week could Mom teach the lesson?'

"His words and my feelings told me that in trying to do right, I had done wrong. I had taught ideas, but I hadn't taught my family. . . .

"I have learned a few things since then. I still don't let the children get very far out of line—nor do they seem to want to—but I've found better methods of discipline. I've determined to control myself, and, with

13-c, Gospel study should be part of family home evening.

the help of prayer, I've done it. I simply refuse to get upset during family home evening."

This father finished the account of his experience by sharing the following advice:

"Be pleasant. Save your best and friendliest behavior for home. . . .

"In our home, family home evening is not like the formal classes at the chapel. No law says we must sit in chairs; we often sit on the floor to make sure everyone feels relaxed. . . .

"Fathers get upset because they feel they must see that the lesson is taught and that the family members pay strict attention. That idea is partially correct, but when it becomes an obsession, family home evenings become unpleasant experiences" (George D. Durrant, *Love at Home, Starring Father* [1976], 44–46).

- How can we use prayer to improve our family home evenings?

- How much time should we spend each week preparing for family home evening? How can better planning improve our home evenings?

Members of the First Presidency asked parents: "Do you spend as much time making your family and home successful as you do in pursuing social and professional success? Are you devoting your best creative energy to the most important unit in society—the family; or, is your relationship with your family merely a routine, unrewarding part of life?"

They continued, saying, "Parents and children must be willing to put family responsibilities first in order to achieve family exaltation" (*Family Home Evening* [manual, 1973], 4).

Family Home Evening Strengthens the Family

- Hold a bundle of sticks or matchsticks in your hand. Tell the class that these represent members of a family. Take one of the sticks out of the bundle and break it in half. Tell the class that when we stand alone we are not as strong as when we are with our family. Then take a string or elastic band and bind the sticks together. Tell the class that the string represents the strengthening influence of the gospel. Show how difficult it is to break the sticks. Explain that we are stronger when we are united as a family and strive together to live the gospel.

Well-planned weekly family home evenings can help us assist family members to overcome the evil influences in the world. Satan is attacking righteousness, using many different temptations to promote sin and wickedness. The youth are his special targets. If we teach them the

13-d, Children need help in developing spiritual sensitivity.

gospel and strengthen them spiritually in the home, they will be more able to withstand the temptations they face in the world.

"In our Home Evenings and other positive family experiences we can fill our souls with the things of God, thus leaving no room for evil to find a place in our hearts or minds" (The First Presidency, *Family Home Evening* [manual, 1972], 4).

In 1915 the First Presidency of the Church gave us this promise: "If the Saints obey this counsel [to hold family home evening], we promise that great blessings will result. Love at home and obedience to parents will increase. Faith will be developed in the hearts of the youth of Israel, and they will gain power to combat the evil influences and temptations which beset them" ("Home Evening," *Improvement Era*, June 1915, 734).

- What blessings have come to your family through family home evening?

The family home evening program can build love and peace in our homes. As this feeling grows, our families will desire to live the gospel, and much of the quarreling and contention in our homes will be elimi- nated. As our families pray, sing, and discuss the gospel together, the Spirit of the Lord can come into our homes and replace any spirit of contention found there.

Elder Marion D. Hanks shared a personal story illustrating this Spirit: "I knelt with my own family, at the conclusion of a great family home evening, the night before our lovely daughter was to be married in the temple. I think she wouldn't mind my telling you that after we had laughed and wept and remembered, she was asked to pray. I don't recall much of her prayer, the tears and the joy and the sweetness, but I remember one thought: she thanked God for the unconditional love she had received. This life doesn't give one very many chances to feel exultant and a little successful, but I felt wonderful that night" (in Conference Report, Oct. 1971, 119; or *Ensign*, Dec. 1971, 106).

- How can regular family home evenings bring more love and peace into our homes? How can they help family members fight the forces of evil? (Write the ideas on the chalkboard.)

- Ask the assigned class members to share special family home evening experiences they have had.

Conclusion

Family home evening is part of the Lord's plan to help us return to Him. It is a time set aside for us to teach our children the principles

13-e, Family home evening should involve all family members.

of the gospel and to help our families draw closer in love and understanding. These times together can help us strengthen our family and teach us how to live together in greater love and harmony. Our family members will thus be better able to combat the influences of evil in the world.

"Again most earnestly we urge parents to gather their children around them in love and patience and understanding, and instruct them in truth and righteousness. . . . The home is the first and most effective place for children to learn the lessons of life" (The First Presidency, *Family Home Evening* [manual, 1975], 3).

Challenge

If you are not holding regular family home evenings, begin this week. Prayerfully plan them to meet the needs of your family. Involve all family members in family home evening as much as possible.

Additional Scriptures

- Mosiah 4:14–15 (parents to teach children truth)

- Doctrine and Covenants 68:25 (parents to teach children doctrine)

Teacher Preparation

Before presenting this lesson:

1. Prepare a bundle of small sticks or matchsticks to perform the object lesson suggested in the lesson.

2. Ask a few class members to prepare to tell briefly of special family home evening experiences they have had.

3. Assign class members to present any stories, scriptures, or quotations you wish.

HAVING FUN TOGETHER AS FAMILIES

Lesson 1 4

The purpose of this lesson is to encourage us to strengthen our families by having fun with them.

Introduction

- Show visual 14-a, "Having fun together strengthens families."

- Ask the two assigned class members to share their happiest family experiences. Point out that an important part of gospel living is doing things together as a family.

Elder Marion D. Hanks told the following story:

"Young people want and deserve parents and a family they can be proud of. . . . The influence of a good family is well-captured by this account from an unknown source:

" 'It was a gorgeous October day. My husband Art and I were down at the boat landing helping our friend Don drag his skiff up on the beach. Art remarked wistfully that it would be a long time before next summer, when we could all start sailing again. "You folks ought to take up skiing like our family and have fun the year round," Don said.

" ' "Doesn't that get pretty expensive?" I asked.

" 'Don straightened up and smiled. "It's funny," he said. "We live in an old-fashioned house. . . . For years we've been saving up to have the bathroom done over. But every winter we take the money out of the bank and go on a couple of family skiing trips. Our oldest boy is in the army now, and he often mentions in his letters what a great time we had on those trips. You know, I can't imagine his writing home, 'Boy, we really have a swell bathroom, haven't we?' " ' " (in Conference Report, Apr. 1968, 57; or *Ensign*, June 1968, 75).

- How did this family strengthen its unity?

14-a, Having fun together strengthens families.

Most of us like to spend our time doing worthwhile things. Working, magnifying Church callings, relaxing, improving ourselves—all are important and take much of our time. However, these may not be the most valuable activities in our lives. Think about how you would answer the following questions:

- What are the most important activities in my life?

- Do I spend enough time doing the most meaningful activities in my life?

- How could I organize my life so I could have more time for the most important activities?

One of the most important ways to spend our time is with our family. However, daily routines, personal interests, or poor planning may cause us to develop poor habits and waste time that could be spent with our family. Yet despite our circumstances, we must find time to spend with our family and discover ways to improve our family relationships.

- What brings a family closer together? (Answers may include caring, showing love, sharing, and doing things for and with each other.)

Activities That Unify Families

Most of us can remember from our childhood the great joy of sharing experiences as a family. A mother made this observation:

"When I think back on my childhood and my teenage years I recall with an almost reverent attitude those pleasant memories of the things we children and mother and father did as a family. I remember that in those days there wasn't much to do in the community so we had to seek our recreation in our home. I wouldn't trade the memories of our family parties and other family recreation for all of today's theatres, bowling alleys, and restaurants. . . .

"I am determined to do all I can to plan activities for my family that will bring the Lord's Spirit into our home the way the Spirit filled the home of my parents. I want my children to have the great blessing of having the memories that are so dear to me" (*Family Home Evening Manual* [1968], 184–85).

Like this mother, we should try to provide positive memories for our families. But the activities offered by the world outside the home are not always acceptable; many do not build family unity and a closeness to our Heavenly Father. Church leaders recognize a growing need for families to do things together and have counseled us to plan family activities. President David O. McKay, for example, counseled us to make our homes attractive and have more activities there (see *Gospel Ideals* [1954], 485–86). If we do so, our children will be happy and proud to bring their friends home, because home will be a warm, friendly, happy place.

- What are some activities that unify families? (List the suggestions on the chalkboard. Add any of the following to the list: write regularly to someone far away, make a family scrapbook, make up and play a game, have treats after an activity, have a night of singing, have a hobby night, make and fly a kite, each week take turns reading aloud a favorite book, or help another family.)

One father shared how he helped bring his family together:

"When I was called to be a mission president, I was fearful that at a most critical time in the lives of my eight children I might not have sufficient time to be a good father. I was determined that being a father was a more important call from the Lord than being president. That meant that even though I would dedicate myself to the mission, I would *double* my dedication as a father. I knew that in order to preside effectively in the mission, I must first preside well at home. I spent much time with my family, knowing they were the only ones who would still be mine at the end of my mission. If they felt secure and happy in the early days of our mission, things would go from good to better.

"One of the first orders of business was to throw a big rope over a high limb on the huge ash tree that towered over our front yard. [A missionary] climbed the rope and tied it to the limb. Thus the giant mission home swing was born. With the swing came instant neighborhood friends for our younger children.

"A few months after our arrival, we attended a mission presidents' seminar. Each president, asked what he felt was his best idea so far, reported on some program which he felt had enhanced the work. When my turn came, I said, 'The best thing I've done so far is to build a swing.' Everyone laughed. President S. Dilworth Young was amazed and asked, 'What?' I described the swing and explained that my major goal was to be a good father. . . . The swing became my symbol of this setting of priorities. Later came a basketball standard and a sandpile. Our yard became a park where I spent much time with my children and where they settled for three happy years. I believe they will forever remember with joy their time in Kentucky and Tennessee" (George D. Durrant, *Love at Home, Starring Father* [1973], 18–20).

- What did this father do to help build family unity?

- Have a class member read Ecclesiastes 3:1–8.

This scripture tells us that "there is a season, and a time to every purpose under the heaven," including "a time to laugh." No matter how busy we are, we should take time as a family to relax and have fun together. Our homes should be full of laughter and happiness

Even work can be enjoyable if approached in the right way. For example, in families with small children, work such as planting a garden, cleaning the house, or washing the dishes can be approached as a game. This will keep enthusiasm and interest high. Such an approach can help us lead our families toward happy lives that are balanced between work, rest, and play.

Planning Family Activities

Successful family activities are usually planned in advance. The following suggestions can help us plan and carry out family activities:

1. List the activities all family members enjoy. This could be done in a family home evening.

2. Choose an activity from the list.

3. Select a date for the activity. Write it on the family calendar to avoid conflicts.

4. Plan the activity together, involving everyone. Give an assignment to each member of the family.

5. Promote the activity in our family—talk about it with excitement.

6. Save money for the activity, if necessary.

7. Do it!

▪ What else can we do to plan and carry out family activities?

After having an activity, we should think about how to improve our family fun. We should ask ourselves what would have made the activity more successful and what would have brought the family closer together. If we do this, it is less likely that we will repeat our mistakes. We can plan together to make the next activity even better.

We should record our activities in our family records and personal journals and include photographs and special souvenirs, when possible. Remembering the fun we have had together can strengthen our love for one another.

Fathers should also plan to spend time alone with each family member. This is a good way for a father to develop closeness with his children. Children feel important and loved when their fathers make the effort to spend time with them alone.

Spontaneous activities can also bring families closer together. Such activities are valuable; we should take advantage of them.

Activities Strengthen Families

The following story shows what children want most from their fathers:

"Three hundred twenty-six school children of a district near Indianapolis were asked to write anonymously just what each thought of his father.

"The teacher hoped that the reading of the essays might attract the fathers to attend at least one meeting of the Parent-Teachers Association.

"It did.

"They came in [inexpensive] cars and [luxurious] cars. Bank president, laborer, professional man, clerk, salesman, meter reader, farmer, utility magnate, merchant, baker, tailor, manufacturer, and contractor, every man with a definite estimate of himself in terms of money, skill, and righteousness or looks. . . .

"The president picked at random from [a] stack of papers. 'I like my daddy,' she read from each. The reasons were many: he built my doll house, took me coasting, taught me to shoot, helps with my school-work, takes me to the park, gave me a pig to fatten and sell. Scores of essays could be reduced to: 'I like my daddy. He plays with me.'

"Not one child mentioned his family house, car, neighborhood, food, or clothing.

"The fathers went into the meeting from many walks of life; they came out in two classes: companions to their children or strangers to their children.

"No man is too rich or too poor to play with his children" (Bryant S. Hinckley, *Not by Bread Alone* [1955], 84).

Playing together as a family often gives us the chance to teach gospel principles. Beginning our activities with family prayer will teach our children the value of prayer. Settling differences that occur when we play will teach them how to get along with others and to be consider-ate of others' feelings. Helping each other and working together as a team will teach responsibility and cooperation. Having fun together will help all family members build positive, happy attitudes.

Over the years, family activities often become family traditions. Some families have family reunions; others go on vacations, visit the temple, or go fishing or hunting; still others form family musical groups or develop hobbies together. There are many good traditions families can establish, and they are all valuable because they help bind families together.

- Invite a few class members to tell how playing together has strengthened their families.

Some of us become so involved with work and Church activities that we neglect our families. This is not pleasing to our Heavenly Father. One such man, who spent most of his life in church service, realized one day that he was losing his son. He had not spent much time with him, and consequently they were not close as fathers and sons should be. When he tried to teach his son to live the gospel, his son rebelled and became inactive in the Church.

But this good father had the wisdom to make time for his son, as he had with the older children before he became so busy. He did not preach to him; instead, he started playing with his son. He began to do what his son liked to do. They went to ball games together. They hunted and fished together. They camped out together.

After three years of such activity together, during which time the two became very close, the son came back into Church activity. He later accepted a call to serve a mission. This father learned that one way to reach a son is to do things with him.

Conclusion

Our family is one of the most important things in our life. It is important, therefore, that we do that which will help us become eternal families. Setting aside time to play together and build each other will help us do this.

- Bear your testimony of the importance of playing with your family.

Challenge

Organize a family activity that will be fun for all family members. This planning could be done during family home evening. Organize a family calendar that includes specific activities you will do together each month.

Teacher Preparation

Before presenting this lesson:

1. Ask two class members to prepare to tell briefly about their happiest family experiences.

2. Be prepared to bear your testimony of the importance of playing with your family.

3. Assign class members to present any stories, scriptures, or quotations you wish.

SHARING IN FAMILY WORK

L e s s o n   1 5

The purpose of this lesson is to help us develop positive attitudes about work and to encourage this attitude among our family members.

Introduction

"[A newspaper printed] an interview with a retired shepherd whose age [was] listed at 165. His name [was] Shirali Mislimov. He was born and has lived all his life in the Caucasus Mountains . . . between the Black Sea and the Caspian Sea. . . .

"Mislimov still chops wood. 'I am convinced an idler cannot live long,' he told his interviewer. . . .

"The article said that the old man still 'digs around trees in an orchard, which he has replanted several times in his lifetime.'

" '*Constant work,* mountain air, and moderate eating helped me reach such an advanced age,' said Mislimov, who neither drinks nor smokes" (Wendell J. Ashton, "The Sweetness of Sweat," *Ensign,* July 1971, 35; italics added).

Elder Neal A. Maxwell told how he learned the importance of work in his youth: "I was blessed with parents who, as devoted Church members, taught me many things about the gospel early in my life, including the importance of the gospel of work. They were both hard workers and tried to save what money they had. . . . It was easy for me to learn to like to work because I had parents who worked without complaining" ("Gospel of Work," *Friend,* June 1975, 6).

President David O. McKay said, "Let us realize that the privilege to work is a gift, that the power to work is a blessing, that love of work is success" (quoted by Franklin D. Richards, "The Gospel of Work," *Improvement Era,* Dec. 1969, 101).

- Why is our attitude about work important? How does our attitude affect the job we do? How can our attitude about work influence our children?

Work for the Entire Family

■ Show visual 15-a, "Every family member should share in family work."

Regardless of who we are or where we live, we all have work to do. Fathers generally provide food, clothing, and shelter for their families. Mothers usually manage the home and train the children. All family members are responsible for household duties. Children should understand that they are an important part of the family and that their help is needed.

■ What are some routine tasks at home that we and our children are responsible for? (Answers could include repairing and maintaining yards and buildings, caring for animals, removing trash, preparing meals, tending children, sewing, shopping, and cleaning.)

Sometimes we may have to create or find work for children. Elder Loren C. Dunn told how his father solved this problem:

"While we were growing up in a small community, my father saw the need for my brother and me to learn the principle of work. As a result, he put us to work on a small farm on the edge of town where he had been raised. He ran the local newspaper, so he could not spend much time with us except early in the morning and in the evening. That was quite a responsibility for two young teenagers, and sometimes we made mistakes.

"Our small farm was surrounded by other farms, and one of the farmers went in to see my father one day to tell him the things he thought we were doing wrong. My father listened to him carefully and then said, 'Jim, you don't understand. You see, I'm raising boys and not cows.' After my father's death, Jim told us his story. How grateful I was for a father who decided to raise boys, and not cows. In spite of the mistakes, we learned how to work on that little farm, and I guess, although they didn't say it in so many words, we always knew we were more important to Mother and Father than the cows or, for that matter, anything else" (in Conference Report, Oct. 1974, 12; or *Ensign*, Nov. 1974, 11).

Organizing and Assigning Work

All family members benefit from work done at home, and so they should be willing to do their share. Each family member should be assigned duties that fit his or her abilities. This will prevent idleness and get all the work done. Even little children can be given simple tasks.

When organizing and assigning family work we should meet with our family members and include them in the decision-making process. We may do this during family home evening, or we may hold a special

15-a, Every family member should share in family work.

family meeting. However we manage it, all family members should be involved in the organizing, since all will be expected to do their share of the work.

One way to organize housework is to make a list of all the work that must be done, listing the tasks in order of importance or difficulty. Then a family member's name can be placed on the assignment sheet next to each work item. When the list is complete, it should be posted where all can be reminded of their duties. If a family member cannot read, pictures can be drawn to symbolize words and names.

- Display a poster of the following sample list, or refer to the information on the chalkboard:

Family Responsibilities	
Clean yard Shop	Father
Mend and launder clothing Prepare meals	Mother
Milk the cow Feed the animals Carry out garbage	John
Wash dishes Tend younger children	Mary
Clean cooking area Gather fuel	Sarah

To provide a refreshing change and a variety of experiences, family members may want to exchange duties from week to week or month to month. If this is done, the assignment list should be replaced with a new one. Of course, this chart is only one method of organizing family jobs.

- Invite a few class members to share how they organize family jobs.

One family who used this method found that it gave them a way to teach personal responsibility to their children. During a family home evening the family made a list of household jobs. The six-year-old boy

134

agreed to care for the yard in front of their house. This meant he had to water the plants, pull the weeds, and trim the grass.

A few days later the father noticed paper lying around and the lawn looking neglected. He thought of doing the boy's job. It would be easy to do. But he knew if he did, he would take back the responsibility he had given. So he left the yard as he found it.

The next night the yard looked worse. His son was simply not doing his job. His neighbors' clean yards made his own yard look worse. The father thought of the expense if the plants should die. He even wondered if he had given too big a job for a six-year-old. But again, he decided his son was more valuable than things, and he refused to take over.

Instead, the father asked his son if the two of them could walk around to see how things were going. The son agreed. After they walked around the yard, the boy said, "Oh Dad, it's so hard!" The father said, "Would you like me to help you?" "Oh yes!" his son said. "Wait here." The boy ran into the house, brought out two bags, and asked his father to clean up part of the yard while he cleaned the rest. A few minutes later they finished.

Within two more weeks that son had become completely responsible for the yard. He knew if he did not take care of it, no one would. He knew that his father depended on him and trusted him. (Adapted from Stephen R. Covey, *Spiritual Roots of Human Relations* [1970], 145–46.)

- How did this father help his son fulfill his responsibility? In addition to providing personal help, what else can we do to make routine tasks more pleasant? (We can give small rewards to encourage children to finish their projects.)

Teaching responsibility and sharing the workload is important. Organizing the family so all have specific duties can help parents to do this. However, we must not forget to also leave time for rest and relaxation. Elder Franklin D. Richards reminded us to schedule time for relaxation as well as work: "In searching for ways to develop a love of work, we must not overlook the matter of relaxation. Although work is absolutely essential to achievement, relaxation and proper rest are likewise necessary. [The power to pace oneself] is an important factor in developing a love of work. The Lord expects each of us to work out a proper balance between work and relaxation as well as the physical and spiritual aspects of life" (*Improvement Era*, Dec. 1969, 103).

The Value of Working Together

- What is the value of working together as a family? (List the responses on the chalkboard. Be sure to include the following:

we will experience joy in seeing the results of our combined labor, we will feel closer to our families, our children will learn to cooperate and share responsibility, we will experience joy as parents because we are obeying the will of the Lord, and each family member will benefit from learning to work.)

"In one Latter-day Saint family where the father was a physician, the parents were concerned that their children learn the value of work. They realized that they were passing up an opportunity for their children's growth by hiring a custodian to clean the office.

"The children, excited about the opportunity to earn a regular income, took over the task of cleaning the office each morning. Teamwork became an important factor. The girls in the family would clean the office one morning while the boys stayed home to assist with household duties; then on the following morning they would rotate duties. . . .

"As a result of the project: (1) the children became familiar with their father's vocation. . . . (2) The children felt that they were a part of their father's business, and they felt a personal pride in his work. (3) The children had a regular work project with daily tasks to perform and a feeling of responsibility for seeing that the job was done. (4) The children developed teamwork. . . . (5) The children had a regular income" (Elwood R. Peterson, "Family Work Projects for Fun and Profit," *Ensign*, June 1972, 8).

▪ What is the law of the harvest? ("We reap what we sow." Write this phrase on the chalkboard.)

Each task we perform has its own natural reward. As we plant gardens and care for them, we enjoy the fruits of our labor at harvesttime. As we build and repair our homes, we live in greater comfort and security. As we keep our clothing clean and attractive, we enjoy greater comfort and set a good example of cleanliness. As we prepare nutritious food and keep dishes clean, we enjoy better health.

One of the goals of family work is to develop character and learn to work. Individuals become dependable as they take on responsibility and enjoy the satisfaction of a job well done. President Spencer W. Kimball said: "I hope that we understand that, while having a garden, for instance, is often useful in reducing food costs and making available delicious fresh fruits and vegetables, it does much more than this. Who can gauge the value of that special chat between daughter and Dad as they weed or water the garden? How do we evaluate the good that comes from the obvious lessons of planting, cultivating, and the eternal law of the harvest? And how do we measure the family togetherness and cooperating that must accompany successful canning? Yes, we are laying up resources in store, but perhaps the greater good is contained in the lessons of life we learn as we *live providently* and extend to our children their pioneer heritage" ("Welfare Services: The Gospel in Action," *Ensign*, Nov. 1977, 78).

The following incident shows how one family member learned the value of working with her family:

"During the mid-summer months there were acres of sugar beets to be thinned. This means that we had to dig up some of the small vegetables to make more room for the beets to grow larger. We loved to eat the sweet roots of the beets that we thinned, but we got awfully tired of bending over all day thinning them out. One day I tried to stay at the house and not have to go down those long beet rows on my hands and knees. I told my father that my head ached—which I'm quite sure it did—but he didn't give me permission to rest. So we all walked out into the field and began to work.

"After thinning for a while I complained that my head ached. My father apparently didn't believe me because I wasn't sent to the house. Again and again I complained of my head aching. . . . At last my father said, 'All right, you go to the house and tell your mother to come and thin beets in your place.' This horrified me—I couldn't think of my mother coming into the field and doing my work. I told my father that I preferred to stay and work: as I worked, my head quit hurting and I didn't complain again."

- What did this girl learn from her experience? (Answers may include the importance of work, doing her share, respect for her parents.)

Conclusion

Elder Neal A. Maxwell said:

"I do not believe people can be happy unless they have work to do. One can really be more of a slave to idleness than to work. Work also keeps us humble and reminds us of how all our blessings come to us from our Heavenly Father. . . .

"The gospel of work is a very important teaching of the Church. If we learn to work early in life we will be better individuals, better members of families, better neighbors, and better disciples of Jesus Christ, who Himself learned to work as a carpenter" (*Friend*, June 1975, 7).

Challenge

Be cheerful and uncomplaining about your work. Plan, organize, and prepare a family work schedule this week that assigns family members their duties.

Additional Scriptures

- Proverbs 6:6–11 (example of the ant)

- Ephesians 4:28 (counsel to be self-reliant and charitable)

- 1 Thessalonians 4:9–12 (Saints to work with their own hands)

- 2 Nephi 5:17 (Nephites encouraged to be industrious)

- Doctrine and Covenants 42:42 (the idle not to eat the bread of the laborer)

- Joseph Smith—History 1:55 (Joseph Smith labored)

Teacher Preparation

Before presenting this lesson:

1. Read *Duties and Blessings of the Priesthood, Part A,* lesson 23, "Developing and Improving Employment Skills."
2. Read *Gospel Principles* chapter 27, "Work and Personal Responsibility."
3. Prepare the poster suggested in the lesson, or write the information on the chalkboard.
4. Assign class members to present any stories, scriptures, or quotations you wish.

HOME GARDENING

L e s s o n   1 6

The purpose of this lesson is to help us improve our skills in growing family gardens.

Introduction

President Spencer W. Kimball said: "We encourage you to grow all the food that you feasibly can on your own property. Berry bushes, grapevines, fruit trees—plant them if your climate is right for their growth. Grow vegetables and eat them from your own yard. Even those residing in apartments or condominiums can generally grow a little food in pots and planters. Study the best methods of providing your own foods. Make your garden . . . neat and attractive as well as productive. If there are children in your home, involve them in the process with assigned responsibilities" (in Conference Report, Apr. 1976, 170–71; or *Ensign,* May 1976, 124).

The Rewards of Home Gardening

There are many good reasons to have gardens:

Family Unity

Families who work together in a home garden build family unity because they share a common purpose. President Kimball said: "We hope you are making this [gardening project] a family affair, with everyone, even the little ones, assigned to something. There is so much to learn and harvest from your garden, far more than just a crop itself" (in Conference Report, Apr. 1978, 120; or *Ensign,* May 1978, 79).

Appreciation of Work

A home garden helps children learn the value of work. After they have helped the family plant a garden and care for it, they will enjoy seeing the results that come from their hard work.

Self-Sufficiency

Growing a garden helps us develop confidence as we become better prepared to take care of our own needs. We know that if problems come we can meet them because we have preserved fruit, grown a garden, and planted fruit trees and berry bushes. An added blessing is knowing that we can also help others in need.

Instruction and Pleasure

A garden reminds us of the beauties of this world our Heavenly Father created for us, and it can give us hours of instruction and pleasure as we witness the miracle of growth. President Spencer W. Kimball said that gardening will "remind us all of the law of the harvest. . . . We do reap what we sow. Even if the plot of soil you cultivate, plant, and harvest is a small one, it brings human nature closer to nature as was the case in the beginning with our first parents" (in Conference Report, Apr. 1976, 117; or *Ensign,* May 1978, 77–78).

Health

The Lord loves us and wants us to be healthy. Growing and eating our own fresh vegetables and fruits will help us maintain good health. Also, food we get from our gardens is usually fresher and better tasting than the food we buy.

Reduced Expenses

Home gardening can reduce the cost of living. Eating the food we grow ourselves enables us to save the money we would have spent on food grown by others.

- What else can we learn from planting and harvesting a garden?

Beginning with a Plan

Before we actually plant our gardens, we must make the following decisions:

Where Do We Plant?

- Show visuals 16-a, "A home garden can produce many kinds of food"; 16-b, "Gardens can be planted almost anywhere"; and 16-c, "Vegetables and fruits can be grown in pots if land is unavailable."

A garden deserves the best location possible because it will become a valuable piece of land. A sunny location that receives at least six hours of sunlight each day is best for a garden plot.

The garden should be easily accessible from the home. It should not be so steep that the water will wash away the soil and seeds. If the garden must be on a steep slope, the furrows, or trenches in the earth, should run *across* the slope, not up and down.

Soil is also important. If it is too sandy, it cannot hold water. If it is too full of clay, the water puddles on top and penetrates slowly. We can solve either problem by adding the opposite kind of soil and by adding

16-a, A home garden can produce many kinds of food.

compost. If there is not enough rainfall in the area, water for irrigation will be needed.

Those who live in apartments face special problems because of space limitations. These people can garden in pots and planters or borrow or rent land. This is what two families in Germany did in order to have a garden. Writing of their experience to President Spencer W. Kimball, they said:

"We are two families in the Frankfurt Mission, and we [are writing to] tell you about our garden.

"It was not very easy to find a piece of land in a large city like Frankfurt—it is a tiny garden—and when we rented it, it looked like a wilderness, with a broken fence, a broken cottage, and wild grass all over. It did not discourage us.

"First we made a new fence, repaired the cottage, and [dug] the whole garden. In the springtime we planted vegetables and the neighbours told us that [they] would not grow. There is a little stream where we can go on our bikes [carrying cans with us], and this way we carry our water. We prayed to the Lord that he would bless our garden. The Lord did answer our prayers. Every kind of vegetable came. It is so wonderful to see the plants grow" (quoted by Spencer W. Kimball, in Conference Report, Oct. 1976, 5; or *Ensign,* Nov. 1976, 5).

What Do We Plant?

A second decision we will have to make is what to plant. Some garden plots have plenty of space; others have only a little. If space is limited we must choose crops that grow upward on stakes or fencing, like berry vines, pole beans, or tomatoes. We can also conserve space by planting seeds that bear heavily, like squash and tomatoes, rather than planting seeds that produce only one fruit or root apiece, like radishes.

Although we may need to preserve space, we should choose foods that will give our family members the nutrients they need. We should also plant only those foods they like and will eat. Legumes such as lentils, soybeans, peas, and nuts; fruits and leafy vegetables; root vegetables; and grains provide a variety of nutrients from different food groups. Of course, in making our selections we should only choose foods that grow well in our climate and soil.

- Display a poster listing the specific fruits, vegetables, legumes, and grains that grow in your area, or refer to the information on the chalkboard. You may want to discuss which of these crops produce the most food in the least amount of space.

16-b, Gardens can be planted almost anywhere.

We should draw a map of our gardens as we are planning our crops so we can alternate the foods each year. If the same plants are grown in the same spot year after year, their quality will deteriorate.

■ Show visual 16-d, "A sample garden layout."

When Do We Plant?

Another decision we must make is when to plant. Different foods grow best under different conditions. Some crops grow better in a dry season, whereas others prefer a wet season. Some crops grow best in cooler weather, like beets, cabbage, carrots, lettuce, onions, peas, and spinach. Others grow best in warmer weather, like beans, corn, melons, squash, and tomatoes. We must know when to plant the crops that grow best in our area.

■ Display a poster listing the planting times for specific crops in your area, or refer to the information on the chalkboard.

Preparing the Garden Site

Four to six weeks before planting time, clear the garden site of weeds, stumps, stones, trash, and twigs, and loosen the soil with a shovel or hoe so that water can penetrate easily. The soil will be right for planting if it is crumbly but not in clods.

Most soil can be improved. Compost, which is well-rotted plant and animal waste, will improve the texture of both sandy and clay soil. Compost also helps produce more and better crops because it adds nutrients to the soil. Properly prepared compost, however, cannot be made and added to the soil in the same day. Making compost often takes four to six months. Because of this, some people make a compost heap every year and add it to their garden the following year.

Making compost is not difficult. First, locate a spot for the compost. This may be a pit, an open area away from drinking water, or a three-sided corral made of wood or wire fencing on top of the ground. Next, spread a six-inch layer of organic refuse such as grass clippings, leaves, chopped corn cobs, straw, vegetable or fruit peelings, or leftover vegetable foods over the spot, being careful to keep cans, metal objects, bones, fat, or other material that does not decompose quickly out of the heap. To this layer add livestock or poultry waste (manure) or commercial fertilizer. Waste from cows, chickens, sheep, goats, horses, and pigs makes good compost. Never use waste from humans or carnivorous animals; these waste materials contaminate the soil.

■ Show visual 16-e, "The compost heap."

16-c, *Vegetables and fruits can be grown in pots if land is unavailable.*

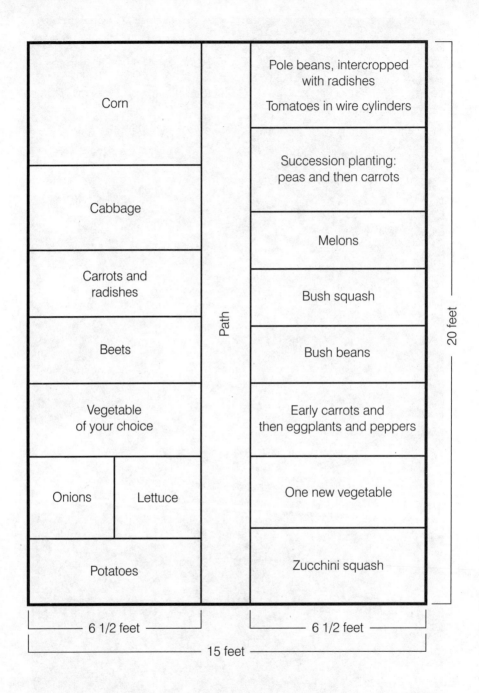

16-d, A sample garden layout

Finish the compost heap by covering the layer of refuse with a two-inch layer of soil. Then indent the top of the heap to form a basin that will collect water. As you collect more refuse, cover each six-inch layer of refuse with two inches of soil. Moisten each layer when you add it to the heap.

Always keep the heap moist but not wet, and turn it with a pitchfork every week or so to let air into the center. The heap will decompose most rapidly if the center is "cooking" at about 160° F. If the compost heap is not hot in the center, add more nitrogen in the form of cotton-seed meal or blood meal, or use a nitrogen fertilizer, if available. When the heap has lost its odor, the compost is ready to be added to the soil.

▪ Invite a few class members to describe how they make compost.

Planting the Garden

In areas where the growing season is short, you can start a garden indoors in potting soil. If you start your garden outdoors, plant the seeds in straight rows so you can distinguish young vegetables from weeds.

Plant rows of the same crop such as corn every week for several successive weeks so that the crop does not mature all at once. Seeds vary in size, so they cannot be planted to the same depth. Normally seeds should be planted no deeper than three times their diameter. Space the seeds far enough apart from each other in each row so that as they sprout and grow the plants have room to mature to their full size. Tap the soil firmly over the seeds, and leave enough room between the rows of seeds to allow the soil to be loosened around the plants while they are growing.

After the seeds are planted, keep the ground moist. If the ground dries out, the seeds will not sprout.

Tending the Garden

All of your planning, preparing, and planting will have little benefit if you do not care for the garden afterward. Such care includes the following:

Water

Water the garden heavily at least once a week where there is not enough rainfall. The soil should be wet seven inches deep just after watering. To prevent the ground from becoming baked, try not to water during the hottest part of the day.

Cultivate

Weeds rob water and nutrients from plants. Pull weeds out by hand, or dig them out with a hoe. After your plants have sprouted, a thick

Layer 1: organic material
Layer 2: soil
Layer 3: organic material
Layer 4: soil

16-e, The compost heap

mulch may prevent weeds from growing, but you must still loosen the soil each week. Using the hoe, pull the mulch to one side, loosen the soil, and then replace the mulch.

Mulch

When the plants get several inches high, remove any remaining weeds, and place sawdust, shredded newspapers, grass, leaves, or straw two or three inches high around the plants and between the rows. This mulch prevents the soil from drying out or getting too warm. Many people who use mulch find they weed less often.

Control Insect Damage

Insects damage plants and can even ruin entire crops. You can remove insects by hand, wash them off, or kill them with insecticide. If you use an insecticide, you must wash the food before eating it.

Harvest the Crops

▪ Show visual 16-f, "A good harvest is the result of good gardening."

Fruits and vegetables picked just before they are cooked, eaten, or preserved will taste best and have the highest nutrition. Some crops such as cucumbers produce better if you harvest them often. Crops should not be allowed to become overripe, wilted, or dried out. Harvest leafy vegetables when they are young and tender.

▪ How can we motivate ourselves to care for a garden after we have planned, prepared, and planted it?

Conclusion

We can show that we love and trust the Lord by doing what His prophets ask us. One thing they have asked us to do is to plant a garden. If we each plan, prepare, and care for a garden, keeping it orderly and producing well, we will be blessed.

Challenge

Work cooperatively with your family members to plant and care for a garden.

Additional Scripture

▪ Doctrine and Covenants 59:16–20 (God gave us the good things of the earth)

Teacher Preparation

Before presenting this lesson:

1. Learn from your library, local agricultural advisers, or experienced gardeners:

16-f, A good harvest is the result of good gardening.

a. Which crops produce best in your area.

b. Which of these crops produce the most food in the least amount of space.

c. Planting dates for each of these crops.

2. Prepare the posters suggested in the lesson, or write the information on the chalkboard.

3. Assign class members to present any stories, scriptures, or quotations you wish.

PERSONAL
DEVELOPMENT

PERSONAL AND FAMILY GOALS

Lesson 17

The purpose of this lesson is to help us set and achieve personal and family goals.

Introduction

When President Spencer W. Kimball was 14 years old, a Church leader visited his stake conference and told the congregation that they should read the scriptures. In recalling the experience, President Kimball said:

"I recognized that I had never read the Bible, [so] that very night . . . I walked to my home a block away and climbed up in my little attic room in the top of the house and lighted a little coal-oil lamp that was on the little table, and I read the first chapters of Genesis. A year later I closed the Bible, having read every chapter in that big and glorious book. . . .

"I found that there were certain parts that were hard for a 14-year-old boy to understand. There were some pages that were not especially interesting to me, but when I had [finished reading], I had a glowing satisfaction that I had made a goal and that I had achieved it" (in Conference Report, Apr. 1974, 126–27; or *Ensign*, May 1974, 88).

A goal is something we desire to achieve. In our premortal life, as spirit children of our Heavenly Father, we learned that this life was to be a time to progress toward becoming like our Heavenly Father. This progress should be our primary goal in life. To reach that goal we need to set and achieve secondary goals. Setting such goals will also help us live a full and abundant life.

Selecting Personal and Family Goals

The first step in selecting a goal is to think about the way we are living and decide how to improve. We can then select personal and family goals to help us improve. If we want to become stronger spiritually, for example, we should examine our spiritual strength and set appropriate goals for improvement. In doing so, we might consider the following questions:

Do I pray as often as I should?

Do I know what the prophet says, and do I follow his counsel?

Do I read the scriptures regularly?

Do I faithfully carry out my priesthood assignments?

Am I honest in paying tithes and offerings?

Do I think clean and worthy thoughts at all times?

Does our family hold family home evening every week?

Has our family been sealed in the temple?

Is our family preparing others to receive the gospel?

We should also consider the progress we hope to make in our education, occupation, and other areas. As we consider each area of our lives, we should determine how we need to improve. We should then set goals to help us do so. Each goal should be challenging, but it should also be something we are able to do.

- Invite class members to list and discuss reasonable goals in the following areas: prayer, scripture study, family home evening, temple marriage, family history, home teaching, missionary work, tithing, thinking clean thoughts, education, and occupation.

It takes time and effort to do these things. Consequently, we should begin by choosing only one or two goals to work on. As we improve in one thing, we can concentrate on another. Perfection is something we work toward step by step all our lives and into eternity; it does not happen just because we have set that as our goal.

To set personal goals we must consider our desires and abilities and pray for inspiration from the Lord. We may also want to ask a spouse, parent, Church leader, or trusted friend for advice in setting goals. We should decide what we want to do, how we want to do it, and when we want to finish it.

President N. Eldon Tanner told of an experience he had with a grandson who set a personal goal:

The grandson said: " 'Grandpa, I have been a hundred percenter ever since I was ordained a deacon a year ago. . . . I haven't missed a sacrament meeting, Sunday School, or priesthood meeting. . . . '

"I congratulated him and said, 'John, if you will continue to be a hundred percenter until you are old enough to go on a mission, I will finance your mission.' He smiled and said, 'I'll do it.'

17-a, Family scripture study offers many rewards.

"I thought I was perfectly safe, but he set about to be a hundred per-center. I remember on two occasions how he disciplined himself in order to accomplish his undertaking. One time his uncle invited him to go for a trip with him and his boys where they would be gone over Sunday. John said, 'Is there any place I can attend my meetings on Sunday?' and as he was told there was not, he said, 'No, I can't go. I am going to be a hundred percenter,' and therefore sacrificed a lovely trip to the ocean and an island on which they were going to celebrate.

"Another time near a weekend he broke his leg. The first thing he asked his doctor was, 'Will I be able to attend Church on Sunday? I have to be a hundred percenter.' He came, of course, on crutches.

"When he became 19 years of age, he said, 'Grandpa, I have been a hundred percenter ever since we made that deal.' I was very happy to finance him on his mission. This achievement has been a great influence in his life" (in Conference Report, Apr. 1975, 113; or *Ensign*, May 1975, 77).

- How long had John worked to achieve his goal? (Six years.) How do you think he felt when he achieved his goal?

To set a family goal, family members should discuss their desires and feelings with each other. Each should take part in establishing the goal, with the father leading the discussion, if possible. Prayer will help in setting the goal.

Elder J. Thomas Fyans told how one family selected its goals:

"Three thousand miles from [Salt Lake City, Utah,] lives a family who will again do a very special thing following this conference. When the *Ensign* arrives with the conference addresses at their home, the family will immediately read the messages, with the older children reporting on selected addresses.

"But they will do more than read. In family home evenings they will select family and personal goals based upon the conference messages. Their goals are practical: 'Remember grandmother in our daily prayers, memorize a Church hymn, review our family preparedness, do the Lord's thing in his way—not ours, bring a nonmember to church.' They will discuss their goals, pray about them, and review them frequently. Is there any wonder why the father says: 'Our family regards general conference as the Lord's list of things we should be concentrating on. It has meant more to us and our children than words can say' " (in Conference Report, Oct. 1974, 89–90; or *Ensign*, Nov. 1974, 65).

17-b, Prayer can draw families closer together.

Goals Assist Our Eternal Progress

- Ask class members to think for a moment about their eternal goals. Invite a few of them to share some of their goals with the class. List these goals on the chalkboard.

As we set goals that help us be more like the Savior and Heavenly Father, we will become worthy to have eternal life with our families. President Joseph Fielding Smith said: "But here [on earth] we lay the foundation. Here is where we are taught these simple truths of the gospel of Jesus Christ, in this probationary state, to prepare us for that perfection. It is our duty to be better today than we were yesterday, and better tomorrow than we are today" (*Doctrines of Salvation,* comp. Bruce R. McConkie, 3 vols. [1954–56], 2:18).

- Show visuals 17-a, "Family scripture study offers many rewards"; 17-b, "Prayer can draw families closer together"; and 17-c, "Family home evening can build spirituality."

We need to select and achieve goals that will help us prepare for eternal life and draw nearer to Heavenly Father. For example, we may set goals to read the scriptures daily, have family prayer, or have family home evening.

- What other goals can help us prepare for eternal life and draw nearer to God?

The following story illustrates how goals help us progress toward eternal life:

When Jerry first met the missionaries, he was 24 years old and very depressed. He had been trained as a teacher but was not working in a job related to teaching. He was not married and saw no real purpose in life. Morning after morning he would ask himself, "Why go through another day?"

One day an old friend who had joined the Church invited him to meet with the missionaries. The elders challenged him to read and pray about the Book of Mormon. As he studied the gospel of Jesus Christ, Jerry felt that life really did have a purpose. As he prayed, he soon knew that the Book of Mormon was true and that he wanted to follow the Savior. Because he wanted to be baptized, he changed his life and began to live the gospel.

After his baptism, Jerry accepted a call from the bishop and was completely faithful in his priesthood duties. He felt a great desire to help others and soon found a job as a teacher of young children. Then he met and married a beautiful young lady, who was also a recent convert.

17-c, Family home evening can build spirituality.

They set a goal to go to the temple and were subsequently sealed together for all eternity. Since then they have found great happiness in following the Lord's plan.

Achieving Our Goals

- Have a class member read 2 Nephi 32:9.

Nephi tells us to pray before we try to accomplish anything. One of the most important parts of setting a goal is committing ourselves to achieve the goal. As we pray to our Heavenly Father, we should ask for His help. We should promise that we will do everything we can to achieve our goals.

- What can we do to remind ourselves of our goals? (Be sure to mention the following ideas: we can write our goals in a journal, write them on a piece of paper that we will see every day, or discuss them regularly with our family.)

All the righteous desires and goals we may have will not help us unless we work to achieve them. The Lord said, "All victory and glory is brought to pass unto you through your diligence, faithfulness, and prayers of faith" (D&C 103:36). As we work diligently, obey the commandments, and pray, we can accomplish our righteous goals. Each day is an opportunity to come a little closer to achieving our goals. We can also make special efforts to help family members reach their goals.

Often we must sacrifice to reach a goal. President Spencer W. Kimball once explained how he was able to achieve one of his goals through sacrifice:

"After my mission I wanted to attend college, but my family could not afford to send me. So I took a job in the freight yards of the Southern Pacific Railroad in Los Angeles to earn money for school. I worked fourteen hours a day moving freight between warehouses and boxcars on a two-wheeled hand truck. Often I had a thousand-pound load on the hand truck. I'm sure you can understand why I was tired at the end of the day.

"I was living with my sister two or three miles away. The streetcar fare was ten cents, and I trudged the whole distance each way in order to save twenty cents a day. I wanted very much to go to college, and walking that distance made my goal that much nearer. . . . [Through sacrifice] I was able to save enough to return to my home state of Arizona and attend the University of Arizona" ("Decisions: Why It's Important to Make Some Now," *New Era*, Apr. 1971, 2–3).

Conclusion

Elder O. Leslie Stone said: *"We should all constantly evaluate our progress. To live righteous lives and accomplish the purposes of our creation, we must constantly review the past, determine our present status, and set goals for the future. Without this process there is little chance of reaching one's objectives"* (in Conference Report, Apr. 1978, 87; or *Ensign,* May 1978, 57).

Setting worthy goals, planning and working toward them, evaluating our progress, and then setting new goals are part of the process that will bring us nearer to eternal life. Heavenly Father is pleased when we set righteous goals, and He will help us achieve them.

Challenge

Prayerfully select a personal goal. You might want to set a goal in one of the following areas: prayer, scripture study, family home evening, temple marriage, family history work, missionary work, tithing, the cultivation of clean thoughts, or home teaching.

Write your goal in your journal or on a piece of paper that you will see often. Commit yourself to achieve the goal. Pray for help and commit to the Lord that you will do your best.

Discuss with your family a goal you can achieve together, and then work toward achieving it.

Teacher Preparation

Before presenting this lesson:

Assign class members to present any stories, scriptures, or quotations you wish.

DEVELOPING AND TEACHING SELF-MASTERY

L e s s o n   1 8

The purpose of this lesson is to help us develop greater self-mastery and to teach us how to help our children develop this strength.

Introduction

A story is told about how Arabian horses are selected and trained. Because these horses are used in important service, they must have unquestioning obedience to their masters. Early in their training they are taught to respond instantly to the master's command. Then they are given a test to see how they behave under pressure. For a long period of time they are kept in an enclosure away from water that is available just outside the gate. After a period of time the gate is opened, and the horses run for the water. Just before they reach the water, however, the master blows a whistle. Because of their thirst, some of the horses pay no attention. But others immediately turn and go to the master. These obedient horses have learned discipline and are accepted for the most important jobs. The others are used in less important work. (Adapted from Sterling W. Sill, *Leadership* [1958], 1:62–63.)

The Lord has given us our agency. Thus, we are free to make choices. These choices determine our future: As we choose righteousness, we prove ourselves worthy to serve in the kingdom of God. But to choose righteousness, we, like the horses, need training, discipline, and obedience. These things help us control our appetites and passions and teach us to follow the promptings of our Master, even when we are tempted.

- Read Proverbs 16:32.

Self-Mastery Is Necessary for Eternal Progression

Self-mastery is the power within us to control our desires and actions. Such power is necessary to return to live with Heavenly Father. It requires continual effort on our part, but as we develop self-mastery, we become better prepared to make correct decisions.

Self-mastery is especially important for us as priesthood bearers. We cannot effectively counsel and serve others unless we are striving to

163

master ourselves. As we strive for self-mastery we are an example to our children and others.

When we are baptized we begin a new life devoted to following the Savior. But to follow Him we must overcome worldliness, weakness, and imperfection. The Savior taught, "If any man will come after me, let him deny himself, and take up his cross, and follow me" (Matthew 16:24). He also taught, "Enter ye in at the strait gate: for wide is the gate, and broad is the way, that leadeth to destruction, and many there be which go in thereat: Because strait is the gate, and narrow is the way, which leadeth unto life, and few there be that find it" (Matthew 7:13–14).

Entering into the narrow way requires self-restraint and self-denial. It means overcoming temptations. But the Lord promises to reward us for mastering ourselves and following His commandments.

Self-Mastery Makes Us Free

Heavenly Father has given us commandments because He loves us and wants to protect us from sorrow. Following His commandments will make us free.

Developing self-mastery will help us form positive habits such as arising early, studying the scriptures daily, and fulfilling our assignments promptly. Such habits can free us from confusion. Following are other principles that bring us freedom when we obey them:

Tithing

By obeying the law of tithing, we learn to overcome selfish desires.

The Word of Wisdom

By living this law we can be free of the harmful effects of tobacco, alcohol, and drugs.

Chastity

Keeping our actions and thoughts within the boundaries the Lord has set frees us from sorrow and regret.

- What other gospel principles bring us freedom when we follow them? How do they free us?

Gaining Self-Mastery

- Read Alma 37:32–37. What does this scripture teach us about self-mastery? (We should feel disgust for sin and iniquity, repent, have faith in Christ, be humble, make the effort to withstand every temptation, never become weary of good works, learn wisdom, keep the commandments of God, pray, and counsel with the Lord in all our doings.)

Gaining self-mastery is a lifelong process. It requires a knowledge of ourselves and of gospel principles. It means setting goals to live those principles and relying on the Lord for strength and support as we do our best to reach those goals.

■ Display a poster of the following list, or refer to the information on the chalkboard:

How to Gain Self-Mastery

1. Know yourself.

2. Set righteous goals.

3. Rely on the Lord through prayer and scripture study.

Know Yourself

As we gain experience and learn more about the gospel, we come to recognize our strengths and weaknesses. With this recognition comes a desire to overcome bad habits and feelings and a motivation to improve strengths we already have.

President David O. McKay said that some of the evils we find in ourselves are jealousy, hatred, envy, and animosity. Of them he said: "All such evils you must overcome by suppression. That is where your control comes in. Suppress that anger! Suppress that jealousy, that envy! They are all injurious to the spirit" (*Gospel Ideals* [1954], 356).

Overcoming these feelings is not easy; it takes time to change. But as we make the effort and depend on Heavenly Father's help, we will develop the patience and courage to overcome the evils we find in ourselves.

Set Righteous Goals

A good way to gain self-mastery is to set and achieve goals. If we have a goal firmly set in our minds and work to accomplish our goals with the Lord's help, we will achieve self-mastery. This process requires endurance, but the Lord has told us that we must endure to the end in righteous living to achieve the goal of exaltation, or eternal life (see D&C 14:7).

■ Ask the class members to ponder for a moment the goals they are presently working toward.

Rely on the Lord through Prayer and Scripture Study

It takes faith in Jesus Christ to overcome our temptations and achieve our eternal goals. Regular prayer and scripture study promote this faith and help us gain the strength to overcome our problems. In addition, the lives of the Lord's servants detailed in the scriptures set examples for us to follow; they help us realize that if others have gained self-mastery, we can gain it too.

- Invite class members to tell how they have gained self-mastery through reading the scriptures and praying.

Helping Children Develop Self-Mastery

- Show visual 18-a, "Wise parents teach their children self-mastery."

Our homes should be places where our children can learn self-mastery. The following four principles can help us teach our children self-mastery.

- Display a poster of the following list, or refer to the information on the chalkboard:

How to Teach Children Self-Mastery

1. Establish and enforce rules early.
2. Teach children the principles of the gospel.
3. Give children responsibility.
4. Discipline with love.

Establish and Enforce Rules Early

President David O. McKay taught that a child should learn obedience at an early age. If parents do not teach their children obedience early, they may have difficulty doing so later on. He stressed that we should let the child be free to develop; but if the child goes beyond the established rules, we should be gentle, yet firm, in our restraint. (See *Stepping Stones to an Abundant Life*, comp. Llewelyn R. McKay [1971], 38.)

President N. Eldon Tanner also discussed the importance of teaching children while they are young: "While we are teaching [our children], we have the responsibility to discipline them and to see that they do what is right. If a child is [covered] with dirt, we do not wait until he grows up to decide whether or not he will bathe. We do not let him

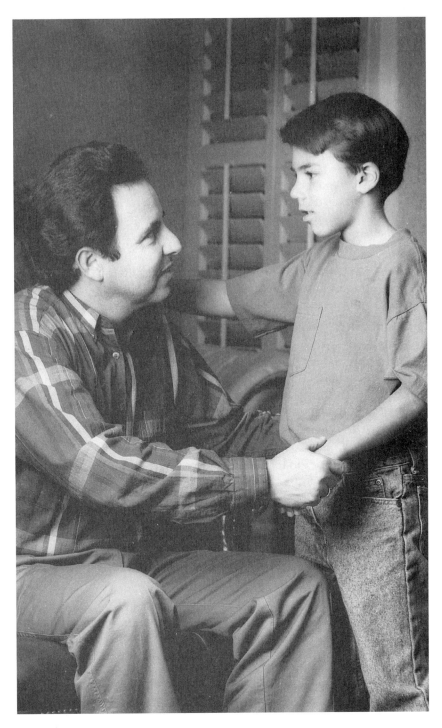

18-a, Wise parents teach their children self-mastery.

wait to decide whether or not he will take his medicine when sick, or go to school or to church" (*Seek Ye First The Kingdom of God,* comp. LaRue Sneff [1973], 87).

Teach Children the Principles of the Gospel

President N. Eldon Tanner said: "Parents also should teach their children early in life the glorious concept and fact that they are spirit children of God, and [that] choosing to follow the teachings of Jesus Christ is the only way to enjoy success and happiness here and eternal life hereafter. They must be taught that Satan is real and that he will use all agencies at his disposal to tempt them to do wrong, to [try to] lead them astray, make them his captives, and keep them from [the] supreme happiness and exaltation they could otherwise enjoy" (*Seek Ye First The Kingdom of God,* 87).

If we want to teach our children gospel principles, we must also set proper examples for our children to follow. If we fail to control our appetites and passions, we cannot expect our children to control theirs.

Give Children Responsibility

Elder L. Tom Perry said: "We must be . . . certain that our teaching is adequate and that we have instilled a faith and trust in the Lord in [our children's] lives. We must be certain that they have been trained properly, and as they start to mature spiritually, we need to give them opportunities to express the strength that is growing within them. We need to give them our faith and trust and then give them responsibility" (in Conference Report, São Paulo Area Conference 1975, 12).

There are many ways to teach children responsibility. Elder F. Enzio Busche gave one example:

"We try to guide our children toward self-respect . . . and mostly leave it up to them to judge themselves. We have experienced the fact that one is not as good a teacher when one discovers and points out mistakes . . . as when one helps a child to discover for himself that he is doing wrong. When a child can comprehend his mistakes himself, the first step to change has already been taken.

"I remember once how we asked our son, after a transgression, to set his own punishment. He decided that he should not be allowed to watch television for one month. That seemed to us to be considerably too severe, but how happy we were to hear from his grandmother that while visiting her he had insisted she was wrong to encourage him to watch a certain television program, even though his parents would never know. I don't think there can be a greater joy for parents than to see a child handle himself well in a difficult situation" ("Provoke Not Your Children," *Ensign,* Mar. 1976, 42).

- What did Elder Busche do to help his children develop self-mastery? (He helped them gain self-respect by discovering their own mistakes. He encouraged them to discipline themselves.)

Before we give our children responsibilities, we as parents must ensure that they are ready for them. President Tanner explained: "Children do not learn by themselves how to distinguish right from wrong. Parents have to determine the child's readiness to assume responsibility and his capacity to make sound decisions, to evaluate alternatives, and [to experience] the results of doing so" (*Seek Ye First The Kingdom of God*, 87).

Discipline with Love

When we discipline our children, we should do so with firmness but not cruelty. We should clearly state our expectations of them and give appropriate punishments. After we discipline our children, we should show an increase of love toward them.

- Read Doctrine and Covenants 121:43–44. Why should we show an increase of love to children after disciplining them? (So they understand that we love them and that we discipline them to ensure their well-being, and so they do not think we are their enemy)

- Discuss the following examples with the class. Emphasize that the solutions require self-mastery. You may want to ask for personal examples from class members instead of listing these examples.

1. Sven and Inger have three teenage children who argue and quarrel constantly. How could they help their children stop quarreling and develop self-mastery?
2. John and Elsie want to have family prayer in their home each day, but work schedules, school schedules, and other duties interfere. Family members feel that it is impossible to get together for family prayer. What can John and Elsie do to help the family develop the self-mastery to have family prayer?
3. The Unga family recognizes the need to pay tithing, but the family members never feel that they have enough money to meet their other expenses. However, they always seem to have enough money for recreation, new clothing, and nonessential items as they desire them. How can these family members develop the self-mastery to pay tithing?

- How will individuals who have mastered themselves act toward others in their family?

Conclusion

Using our God-given agency and working diligently, we must develop self-mastery if we want to prepare ourselves and our families to meet challenges. We must be able to make proper choices and to control our desires and emotions if we are to prepare to return to our Father in Heaven.

- Bear your testimony that as family members consciously develop self-mastery, they can overcome many of the problems in their lives.

- Sing "Choose the Right" (*Hymns,* no. 239), or read the words, found below.

Choose the Right

Choose the right when a choice is placed before you.
In the right the Holy Spirit guides;
And its light is forever shining o'er you,
When in the right your heart confides.

[Chorus] Choose the right! Choose the right!
Let wisdom mark the way before.
In its light, choose the right!
And God will bless you evermore.

Choose the right! Let no spirit of digression
Overcome you in the evil hour.
There's the right and the wrong to ev'ry question;
Be safe through inspiration's pow'r.

[Chorus]

Choose the right! There is peace in righteous doing.
Choose the right! There's safety for the soul.
Choose the right in all labors you're pursuing;
Let God and heaven be your goal.

[Chorus]

Challenge

Select a problem in your life or in your family. Follow the steps outlined in the lesson to master the problem. Read the scriptures for appropriate models in developing self-discipline.

Additional Scriptures

- Proverbs 25:28 (rule your own spirit)

- James 1:26 (control your speech)

- Alma 38 (Alma's counsel to Shiblon to observe meekness and self-control)

Teacher Preparation

Before presenting this lesson:

1. Study *Gospel Principles* chapter 4, "Freedom to Choose."

2. Prepare the posters suggested in the lesson, or write the information on the chalkboard.

3. Prepare to have the class sing at the conclusion of the lesson "Choose the Right" (*Hymns,* no. 239), or plan to read the words in class.

4. Be prepared to bear your testimony that as family members consciously develop self-mastery, they can overcome many personal problems.

5. Assign class members to present any stories, scriptures, or quotations you wish.

DEVELOPING
OUR TALENTS

Lesson 1 9

The purpose of this lesson is to motivate us to improve our talents and to inspire our family members to do likewise.

Introduction

Heavenly Father has given each of us talents, and He wants us to use them. In a parable recorded in Matthew, the Lord told of a man who was about to leave on a long trip. Before leaving he called his servants together and entrusted his goods to them. To one servant he gave five talents (in this parable, *talents* means money); to another, two; and to another, one. To each man he gave talents according to his ability.

While the master was away, the servant with five talents put them to use and made five more talents. The servant with two talents put them to use and made two more. But the servant with one talent hid it in the ground.

Later the master returned and asked his servants to account for their talents. To the servants who had doubled their talents he said, "Well done, thou good and faithful servant: thou has been faithful over a few things, I will make thee ruler over many things: enter thou into the joy of thy lord" (Matthew 25:21). But the master called the servant who hid his talent "wicked and slothful." He said that he would take the talent from him and give it to the servant with 10 talents. (See Matthew 25:14–30.)

The Lord told this parable to teach the importance of using our abilities, or talents, wisely. More was expected from the man given many talents than from the man with fewer talents, yet all were expected to increase the talents they were given. Even the man with one talent was expected to use it wisely.

President Spencer W. Kimball said: "God has endowed us with talents and time, with latent abilities and with opportunities to use and develop them in his service. He therefore expects much of us, his privileged children" (*The Miracle of Forgiveness* [1969], 100).

Everyone Has Talents

Each of us is blessed with talents from God. The talents we have been given may be personal, artistic, or creative. We should use these gifts to serve others and to bring joy to our lives.

- Display a poster of the following list, or refer to the information on the chalkboard. Invite class members to identify and ponder their own talents (the talents do not have to be listed here).

Personal Talents	**Artistic and Creative Talents**
Having self-control	Singing
Being patient	Painting
Having courage	Carving wood
Being kind	Working with ceramics
Having a sense of humor	Sculpting
Being a good listener	Baking
Forgiving easily	Gardening
Inspiring confidence in others	Writing
	Composing songs
Having faith	Dancing
Loving others	Storytelling
Having a strong testimony	Acting
Being active in the Church	Playing a musical instrument
Supporting Church leaders	Being athletic
Seeing good in others	Sewing
Being cheerful	Weaving

The Lord told Joseph Smith:

"For all have not every gift given unto them; for there are many gifts, and to every man is given a gift by the Spirit of God.

"To some is given one, and to some is given another, that all may be profited thereby" (D&C 46:11–12).

This scripture refers to spiritual gifts the Lord has given us. It says that we all have been given talents to help others and to improve ourselves. One Church member explained:

"Our greatest possibility for expansion and development comes in the area of our talents, our virtues, and our abilities. . . .

"If you desire a strong back, all you need to do is carry a great load. By this same procedure, we may expand the abundance of our own abilities to almost any dimension" (Sterling W. Sill, "A Hundred-Hundred Marriage," *Ensign,* Mar. 1971, 34–35).

Working to Discover Our Talents

The Apostle Paul told his young friend Timothy, "Neglect not the gift that is in thee" (1 Timothy 4:14). We should also follow Paul's advice, but if we are to develop our gifts, we must first discover what they are.

To discover our talents, we should first pray to Heavenly Father, asking for His guidance in recognizing them.

Second, we should receive a patriarchal blessing (see *Duties and Blessings of the Priesthood, Part A,* lesson 10, "Patriarchs and Patriarchal Blessings"). Special gifts are often revealed in these blessings. President Spencer W. Kimball said, "It is our great hope that every person . . . will be given the opportunity of having a patriarchal blessing" (*Church News,* 8 Oct. 1977, 3). Although patriarchs function only in organized stakes, a worthy member in a developing area of the Church may receive a patriarchal blessing from the patriarch in the nearest stake.

Third, other people can help us recognize our talents. The following story, told by Elder Franklin D. Richards, shows how President Spencer W. Kimball helped a man recognize one of his talents:

"A few years ago President Kimball and I were in Cusco, Peru, on a Sunday and attended the branch Sunday School. A young missionary from North America was playing the piano. After the service President Kimball asked if any of the local members could play the piano. The branch president told him that one of his counselors could play two hymns. President Kimball then asked that the man play the two hymns for sacrament meeting and he did so. Afterwards President Kimball suggested that he continue to develop his musical talent and play the piano for all Church services" (in Conference Report, São Paulo Area Conference 1975, 24).

The man in this story probably had never recognized his talent. It took someone to point out his talent to him before he started to develop it.

A fourth way we can recognize our talents is through Church service. As we seek the Lord's help in our callings, He will help us discover the talents we need to fulfill our responsibilities. Elder Franklin D. Richards said: "Frequently persons asked to accept a position in the Church are prone to say, 'Oh, I can't do that. I haven't as much experience or education as someone else that may have been serving.' But with faith, study, work, and prayer, the Lord will make it possible for us to accomplish things that seem impossible" (in Conference Report, São Paulo Area Conference 1975, 23).

- What else might help us discover our talents?

Developing Our Talents

Once we have discovered our talents, it is our duty to develop and use them. Doing this may require much work and practice. Sometimes we look at others' talents and think they came to them with very little effort. We do not realize that often people have put much effort into developing their talents.

One man who worked hard at developing his talents was President Heber J. Grant. Explaining how he developed them, he said:

"I could not throw the ball from one base to another; . . . I lacked strength to run or bat well. When I picked up a ball, the boys would generally shout, 'Throw it here, sissy!' So much fun was engendered on my account . . . that I solemnly vowed that I would play base ball [on the team] that would win the championship of the Territory of Utah. . . .

"I saved a dollar, which I invested in a base ball. I spent hours and hours throwing the ball at [Bishop Edwin D. Woolley's] barn. . . . Often my arm would ache so that I could scarcely go to sleep at night. But I kept on practicing, and finally succeeded in getting into the second [team] of our club. Subsequently, I joined a better club, and eventually played [on the first team] that won the championship of the Territory. Having thus made good my promise to myself, I retired from the base ball arena" ("Work, and Keep Your Promises," *Improvement Era*, Jan. 1900, 196–97).

President Grant also worked at his talent in penmanship. He "resolved that some day he would be a bookkeeper in the Wells Fargo and Company's bank." A good bookkeeper had to write well, so he started working to become a penman. One author wrote: "At the beginning his penmanship was so poor that when two of his [friends] were looking at it one said to the other, 'That writing looks like hen tracks.' 'No,' said the other, 'it looks as if lightning had struck an ink bottle.' This touched Heber's pride and, bringing his fist down on his desk, he said, 'I'll some day be able to give you fellows lessons in penmanship'; and he was" (Bryant S. Hinckley, *Heber J. Grant: High-lights in the Life of a Great Leader* [1951], 39–40).

President Grant himself was fond of saying, "That which we persist in doing becomes easier for us to do; not that the nature of the thing itself is changed, but that our power to do is increased" (in Conference Report, Apr. 1901, 63).

Developing our talents may also require us to overcome the fear of using them. The Lord said: "With some I am not well pleased, for . . . they hide the talent which I have given unto them, because of the fear of man. . . . And it shall come to pass, if they are not more faithful unto me, it shall be taken away, even that which they have" (D&C 60:2–3).

Overcoming our fear is never easy to do, but the Lord has given us some counsel that can help: "If ye are prepared ye shall not fear" (D&C 38:30). If we are prepared, we usually feel confident that we can do what we have prepared ourselves to do. Such confidence overcomes fear.

Preparation results from study and practice. We are counseled to "seek learning, even by study and also by faith" (D&C 88:118). If our desire is strong, weak talents can be strengthened by study, practice, and training.

If we fail to develop the talents the Lord has given us, they will be taken from us. One Church member explained: "The Lord grants us our [talents and abilities] on a kind of lend-lease basis where he takes back everything that is not used. These are terms similar to those under which he gave manna to the children of Israel in the wilderness. Each day an abundance of manna covered the ground and the people gathered as much as they desired, but that which was not used spoiled. So it is with our abilities. Most of us never get strong backs or have great minds because the burdens we have given them to bear have never been heavy enough. All of our potential that is not used is lost" (Sterling W. Sill, *Ensign*, Mar. 1971, 35).

- Ask the assigned class member to tell how he recognized and developed one of his talents.

Helping Our Family Members Develop Their Talents

- Show visual 19-a, "Parents should nourish their children's talents."

We should help our family members recognize and develop their talents and teach them to use their talents to serve the Lord.

Following are ways we can help family members develop their talents:

- Display a poster of the following list, or refer to the information on the chalkboard:

19-a, Parents should nourish their children's talents.

**Helping Family Members Develop
Their Talents**

1. Encourage each family member to receive a father's blessing or a priesthood blessing.
2. Establish good family attitudes about talents.
3. Help family members select talents to develop.
4. Encourage family members to pray for strength, courage, and inspiration in developing their talents.

Encourage Each Family Member to Receive a Father's Blessing or a Priesthood Blessing

▪ Show visual 2-c, "Priesthood blessings are available to all family members," or 12-a, "Father's blessings can strengthen family members."

Fathers can give family members blessings to help them gain the desire and ability to develop their talents. If an individual cannot receive a father's blessing, he or she may receive a priesthood blessing for the same purpose from a home teacher or other priesthood leader.

Establish Good Family Attitudes about Talents

We must teach and show by our example that it is good to develop talents. We should also praise our family members when they achieve and comfort them when they fail. We should never criticize them.

Help Family Members Select Talents to Develop

Outline with family members an active program of talent development, and then schedule time for them to practice and demonstrate these talents. A good time for them to demonstrate their talents is during family home evenings.

Encourage Family Members to Pray for Strength, Courage, and Inspiration in Developing Their Talents

If in our family prayers we ask the Lord to help family members develop and use their talents, they will be inspired to pray for these blessings also.

Conclusion

God has granted talents to each of us. In appreciation and by commandment, we must discover and develop them, remembering this counsel as we do so: "Seek ye earnestly the best gifts, always remembering for what they are given; For verily I say unto you, they are given for the benefit of those who love me and keep all my commandments, and him that seeketh so to do" (D&C 46:8–9).

Challenge

Establish a good family attitude about developing and using talents. Outline a plan to develop one of your talents. If you are a father who holds the Melchizedek Priesthood, give each family member a blessing to help him or her discover personal talents. Then help family members select one or two talents they would like to develop. Encourage them to pray for strength, courage, and inspiration in developing their talents.

Additional Scriptures

- Luke 12:47–48 (to whom much is given much is required)

- Ether 12:35 (talents to be taken away if not shared)

Teacher Preparation

Before presenting this lesson:

1. Read *Gospel Principles* chapter 34, "Developing Our Talents."

2. Ask a class member to be prepared to share how he recognized and developed one of his talents.

3. Prepare the posters suggested in the lesson, or write the information on the chalkboard.

4. Assign class members to present any stories, scriptures, or quotations you wish.

DEVELOPING LEADERSHIP

Lesson   2 0

The purpose of this lesson is to help us understand basic leadership principles.

Introduction

- What is leadership? (The ability to lead others)

The Church needs good leaders—men and women who can care for its rapidly growing membership, can conduct the business and maintain the order of the Church established by the Lord, can help others keep the commandments, and will stand firm for the cause of truth throughout the world.

Church leaders who strive to make the world better through living and teaching gospel principles are entitled to knowledge and inspiration. When we are led by such leaders, our homes, families, communities, and nations are strengthened. Our duty as priesthood bearers is to prepare ourselves to be inspired leaders, for our leadership may affect others throughout their lives.

Bishop Victor L. Brown expressed gratitude for the leaders in his early life. He said:

"I remember with some clarity the thrill of passing the sacrament as a deacon in the Cardston Second Ward, Alberta Stake, in Canada. . . .

"I remember how I considered it an honor to participate in such a sacred service. I remember so well how my parents taught me that my hands and heart should be clean and pure so that I would be worthy to participate in this ordinance.

"The greatest of all lessons was the example my father and mother set for me. Next was the example of my deacons quorum adviser, who was also my Scoutmaster. [He] was the epitome of what leaders of boys should be. Every boy under his leadership felt his great love. His influence was not limited to Sunday morning or Tuesday evening; it was felt all through the week. I shall ever be grateful to my deacons adviser for the lessons of life he taught me as a twelve-year-old deacon, lessons that have helped me from that day until now" (in Conference Report, Apr. 1972, 101; or *Ensign,* July 1972, 89–90).

- For what leaders was Bishop Brown grateful? Why were they effective leaders?

- Have class members think about the following questions: What am I doing to prepare for leadership callings? What kind of a leader am I now? What kind of influence do I have on others?

What Is a Leader?

- Show visual 20-a, "Like a true shepherd, a leader shows others the way, inspiring them to follow him."

Elder Bruce R. McConkie said: "The house of Israel is the choice sheepfold of the Lord, and those appointed to care for the sheep are the Lord's *shepherds.* Thus anyone serving in any capacity in the Church in which he is responsible for the spiritual or temporal well-being of any of the Lord's children is a shepherd to those sheep. The Lord holds his shepherds accountable for the safety (salvation) of his sheep. (Ezek. 34.)" (*Mormon Doctrine,* 2nd ed. [1966], 710).

A true shepherd leads his sheep. He goes before them, giving directions. They know his voice and follow him. He knows and loves each one. He watches for approaching dangers and is ready to risk his life for his sheep. (See James E. Talmage, *Jesus the Christ,* 3rd ed. [1916], 417.)

Like a true shepherd, a leader inspires others to follow him and to fulfill their own duties. He shows the way by living the principles he teaches and by understanding and responding to others' needs. A leader recognizes and solves problems, sets and achieves goals, and evaluates his own and his followers' actions and makes and suggests improvements.

President Harold B. Lee, speaking of the time when he became President of the Church, explained what true leadership is: "Somehow the impressions that came to me were, simply, that the only true record that will ever be made of my service in my new calling will be the record that I may have written in the hearts and lives of those with whom I have served and labored, within and without the Church" (in Conference Report, Oct. 1972, 19; or *Ensign,* Jan. 1973, 24).

Qualities of a Good Leader

The Lord revealed in the scriptures the qualities that make a good leader.

- Ask a class member to read Doctrine and Covenants 121:41–45. What leadership qualities does the Lord identify in this passage? (List the responses on the chalkboard.)

*20-a, Like a true shepherd, a leader shows others the way,
inspiring them to follow him.*

As the Lord indicates in this scripture, leaders should have the following qualities:

Persuasiveness

Persuasion is trying to convince others to do something. It is the opposite of ordering or forcing. One priesthood leader used persuasion to help a home teacher fulfill his assignment. The leader met with the home teacher and calmly explained that five families were being completely "cut off" from any communication with the bishop when the home teacher did not do his duty. He told the brother that if he did not want to do his assignment, another could be asked to replace him. The leader stressed, however, that he wanted the brother to fulfill his assignment. The home teacher reacted positively to this persuasion and greatly improved his work.

Long-Suffering

An effective leader endures his challenges, relying on the Lord for strength. He is also patient when working with others, especially with members of his own family.

Gentleness

Gentleness is being considerate. It is treating others' feelings tenderly. It is love.

Meekness

Meekness is being teachable and patient. The meek are those who are willing to learn and ask for God's help. Because of this meekness, others love and appreciate them.

Love Unfeigned

Unfeigned love is sincere love. It is true concern for others that is reflected in expressions and actions that show "I really care how you feel," "I understand you," and "I want to help."

Kindness

Kindness is showing sincere love, care, and respect for others. A kind leader gets to know others and is sensitive to their needs. He makes time to counsel with individuals privately.

Charity

A good leader must have charity, the pure love of Christ, for *all* people. This love includes sacrificing for the well-being of others.

- Invite a class member to read Moroni 7:44–48.

One father, teaching his sons to become good leaders, said: "From the prophets and from the Prince of Peace, learn how to lead, beginning with yourselves. Stand on your own feet. Stand tall. Hold your heads high as though you are truly sons of God, which you are. Walk among men as holders of powers beyond your own, which you have, through the priesthood. Move on the good earth as though you are partners of the Lord in helping to bring immortality and eternal life to mankind, which you are. Walk quietly, . . . but walk fearlessly, in faith. Don't let the ill winds sway you. Walk as leaders with the priesthood in the government of God. Walk with hands ready to help, with hearts full of love for your fellowmen. But walk with a toughness in righteousness" (Wendell J. Ashton, in Conference Report, Apr. 1971, 61; or *Ensign,* June 1971, 58).

Leadership Responsibilities

If we are to become good leaders, we should also do the following:

- Write these qualities on the chalkboard as they are discussed.

Learn Our Duties

The Lord has instructed us as priesthood holders to learn the duties of our callings and to carry out these duties (see D&C 107:99). We can learn our duties by studying the scriptures and the guidebooks, handbooks, and manuals provided by the Church. We can talk with others who hold or have held the same position. We need to attend all our leadership meetings and personal interviews. We also need to pray and sometimes fast for help in learning our duties.

Fulfill Our Stewardship

Stewardship has two parts: delegation of authority and accountability.

Delegation of authority

As leaders we must learn to delegate authority to others. This means giving others the responsibility to do tasks under our direction and then allowing them to do the work. President Harold B. Lee said: "Let them do everything within their power, and you stand in the background and teach them *how* to do it. I think therein is the secret of growth, to fix responsibility and then teach our people *how to carry* that responsibility" (quoted by N. Eldon Tanner, "Leading As the Savior Led," *New Era,* June 1977, 6).

We as leaders help those under our direction realize the importance of their callings. Leadership is not bossing; leadership is offering and giving help and direction; leadership is inspiring and encouraging those to whom we have given responsibility. (See Matthew 23:11.)

Accountability

The Lord said, "It is required of the Lord, at the hand of every steward, to render an account of his stewardship, both in time and in eternity" (D&C 72:3). When we give assignments to others, we should clearly define the responsibilities of the assignments, leaving the people free afterward to complete them as they see best. However, we should give them a specified time to report to us on their progress.

This kind of report, or accounting, should always be made to one's leaders. In the Church this is often done through personal interviews. During the interview, leaders can give counsel and evaluate how well the task was done. In doing so, however, the leader should always remain positive and helpful, offering praise and encouragement when appropriate.

This, then, is the way we fulfill a stewardship as a leader in the Church: (1) assign a task, (2) allow the individual to carry it out, (3) offer assistance, (4) receive a report, and (5) evaluate the service and commend the individual for it.

Be Good Fathers

Our most important leadership role is as fathers. President Joseph F. Smith instructed fathers on how to lead their families well: "Fathers, if you wish your children to . . . love the truth and understand it, if you wish them to be obedient to and united with you, love them! and prove to them that you do love them by your every word or act to them. . . . When you speak or talk to them, do it not in anger; do it not harshly, in a condemning spirit. Speak to them kindly. . . . Soften their hearts; get them to feel tenderly towards you. Use no lash and no violence, but . . . approach them with reason, with persuasion and love unfeigned" (*Liahona: The Elders' Journal,* 17 Oct. 1911, 1:260–61).

Sustain Our Authorities

A good leader is also a good follower of those in authority over him. Good followers earn the trust and confidence of both their leaders and those they lead. We should all support our leaders by accepting and fulfilling the assignments they give us.

- Who are our leaders? (Parents, teachers, group or quorum leaders, bishop or branch president, stake or mission president, and General Authorities of the Church)

- Bear your testimony about someone you feel is an effective Church leader.

Conclusion

We must develop our leadership skills if we are to magnify our Church callings. Obeying God's commandments, following our leaders' counsel, and faithfully serving in our callings will help us develop these skills and build the Lord's kingdom (see D&C 64:29–34).

As priesthood holders we will always be leaders. This is especially true for every father who holds the priesthood: he will always have a leadership position in the Church by being the patriarch to his family. Those fathers who have been sealed to their families in the temple will hold this position eternally if they keep their covenants.

Challenge

Thoughtfully review the leadership qualities presented in this lesson. Work to develop them in your own life by obeying the commandments, following your leaders' counsel, and serving faithfully in every calling and assignment.

Additional Scriptures

- 2 Timothy 1:7 (God has given the spirit of love)

- 1 Nephi 3:7 (God will help us accomplish our tasks)

- Mosiah 18:8–11 (the faithful should help others)

- Alma 38:11–12 (ways to lead and serve)

Teacher Preparation

Before presenting this lesson:

1. Be prepared to bear your testimony about someone who is an effective Church leader.

2. Assign class members to present any stories, scriptures, or quotations you wish.

LEADERSHIP: INSPIRED DECISION MAKING

L e s s o n   2 1

The purpose of this lesson is to help us improve our ability to make inspired decisions.

Introduction

Basic to our existence as children of God are the need and the right to make decisions. Decision making, however, is a challenging experience. We are often concerned about making the right decision and confused about where we can go to receive help in making it.

But we can turn to the Lord for help. He has told us that He is the source of all truth and that through Him we can know the truth of all things. We are His children, and He has not left us powerless in facing life's challenges.

Elder Boyd K. Packer said: "It is critically important that you understand that you already know right from wrong, that you're innately, inherently, and intuitively good. When you say, 'I can't! I can't solve my problems!' I want to thunder out, 'Don't you realize who you are? Haven't you learned yet that you are a son or a daughter of Almighty God? Do you not know that there are powerful resources inherited from Him that you can call upon to give you steadiness and courage and great power?' " ("Self-Reliance," *Ensign,* Aug. 1975, 88).

Help from the Lord

When we left the presence of our Father in Heaven, He blessed each of us with the Spirit of Christ. The scriptures reveal that the Spirit of Christ, sometimes called "the light of Christ" or our conscience, "lighteth every man that cometh into the world" (see John 1:6–9). This light gives us a basic understanding of right and wrong. Following it will lead us to do good and to understand truth.

We are given an additional source of truth when we are confirmed members of the Church. This is the gift of the Holy Ghost, given to "show unto [us] all things what [we] should do" (2 Nephi 32:5).

The Lord has also told us to "feast upon [His] words" for help in our lives (see 2 Nephi 32:3). We may receive the words of Christ through the scriptures, the words of our living prophets (see D&C 1:37–38; 68:2–4), or the promptings of the Holy Ghost.

Elder Neal A. Maxwell said: "We need to feast upon the words of Christ in the scriptures and as these words come to us from living prophets. Just nibbling occasionally will not do. (See 2 Nephi 31:20 and 32:3.) Feasting means partaking with relish and delight and savoring—not gorging episodically in heedless hunger, but partaking gratefully, dining with delight, at a sumptuous spread carefully and lovingly prepared . . . over the centuries" (*Wherefore Ye Must Press Forward* [1977], 28).

As we humbly "feast upon" the words of Christ, we will know better what to do in all areas of our lives. Church leaders who do this, for example, know better what to say, what to teach, whom to call to positions, and how to make other decisions connected with their callings.

How to Make Decisions

Whether or not we presently hold a Church position, each of us is a leader over our own affairs. Therefore, we must learn how to make inspired decisions.

- Display a poster of the following list, or refer to the information on the chalkboard:

Making Inspired Decisions

1. Identify the problem.
2. Pray for guidance and the spirit of discernment.
3. Study the problem.
4. Make the decision.
5. Pray for confirmation.
6. Act—do it.

Following are the steps for making inspired decisions. These steps are given only as general guidelines.

Identify the Problem

We must understand clearly what the problem is before we can solve it. Sometimes it helps to write the problem down.

Pray for Guidance and the Spirit of Discernment

▪ Show visual 21-a, "Prayer is essential to making right decisions."

As we begin to solve our problem, we should seek Heavenly Father's help. This help often comes through one of the gifts of the Spirit: the gift of discernment. This gift, available to those who pray for it, helps us know the truth and make proper judgments (see John 16:13; Moroni 10:5).

Study the Problem

Asking the Lord for guidance is only part of the process. Some feel that because the Lord has said, "Ask, and it shall be given you" (Matthew 7:7), one need only ask to receive the Lord's answer. But we must do more than ask. The Lord has instructed us to study the problem in our minds (see D&C 9:8). Often before the Lord will inspire us, He also expects us to obtain all the available information on the problem and seek counsel from proper and reliable sources. For example, leaders may seek advice from their counselors, husbands may seek advice from their wives, and sons may counsel with their parents. We should also identify possible solutions to the problem and think about the effects of each.

When making a decision, we should gather enough reliable information to make a wise decision. Decisions made on little or unreliable information are often wrong and may bring regret and sadness.

Make the Decision

After we have studied the problem we should select the best possible solution. (Sometimes the decision to be made is not between good and bad, but rather choosing the best thing to do at the time.) We make the decision based on what we feel is best to do after having carefully studied the information we gathered.

Pray for Confirmation

After making a choice, we approach the Lord in prayer and ask if the decision is right. If it is, the Holy Ghost will confirm the decision by giving us a peaceful, reassuring feeling about it (see D&C 6:22–23). Sometimes we will even get a burning in our bosom (see D&C 9:8).

If, for some reason, we have not chosen correctly, the Lord will reveal that our decision is wrong by leaving us with an uncomfortable feeling or serious doubt. The scriptures refer to this as a "stupor of thought" (D&C 9:9). When this occurs, we must have the humility to begin the decision-making process again.

Often, confirmation from the Holy Ghost comes to us as we pray for it. Sometimes, however, we may be unsure what the Lord wants us to do

21-a, Prayer is essential to making right decisions.

and must begin to solve the problem before a spiritual confirmation will come.

Elder Hartman Rector Jr. said that the Lord expects us to "get on our knees and communicate with him. Tell him what we are going to do—make commitments with him—outline our program—and then get up off our knees and go and *do* precisely what we have told him we would do. In the *doing,* the Spirit comes" (in Conference Report, Oct. 1973, 135; or *Ensign,* Jan. 1974, 107).

Occasionally we may have to make a decision that seems too difficult and has no possible answer. When this happens we should remember what President Marion G. Romney experienced: "I have had problems which it seemed I could not solve, and I have suffered in facing them until it seemed that I could not go farther if I did not have a solution to them. After praying and on many occasions fasting for a day each week over long periods of time, I have had answers revealed to my mind in finished sentences. I have heard the voice of God in my mind and I know his words" (*Look to God and Live: Discourses of Marion G. Romney,* comp. George J. Romney [1971], 45).

At times we must fast, study the scriptures, and pray to solve serious problems. Occasionally, even after doing these things and then making and acting on a decision, we may still not receive a confirmation. At such times, we should simply follow our own best judgment, patiently exercising faith that eventually the confirmation will come. We must always remember that God answers our prayers when, in *His* judgment, it is best for us to receive an answer.

Act—Do It

When we get an answer to our prayers we must do what the answer requires us to do. We cannot expect the Holy Ghost to keep helping us if we ignore His promptings. Even if the answer is not what we want or if the effort He asks of us seems too great, we must be willing to do as He directs. Otherwise, we risk losing contact with the Holy Ghost and thus His comfort and direction.

President Spencer W. Kimball was a good example of one who was committed to doing what the Lord asked him to do: "Prominently displayed on President Kimball's desk is a slogan which reads simply, 'DO IT.' With this inspired leader, personal convenience comes second. Everything is done to meet the Lord's convenience. His example for work has become legend and establishes an example for us all to follow" (Robert L. Simpson, in Conference Report, Oct. 1975, 17; or *Ensign,* Nov. 1975, 13).

Some of these steps for making decisions are illustrated by an experience related in our early Church history. Joseph Smith was translating the Book of Mormon, and Oliver Cowdery was acting as scribe. After a time, Oliver desired to do some of the translation himself. The Lord revealed to Oliver His will regarding this matter. It is recorded in Doctrine and Covenants 9, which tells how Oliver tried to translate but was unsuccessful.

- Read Doctrine and Covenants 9:4–9, pointing out the steps of decision making that are mentioned.

Practicing Decision Making

- Have class members work through the following problem by using the steps for inspired decision making discussed earlier. They should assume the role of one of Brother Jones's Church leaders.

Problem: Brother Jones joined the Church five years ago and was ordained to the priesthood. Because of his work schedule, he has been unable to attend any Church meetings and activities since shortly after his baptism. He has three helpful children and a supportive wife. He is a skilled carpenter who takes special pride in his work.

Step 1: Identify the Problem

- Have class members identify the problem.

In working with less-active members, a priesthood leader should first make a confidential list of those who do not fully participate in Church activity. If the list has many names, he should select those he feels would best respond to fellowship, concentrating his efforts on them. When they are activated, they can help him activate other less-active members.

Step 2: Pray for Guidance and the Spirit of Discernment

- Now that we have identified the problem, where can we go for help in deciding how to solve it?

- Why should we use discernment when approaching Brother Jones?

Problems like Church inactivity present special challenges. Before we can make any decisions concerning a less-active individual, we must have the Spirit to help us recognize the person's real needs and discern truth from error (see Jacob 4:13).

Step 3: Study the Problem

- What information would help us decide how to help Brother Jones?

As we study the problem, we should consider the following:

1. Who are his home teachers? How can we involve them more effectively to help Brother Jones back into activity? Should we assign special priesthood holders to help his family?

2. How can we communicate to Brother Jones that we need him?

3. How can he learn that he needs the gospel?

4. What are his interests and talents? How could we use them so he will feel needed and important?

5. Who are his friends? How could they help him?

6. What activities could we involve him in that would not offend him?

7. How can we offer to help him?

- What other information might we consider?

- Discuss a plan we could follow to bring Brother Jones back into Church activity.

Step 4: Make a Decision

As we study the problem, we must decide how to solve it. In deciding how to help Brother Jones, we should develop a plan to show our love and need for him.

Step 5: Pray for Confirmation

- What is the next step after we have decided what to do?

Once we have made a decision, we should ask the Lord whether it is the right one. The Spirit will tell us whether we have decided correctly.

Step 6: Act—Do It

- What is the final step?

The final step is to follow President Spencer W. Kimball's example and act on our plan; we must "do it." As we faithfully follow our plan, serving with diligence and love (see D&C 81:5), the Spirit will touch the heart of Brother Jones, who may, in time, come into full activity.

Conclusion

Heavenly Father sent us to earth to learn and grow and to help Him do His work. In order to serve well and make inspired decisions concerning ourselves and others, we must keep the commandments, seek the companionship of the Holy Ghost, and have faith in Jesus Christ. We must also have faith in ourselves as we carry out our decisions. This takes courage and commitment. We can be confident that when we prayerfully study our problems and their solutions, listen for answers, and then act on those problems in righteousness, the Lord will support us and our influence for good will increase.

Challenge

This week when making a decision, follow the steps outlined in this lesson. Continue to practice this process until it becomes part of your life.

Additional Scriptures

- 1 Kings 3:5–15 (Solomon asks for an understanding heart)

- 1 Nephi 3:7 (the Lord will help us do what He asks us to do)

- Doctrine and Covenants 11:12–14 (put your trust in the Spirit)

Teacher Preparation

Before presenting this lesson:

1. Review lesson 12, "Effective Family Leadership," in this manual.

2. Prepare the poster suggested in the lesson, or write the information on the chalkboard.

3. Assign class members to present any stories, scriptures, or quotations you wish.

STEWARDSHIP AND DELEGATION

Lesson 2 2

The purpose of this lesson is to help us understand and use the principles of stewardship and delegation.

Introduction

Moses was a great leader, but after he led the people of Israel out of Egypt he found it difficult to solve all the people's problems by himself. Every day, from morning until evening, he sat before the people to answer their questions and to resolve their difficulties. But the task was too much for one man. After receiving counsel from Jethro, his father-in-law and a righteous priesthood leader, Moses divided the people into groups of 10, 50, 100, and 1,000. He then appointed a worthy man to lead each group. Thereafter, as the prophet of Israel, Moses spent his time teaching the people the commandments and solving the most difficult problems. The other problems were handled by the leaders he had called. (See Exodus 18:13–26.)

Moses became a more effective leader by organizing the people he served. His use of the principles of stewardship and delegation helped him establish order among the people of Israel and govern them more effectively.

Stewards and Stewardship

A steward is a person who has been given responsibility for someone else or for something belonging to someone else. President Spencer W. Kimball defined a stewardship in the Church: "[It] is a sacred spiritual or temporal trust for which there is accountability" (in Conference Report, Oct. 1977, 124; or *Ensign,* Nov. 1977, 78).

Stewardship in the Church involves three basic principles (see D&C 104:11–17):

- Display a poster of the following list, or refer to the information on the chalkboard:

> ### Basic Principles of Stewardship in the Lord's Kingdom
>
> 1. A steward is entrusted with something that belongs to the Lord.
> 2. A steward exercises agency in caring for his stewardship.
> 3. A steward is accountable for his stewardship.

A Steward Is Entrusted with Something That Belongs to the Lord

The Lord said, "I, the Lord, stretched out the heavens, and built the earth, my very handiwork; and all things therein are mine" (D&C 104:14). The entire earth is the Lord's, and everything on it belongs to Him. Everything we have has been given to us by the Lord. He has entrusted our bodies, our talents and abilities, and our families to our care. We are stewards over these things. When leaders call someone to a Church position or give a priesthood assignment, they are assigning a stewardship.

- Have the class members ponder for a moment the stewardships they have received from the Lord.

A Steward Exercises Agency in Caring for His Stewardship

As children of Heavenly Father, we have the agency to act for ourselves. Therefore, when we receive a stewardship, we are free to care for it in the way we decide. We are free to be faithful, diligent, and obedient; but we are also free to be lazy and disobedient. The Lord said, "I . . . have given unto the children of men to be agents unto themselves" (D&C 104:17).

A Steward Is Accountable for His Stewardship

The Lord expects us to be faithful in our stewardships, but He will not force us to do so. However, at the time of the Judgment we must make an accounting to Him of how we cared for our stewardships. We must also make an accounting to the Lord's representatives—our priesthood leaders—in priesthood interviews. "It is required of the Lord, at the hand of every steward, to render an account of his stewardship, both in time and in eternity" (D&C 72:3).

- Have a class member read Doctrine and Covenants 51:19, 52:13, 72:4, and 78:22. What does the Lord promise to those who are faithful in their stewardships?

Delegation

To delegate means to give another person responsibility and authority to accomplish a certain task for which you are responsible. The assigned task then becomes a stewardship for the person given the task. Moses was an effective leader because he used the principles of stewardship and delegation. Church leaders can also be more effective by using these principles.

Building the kingdom of God on earth is a glorious work, but no one can do it alone. When we are called to lead, we should involve others. A leader who works hard will bless many lives, but a leader who delegates effectively and inspires others to work hard will bless the lives of many more.

Effective delegation in the Church involves four basic principles:

- Display a poster of the following list, or refer to the information on the chalkboard:

> **Basic Principles of Delegation in the Lord's Kingdom**
>
> 1. Select the right person.
> 2. Assign the stewardship.
> 3. Allow the individual to govern himself or herself.
> 4. Hold the individual accountable for his or her stewardship.

Select the Right Person

When we have a task that needs to be accomplished, we should prayerfully select the person to be assigned (see lesson 21, "Leadership: Inspired Decision Making," in this manual).

Assign the Stewardship

After selecting the right person, we should assign the stewardship. The proper way to extend a calling in the Church is to have an interview with the person. It is always appropriate to invite the person's spouse to the interview. Assignments such as welfare projects or administration of the sacrament may be made without conducting an interview.

- What information should a leader give to a person who has just received a new calling or assignment? (The purpose of the organization or project, the duties of the assignment, the specific results the individual will be expected to achieve, and a time for the person to report back on his or her stewardship)

Allow the Individual to Govern Himself or Herself

Each person should be allowed to exercise personal agency in caring for his or her stewardship. A wise leader will offer his help to the assigned person but will never make the decisions for him or her. The leader will also offer support and encouragement.

When asked how he governed the members of the Church, Joseph Smith said, "I teach them correct principles, and they govern themselves" (quoted by John Taylor, in *Millennial Star*, 15 Nov. 1851, 339).

President N. Eldon Tanner wrote: "A leader should never try to do the work of one to whom he has made an assignment. . . . Give them freedom to do their tasks. Never criticize them, but praise success and encourage efforts. . . . We as leaders . . . should give the utmost attention to the personal growth of each individual through teaching correct principles and try to lead that individual to prepare himself for immortality and eternal life. This we should do by example and precept and then be prepared to help and support him in his efforts, but we should let him make his own decisions and govern himself according to the free agency that is his gift" ("Leading As the Savior Led," *New Era*, June 1977, 6).

Hold the Individual Accountable for His or Her Stewardship

Occasionally the leader should interview the assigned person and receive a report about the stewardship. During this interview the leader should help the person evaluate his or her performance and offer help and encouragement. He should also express appreciation for the individual's efforts. Sincere praise for people's actions builds faith and testimony.

President Tanner wrote: "An accounting should always be made to the leader, and he should expect such accounting. In Church administration the basic tool for accountability is [the] personal interview. . . . This can be a very rewarding experience for both parties, where there is an opportunity to give a self-evaluation, and where communication should be open and constructive. It is an ideal setting for offering and receiving help and assistance" (*New Era*, June 1977, 6).

▪ Have the class members consider the following case study:

President Olson needed to call an adviser for the Aaronic Priesthood members in his branch. After much prayer and deliberation he felt inspired to call Brother Johnson, a new convert to the Church. When he met Brother Johnson at priesthood meeting, he made an appointment for Brother and Sister Johnson to meet him in the chapel at 6:30 that evening.

When the Johnsons arrived, President Olson invited Brother Johnson into his office for a brief worthiness interview; then he invited Sister Johnson to join them. After visiting for a few minutes, President Olson offered a prayer. After the prayer he said: "I have invited you here this evening to extend a calling to Brother Johnson. I have prayed about this matter and feel inspired to call you, Brother Johnson, to teach the Aaronic Priesthood class in our branch. I have great confidence that you will be an effective teacher, since I know that the Lord wants you to serve in this position." President Olson then went on to describe in detail the duties of an adviser of the priesthood class.

After making certain that Brother Johnson knew exactly what would be expected of him, President Olson asked if he would accept the call. Brother Johnson said: "I feel very humble in being asked to accept this responsibility, but I have faith that the Lord will help me to do it properly. I will accept this calling and do my best." President Olsen then wrote down the duties for Brother Johnson to take with him and told him how important the brethren in his class were to Heavenly Father.

President Olson then asked Sister Johnson if she would support her husband in this calling. She said that she was very proud of her husband and would support him with all her heart. President Olson expressed his appreciation to the Johnsons and arranged for Brother Johnson to be set apart for his calling the following Sunday. President Olson then set up an appointment to meet with Brother Johnson again in two weeks to receive a report about the calling.

Two weeks later, when Brother Johnson came for the interview, he gave a very good progress report. He said he had learned much about teaching and was trying to be a good teacher. But he said that he still had much to learn. President Olson was pleased. He praised him and said he was doing a fine job. He encouraged him to continue to do his best and to keep learning, and they talked about teaching by the power of the Holy Ghost. They discussed ways that Brother Johnson might help a less-active member of the class. As they set up another reporting interview, President Olson and Brother Johnson each expressed thanks to the other. They both had confidence that Brother Johnson would be a successful teacher.

- How did President Olson follow the principles of delegation? What did he do to help Brother Johnson succeed in his calling?

Conclusion

Stewardship and delegation help us accomplish the Lord's work more effectively. When we receive a calling in the Church, we are entrusted with specific responsibilities in the kingdom of God. These responsibilities are a stewardship, for which the Lord holds us accountable. We are free to care for our stewardships diligently or slothfully, but we will eventually be asked to make an accounting of them.

Effective delegation involves the principles of stewardship. It requires that we assign a stewardship, teach correct principles, allow the person to govern himself or herself, and hold him or her accountable.

As we are faithful in our stewardships and delegate effectively, the Lord's work will go forth. This is how Alma helped the Church prosper in his time.

- Read Mosiah 25:19–24.

Challenge

Identify the stewardships the Lord has given to you. Select one stewardship you can improve in, and set a goal that will help you do so. The next time you need to make an assignment in your family or your Church calling, follow the principles of stewardship. Delegate authority and follow through on the assignment.

Additional Scriptures

- Psalm 24:1 (all things belong to the Lord)

- Matthew 25:14–30 (stewards entrusted with and held accountable for talents)

- Luke 16:10–13 (faithfulness in earthly stewardships)

- Luke 19:11–27 (stewards to be good managers)

- Doctrine and Covenants 59:16–21 (all things made for the prudent use of man)

- Doctrine and Covenants 70:4 (accountability at the Day of Judgment)

Teacher Preparation

Before presenting this lesson:

1. Prepare the posters suggested in the lesson, or write the information on the chalkboard.

2. Assign class members to present any stories, scriptures, or quotations you wish.

CONDUCTING MEETINGS AND INTERVIEWS

Lesson   2 3

The purpose of this lesson is to help us conduct effective meetings and interviews.

Introduction

Nephi tells us that after Christ visited America, the Nephites "did walk after the commandments which they had received from their Lord and their God, continuing in fasting and prayer, and in meeting together oft both to pray and to hear the word of the Lord" (4 Nephi 1:12).

- What meetings do we attend in the Church? Why do we have meetings?

- Display a poster of the following list, or refer to the information on the chalkboard:

Reasons for Meetings

1. To help us keep the commandments of God
2. To build testimonies
3. To teach gospel doctrines and principles
4. To bring us the counsel of modern-day prophets
5. To sustain our leaders
6. To do missionary work
7. To partake of the sacrament
8. To deliver information and correlate the work of the Church
9. To solve problems
10. To inspire and teach
11. To administer ordinances of the gospel, such as baptism

Conducting Effective Meetings

To be effective, meetings must accomplish a definite purpose. Leaders should conduct meetings with order and dignity, encourage participation from those attending, and provide for evaluation and follow-through.

Planning

A meeting is effective when the purpose for which it is held is achieved. This requires planning.

An important aid in planning is an agenda. An agenda is a list of things to be done in the meeting and of those who are to participate. Agendas allow meetings to be presented clearly and effectively. To make an agenda, we must think through what we want to accomplish and then write those objectives down in order of importance so that the most important items are considered first.

- What could we include in an agenda? (List the suggestions on the chalkboard. An example of an agenda for family home evening is at the end of this lesson.)

A short preparation meeting may be held before some meetings such as sacrament and baptismal services. In it the agenda is reviewed with those who will be participating, and a prayer may be offered to ask for the guidance of the Spirit.

The Lord tells us, "It always has been given to the elders of my church from the beginning, and ever shall be, to conduct all meetings as they are directed and guided by the Holy Spirit" (D&C 46:2). When we pray to have the Holy Ghost in our meetings and then act accordingly, the Holy Ghost will be present and help us accomplish the purpose of the meeting. Moroni wrote of the Nephites, "Their meetings were conducted by the church after the manner of the workings of the Spirit, and by the power of the Holy Ghost; for as the power of the Holy Ghost led them whether to preach, or to exhort, or to pray, or to supplicate, or to sing, even so it was done" (Moroni 6:9). Much of this inspiration will come before the meeting as we prayerfully prepare an agenda.

Order and Dignity

When we conduct meetings, we should set a proper example by being clean, well groomed, and appropriately dressed. We should avoid unnecessary talk and maintain dignity.

Participation

Willing, prepared participants make meetings more effective. We should ask the Lord to help us be receptive to the instructions, training, and business of Church meetings. We should go with a desire to participate, learn, and accept the assignments we are given. We should prepare ourselves to participate under the influence of the Holy Ghost.

Evaluation and Follow-Through

After a meeting we should evaluate its effectiveness. Our evaluation could include questions such as these:

Was the purpose of the meeting accomplished?

Could we have made better preparations?

Did we cover all the items on the agenda?

Was there a good spirit in the meeting?

Did the participants understand their assignments and how to accomplish them?

By analyzing our answers to these questions, we can determine how to improve future meetings.

Conducting Effective Interviews

▪ Show visuals 23-a, "Priesthood interviews encourage good relationships," and 23-b, "Effective interviews promote the Lord's work."

Interviews also require special preparation. An interview can accomplish many purposes. It can be used to (1) gather information, (2) deliver information, (3) counsel and motivate, (4) call people to positions, (5) receive reports of stewardships, (6) teach principles and doctrine, or (7) determine worthiness. Because leaders frequently conduct interviews, we should know some basic principles for conducting Church interviews:

Schedule the interviews, and provide sufficient time to conduct them in a dignified, unhurried manner.

Pray to have the Spirit and the power of discernment during the interviews.

Hold them in a place that is quiet and comfortable and allows privacy.

Give full and sincere attention to the individuals. Show a genuine interest in them.

Help them feel comfortable and at ease by being kind and calm.

Make sure they understand any questions we ask.

Keep the interviews on the subject.

23-a, *Priesthood interviews encourage good relationships.*

Let the individuals know we are available for help.

Keep personal information confidential, and assure them we will do so.

Our sincere efforts to listen to the members we interview will help them resolve their concerns. This means trying to understand their concerns and then helping them arrive at decisions for which they feel responsible. They must commit themselves before they can change for the better.

President N. Eldon Tanner explained:

"It is important that those we interview realize that they are *spirit children of God* and that *we love them,* and *let them know that we love them* and are interested in their welfare and in helping them succeed in life. . . .

"Remember, the interview is based on consideration, on sympathy and love. This is so important. Let the people know we love them and are only trying to help them" (in Conference Report, Oct. 1978, 59–60; or *Ensign,* Nov. 1978, 41–42).

Conclusion

The purpose of the Church is to bring souls to Christ, and meetings and interviews can help us do this. Meaningful and profitable meetings and interviews, however, do not just happen. They must be planned, conducted, and evaluated with specific purposes in mind. The Lord says:

"I give unto you a commandment, that when ye are assembled together ye shall instruct and edify each other, that ye may know how to act and direct my church, how to act upon the points of my law and commandments, which I have given.

"And thus ye shall become instructed in the law of my church, and be sanctified by that which ye have received, and ye shall bind yourselves to act in all holiness before me—

"That inasmuch as ye do this, glory shall be added to the kingdom which ye have received" (D&C 43:8–10).

The better we plan and conduct meetings and interviews, the more others will be inspired to live God's laws and commandments.

Challenge

Fathers: Organize and plan an agenda for your next family home evening so you can teach your family the gospel more effectively.

Priesthood leaders: Follow the suggestions in this lesson when given responsibility for conducting meetings and interviews.

All priesthood holders: Prayerfully plan your week. Write an agenda that helps you do what the Lord wants you to do.

23-b, Effective interviews promote the Lord's work.

Additional Scriptures

- Moroni 6:5–6 (Nephites met together often)

- Doctrine and Covenants 20:45 (conduct meetings as directed by the Holy Ghost)

- Doctrine and Covenants 59:9 (go to the house of prayer)

Supplement: Sample Agenda for Family Home Evening

1. Chorister: (name of family member to be chorister)

2. Opening song: (name of hymn or Primary song)

3. Opening prayer: (name of family member to give prayer)

4. Family business: (conducted by head of household)

5. Musical number: (name of family member to give musical number)

6. Lesson from *Gospel Principles* manual: (name of family member to present lesson)

7. Discussion and planning for coming week

8. Closing song: (name of hymn or Primary song)

9. Closing prayer: (name of family member to give prayer)

10. Enjoyable activity: (name of family member assigned)

11. Refreshments: (name of family member assigned)

Teacher Preparation

Before presenting this lesson:

1. Prepare the poster suggested in the lesson, or write the information on the chalkboard.

2. Assign class members to present any stories, scriptures, or quotations you wish.

MAINTAINING GOOD PHYSICAL HEALTH

Lesson 24

The purpose of this lesson is to teach us how to maintain good health and prevent illness.

Introduction

The Lord expects us to understand how to keep our bodies as healthy as possible so we can accomplish our goals and help build His kingdom.

Causes of Illness

▪ What causes illness?

Many years ago people did not know what caused illness. Some believed sickness came because they failed to make proper sacrifices. Others thought it was caused by spells cast by enemies. However, scientists and physicians have learned what causes most health problems, and in the last century especially, many new discoveries have been made to help us maintain good health.

Today we know that most illnesses are caused by germs. Germs are very small organisms that live all around us. They are so small that the eye cannot see them. Some germs are carried through the air; others pass from one person to another; still others pass from animals and insects to people. Human and animal body wastes, especially those from diseased humans or animals, contain many harmful germs that can cause serious illnesses.

Preventing the Spread of Germs

If we want to eliminate illnesses, we need to eliminate the germs that cause them. The following are ways we can reduce or eliminate illness-causing germs:

Clean our home regularly, especially places where germs could live. Prevent insects and animals from getting inside our homes.

Protect food from insects and animals by keeping it properly covered. Where possible, refrigerate perishable foods.

Wash foods carefully to remove as many germs as possible.

Properly dispose of human and animal wastes, since insects and rodents are attracted to them.

Wash our hands before eating, after using the toilet, after changing soiled diapers, and so on.

Brush our teeth after each meal.

Always cover our mouth when sneezing or coughing.

Wear shoes, sandals, or other foot coverings.

Eat properly and rest. Eating proper foods and getting enough rest can help us avoid or overcome illness. Germs are less able to infect a healthy body.

As we maintain good health, we will prevent or eliminate many illnesses. We will also be examples to our children, helping them develop good health habits.

▪ Discuss good health-care practices for infants, older children, and pregnant women.

Protecting Our Health

Health professionals instruct us that, in addition to developing and practicing good health habits, we should protect ourselves from certain illnesses with immunizations. When we are immunized we usually receive an injection of medicine. For some illnesses we need only one injection; for others we may need several injections of the same medication at different time intervals.

In most parts of the world we can receive immunizations from health clinics or doctors. We can be immunized for such diseases as rubeola (measles), mumps, rubella (German measles), diphtheria, pertussis (whooping cough), typhoid fever, smallpox, polio, influenza, tetanus, hepatitis A and B, pneumonia, and varicella (chicken pox).

In addition to immunizations, medicines in the form of liquids or pills have been developed to help prevent and cure illnesses. These should be used carefully according to directions from qualified medical professionals. We should not take medication that has expired or has been prescribed for someone else.

Another good way to prevent illness is to have an annual physical examination by a doctor or other health specialist. Early symptoms of illness can be detected in these regular examinations.

▪ Discuss where to find the nearest health facilities and what immunizations are available locally.

What to Do When Illness Occurs

If serious illness occurs, the best medical help is usually available from a doctor or other health professional. We should not only seek their help when ill, but we should also let them train us in good health practices.

Unfortunately, some people believe that it shows a lack of faith in the Lord to visit a doctor. The Lord expects us to use faith and the power of the priesthood when sick, but He also expects us to use available medical knowledge and services.

Before Spencer W. Kimball became President of the Church, he had severe health problems. Wanting to have the best health possible, he consulted with a doctor. The doctor told him that he had to have a delicate surgical operation for a heart problem. President Kimball put great faith and trust in his doctors and underwent the operation.

On the day President Kimball was ordained and set apart as the President of the Church, he received a letter from Dr. Russell Nelson about his health. Dr. Nelson knew that President Kimball would have questions concerning his health, so in his letter he pointed out that the careful physical examination President Kimball had recently under-gone indicated his body was again in excellent health. The letter stated, "Your surgeon wants you to know that your body is strong; that your heart is better than it has been for years; and that by all of our finite ability to predict, you may consider this new assignment without undue anxiety about your health." . . .

Dr. Nelson's letter continued: "In the performance of that critical oper-ation . . . , I was keenly aware of your apostolic calling, and of my own human frailties, in anticipating one of the most risky and complex operations ever done. This operation turned out to be technically per-fect in every detail, and I acknowledge gratefully the help of the Lord. . . . Most special of all was the fact that, as the operation was nearly completed, it was made known to me that one day you would become the President of the Church." (See Edward L. Kimball and Andrew E. Kimball Jr., *Spencer W. Kimball* [1977], 8.)

We also can enjoy the best possible health if we know the symptoms of illness and receive the proper care when we are ill. If properly diag-nosed early, many illnesses can be treated successfully.

- What symptoms indicate a need to see a medical expert? (Mention each of the following symptoms, and discuss them one at a time: unexplained bleeding and other unusual bodily discharges, sores that do not heal, persistent coughs or labored breathing, long-lasting or high fever, chills, difficulty in passing body wastes, dark spots or a rash on the skin, unexplained weight loss, prolonged serious pain, persistent vomiting or diarrhea, fainting spells or seizures, blurred or changed vision, serious burns or burns over a large portion of the body, soreness or swelling, unconsciousness, or other unusual changes in one's body or its ability to function normally.)

When any of these symptoms afflicts us or others, we should contact a health professional or health clinic immediately. Waiting to get proper medical care can result in severe disabilities, long periods of illness, or even death.

Conclusion

Healthy bodies help us meet the demands of life. Parents must keep themselves healthy and use wisdom and good judgment in caring for their children and teaching them good health practices.

Many resources have been provided so we can maintain good health. The Lord expects us to use these resources to prevent and cure illnesses that afflict us and others. This requires that we use modern medical practices and exercise faith, prayer, and the power of the priesthood. If we do these things, and it is God's will, the sick can be healed.

President Brigham Young taught: "Then let us seek to extend the present life to the uttermost, by observing every law of health, and by properly balancing labor, study, rest, and recreation, and thus prepare for a better life. Let us teach these principles to our children" (*Discourses of Brigham Young,* sel. John A. Widtsoe [1954], 186).

Challenge

Have all your family members immunized if possible. Practice and teach your children good health practices. Survey your living situations, and clean up any germ-infested areas.

Additional Scripture

- Doctrine and Covenants 89 (the Lord's law of health—the Word of Wisdom)

Teacher Preparation

Before presenting this lesson:

1. Contact a local health clinic or health worker. Find out about the following:

    a. Good health-care practices for infants, older children, and pregnant women.

   b. Medical facilities in your area.

   c. Immunizations available locally and how they can be obtained.

2. Assign class members to present any stories, scriptures, or quotations you wish.

LIVING THE WORD OF WISDOM

Lesson 25

The purpose of this lesson is to help us better understand and live the Lord's laws of health.

Introduction

"When Paul C. Kimball, a Latter-day Saint student at Oxford University in England, was asked to coach a young, inexperienced rowing crew, he said he felt 'rather weak. I had never done any coaching.'

"However, he accepted the invitation with one condition: 'If I am going to coach you,' he told the rowers, 'I am going to make you train according to my rules.' His rules were total abstinence from tobacco, alcohol, tea and coffee. It took the boys about a week to decide to accept his condition.

"With their agreement secured, Kimball 'took them in hand and . . . worked with them every afternoon for three hours till February.' That month they entered a series of rowing meets against all the other colleges at Oxford. 'My boys were competing against crews composed of men who had been rowing since they were tiny tots,' Kimball said. 'This group I had was made up of inexperienced boys. But they had trained hard, and not one of them, so far as I know, used a cigarette during this period, or had a cup of tea or coffee, or drank any alcoholic drink.'

"Still, when the day of the race came, no one thought the inexperienced crew had even the remotest chance of winning. When the cannon sounded, starting the mile-and-one-half race up the Thames River, it was expected that the young crew would fall back quickly. But by the time the rowers reached the half-way point, Kimball, who was running along the bank shouting instructions to his crew through a megaphone, noticed that his charges were still running even with their competitors.

"Kimball shouted his last word of counsel: 'Sprint!' They sprinted beautifully and within a minute had stretched out a hundred feet ahead of their nearest competitors. They won the race with ease.

"Each day of the six-day rowing competition, it was expected that Kimball's crew would be defeated. But each day, following the same tactics, they won handily. 'When people asked me how I managed such success with novices, I answered, "I made those boys live right," ' he said. 'When the sprint came, their lungs were clean; their systems were clean; their blood was clean, and their nerves were strong' " (Joseph Walker, "Victory on the Thames," *Church News,* 20 Feb. 1983, 20).

The Lord's Laws of Health

- What are the Lord's laws of health? (The Word of Wisdom, proper rest, and exercise)

Our bodies house our eternal spirits. They will serve the same function in eternity. Our bodies are so important that the Apostle Paul called them "temple[s] of God" (1 Corinthians 3:17). Because our experiences affect our bodies and spirits, we must be careful to keep our bodies clean and healthy.

The Lord's laws of health are meant to preserve our physical, mental, and emotional health. The Lord knows that when we are physically, mentally, and emotionally healthy we can participate in activities that build us spiritually, bless others, and build the kingdom of God.

Many of the Lord's laws of health are found in Doctrine and Covenants 89. This section, called the Word of Wisdom, tells us what to eat and what not to eat. Among the substances we are warned against are strong drinks, hot drinks, and tobacco.

Strong Drinks

Strong drinks are alcoholic beverages such as liquor, wine, and beer. These and all other alcoholic beverages should never be consumed (see D&C 89:5, 7).

Hot Drinks

Hot drinks are defined as coffee and tea. However, our Church leaders have told us not to use any beverage that contains drugs or other ingredients that are harmful or habit forming.

Tobacco

We are not to consume tobacco in any of its forms (see D&C 89:8).

We should always avoid any other substances, including food or drink, that will create unnatural desires or cravings or upset the natural functions of our bodies. Failure to do so will cause us great personal misery.

If we are in doubt about a substance, we should follow the counsel of Elder Joseph Fielding Smith: "If in doubt as to any food or drink, whether it is good or harmful, let it alone until you have learned the truth in regard to it. If anything offered is habit-forming, we will be safe in concluding that it contains some ingredients that are harmful to the body and should be avoided" ("The Word of Wisdom," *Improvement Era,* Feb. 1956, 79).

President Spencer W. Kimball told us to avoid anything or anyone who would influence us to consume any unhealthy substance: "My . . . brothers and sisters, in all love, we give you warning that Satan and his emissaries will strive to entice you to use harmful substances, because they know if you partake, your spiritual powers will be inhibited and you will be in their evil power. Stay away from those places or people which would influence you to break the commandments of God." President Kimball said that if we keep God's commandments, we "will have wisdom to know and discern that which is evil" (in Conference Report, Apr. 1983, 72; or *Ensign,* May 1983, 54–55).

To promote our health and happiness, the Lord created all things of the earth for us to use and benefit from. They are to "please the eye and to gladden the heart; Yea, for food and for raiment, for taste and for smell, to strengthen the body and to enliven the soul" (D&C 59:18–19). The Word of Wisdom suggests some foods that we should make part of our diet. These foods include all wholesome herbs and fruits (see D&C 89:10–11; 49:19). We may also eat the flesh of animals and of fowls of the air and use the skin of animals for clothing (see D&C 89:12–13; 49:18–19); however, we are not to kill animals for mere sport or pleasure and waste the meat (see D&C 49:21). The Word of Wisdom also states that all grain is good for people and animals. Wheat is especially good for us.

- Read Doctrine and Covenants 59:20. How does the Lord say we are to use the resources He has given us?

Although we should make every effort to find out which foods are good for us, we should be careful to avoid extremes in using or refraining from using certain foods. Such action is not justified by the Word of Wisdom (see D&C 49:18).

Other scriptures besides Doctrine and Covenants 89 discuss the Lord's laws of health. One of these reads, "Cease to be idle; cease to be unclean; cease to find fault one with another; cease to sleep longer than is needful; retire to thy bed early, that ye may not be weary; arise early, that your bodies and your minds may be invigorated" (D&C 88:124). We are also told to labor, but not to labor more than we have strength (see Mosiah 4:27; D&C 10:4).

- How does the Lord's caution "cease to be idle" affect good health? (Activity strengthens the body.)

- How does the Lord's admonition "cease to find fault one with another" relate to our good health? (Faultfinding creates emotional distress, and emotional health is necessary to our happiness and spiritual well-being.)

Laws with Promises

- Read Doctrine and Covenants 89:18–21. What does the Lord promise to those who live His laws of health and keep His commandments? ("Health in their navel and marrow to their bones"; wisdom; knowledge; "hidden treasures"; protection from "the destroying angels")

Some of the greatest rewards we receive for obeying the Lord's laws of health are "wisdom and great treasures of knowledge, even hidden treasures" (D&C 89:19).

- What is wisdom? (Discernment in the use of knowledge)

- What are "hidden treasures"? (The most sacred and deep things of God)

These "hidden treasures" are revealed to us by the Holy Ghost: "For the Spirit searcheth all things, yea, the deep things of God . . . which things also we speak, not in the words which man's wisdom teacheth, but which the Holy Ghost teacheth" (1 Corinthians 2:10, 13; see also D&C 88:11–12).

The sacred and deep things we learn will always be with us if we obey God's commandments. The Lord has promised: "Whatever principle of intelligence we attain unto in this life, it will rise with us in the resurrection. And if a person gains more knowledge and intelligence in this life through his diligence and obedience than another, he will have so much the advantage in the world to come" (D&C 130:18–19).

As we receive wisdom, knowledge, and understanding through the Holy Ghost, we can become more like our Father in Heaven. We will become better sons, fathers, husbands, priesthood holders, and disciples of Christ if we use what we have received to bless our own lives and the lives of others.

President Spencer W. Kimball said, "For observing the Word of Wisdom the reward is life, not only prolonged mortal life but life eternal" (*The Miracle of Forgiveness* [1969], 211).

The Old Testament prophet Daniel had a clear and pure understanding of the Lord's laws of health. His story illustrates the blessings we receive when we live these laws.

- Show visual 25-a, "Daniel was blessed for keeping the Lord's laws of health."

25-a, Daniel was blessed for keeping the Lord's laws of health.

After Jerusalem was captured, King Nebuchadnezzar of Babylon wanted certain young people from the captives to be taught his language so they could be servants in his palace. This meant, however, that they were to eat and drink substances that they had been taught not to eat or drink.

Daniel was one of these young men who were chosen. But unlike some of the others, Daniel refused to drink the wine and eat the improper foods that were offered. He asked instead that he be permitted to keep the Lord's laws of health and eat foods he knew were healthful. This was agreed to, as a test. After a while, those who drank the wine and ate the improper foods were compared to Daniel. Because of his obedience, Daniel was healthier than the others and had been given wisdom, knowledge, skill in learning, and visions. (See Daniel 1:3–6, 8, 12–19.)

If we are obedient to the Lord's laws of health and His other commandments, we, like Daniel, will be blessed with these same gifts, probably in mortal life but certainly in eternity. The Lord has told us that "when we obtain any blessing from God, it is by obedience to that law upon which it is predicated" (D&C 130:21). He has also said, "I, the Lord, am bound when ye do what I say; but when ye do not what I say, ye have no promise" (D&C 82:10).

- What other blessings might we receive by obeying the Lord's laws of health?

Conclusion

The Lord's laws of health were given to bless us physically, mentally, emotionally, and spiritually. By living these laws, we are promised many blessings. These blessings will help us strengthen ourselves and our families, serve others, and build the Lord's kingdom.

Challenge

Commit yourself to obey the Lord's laws of health at all times.

Teacher Preparation

Before presenting this lesson:

1. Review *Gospel Principles* chapter 29, "The Lord's Law of Health."

2. Assign class members to present any stories, scriptures, or quotations you wish.

SEEKING
KNOWLEDGE

Lesson   2 6

The purpose of this lesson is to encourage us to seek knowledge.

Introduction

The Savior has commanded us to become perfect, as He and our Father in Heaven are. To become like them, we must learn and grow in the knowledge of the truth.

The Commandment to Seek Knowledge

In the Doctrine and Covenants the Lord commands us to seek knowledge.

- Read Doctrine and Covenants 88:78. According to this verse, what does the Lord want us to learn? (All things that are expedient for us to understand about the kingdom of God)

Of all the knowledge we can gain, the most important is a testimony of Jesus Christ, His divine mission, and His gospel. To gain this testimony, we should continually study the scriptures, pray, and live righteously. All the knowledge we obtain will not matter unless we have understood and obeyed the saving principles of the gospel.

- Read Doctrine and Covenants 88:79. In addition to the gospel, what else does the Lord expect us to study? (List answers on the chalkboard. Answers could include the earth, the heavens, history, current events, predictions of the future, our own country, and other countries.)

President N. Eldon Tanner said, "The Church has always urged us as members to get a good education and to learn everything possible about ourselves, history and geography, science, the universe, and especially the gospel of Jesus Christ" (regional representatives' seminar, 2 April 1971).

Since the Restoration of the gospel, the Church has always encouraged its members to obtain an education. Even in the early days of the

Church the Lord instructed the Prophet Joseph Smith to organize schools for both adults and children (see D&C 55:4; 90:7). Besides gospel study, these schools offered classes in history, languages, grammar, mathematics, and other subjects. Today the Church continues to spend much time, effort, and money to support education. Among its efforts is the Church Educational System, which was established to help meet the members' educational needs.

The Purpose and Blessings of Knowledge

- Read Doctrine and Covenants 88:80. What is the purpose of gaining knowledge? (To magnify our calling and mission)

When we have a knowledge of the people and world around us, we can use that knowledge to help build the kingdom of God. We can find better ways to teach the gospel to more people. In addition, as Latter-day Saints become well respected in their professions, they become examples that may influence others to learn more about the Church.

Education is important not only as a missionary tool but also as a source to build character. President David O. McKay said:

"True education consists not merely in the acquiring of a few facts of science, history, literature or art, but in the development of character. . . . True education trains in self-denial and self-mastery. True education regulates the temper, subdues passion and makes obedience to social laws and moral order a guiding principle of life. . . .

". . . The objective of education is to develop resources in the student that will contribute to his well-being as long as life endures" (*Secrets of a Happy Life,* comp. Llewelyn R. McKay [1967], 46–47).

Gaining knowledge will also help us serve others and our society. We can use our knowledge to provide food, clothing, and shelter for our families; help people overcome sickness and suffering; and make life more productive.

Sometimes, however, as people gain worldly knowledge they become proud of their own wisdom and feel they do not have to follow the counsels of the Lord and His prophets. The Lord has told us that to be educated is good *if* we listen to His counsel. Otherwise we will use our education foolishly. (See 2 Nephi 9:28–29.)

The Importance of Attending School

- Why is it important to attend school? What can we learn by attending school?

Much of our education comes through school, where we learn how to read, write, and do basic arithmetic. We also learn about history, geography, and science. We study the human body, the movement of the stars, and the beauty and purpose of the plants and animals. Education allows us to keep up with advancements in industry, technology, and science.

- Show visual 26-a, "Education is important for young people."

Members of the Church, especially the youth, have always been counseled to do everything necessary to get a good education. This includes receiving the training necessary for employment. Sometimes, however, it is difficult to attend school. We may be concerned about the money, time, or effort required. But because the Lord wants us to be well educated, He will help us attain this goal if we seek His help through prayer and make our best effort. If formal schooling is not possible, we can seek help from those around us who have special knowledge or skills. Such people will usually help us when they see we are willing to learn.

Education Continues throughout Our Lives

- Show visual 26-b, "Education should continue throughout one's life."

We should continue our formal education as long as possible. This can be done by attending a university or a vocational or trade school or through on-the-job training. We can also attend local classes for adults or classes offered by some schools through the mail.

We should continue our education by learning "out of the best books" (D&C 88:118). This requires that we choose reading material wisely. Some books and magazines help us become better people by teaching us about the good and the beautiful. Other books and magazines promote wickedness.

President Spencer W. Kimball warned us that "many . . . evil influences come right into the home—through television, radio, magazines, newspapers, and other forms of literature" (in Conference Report, Apr. 1978, 67; or *Ensign*, May 1978, 45). We must avoid evil influences and instead fill our minds with righteous things. As we read and study about good things, we should ask the Lord to help us understand and remember them.

We can also gain knowledge by attending plays that teach us to have compassion and sympathy for all people and by attending concerts and visiting art museums to increase our love of the beautiful. We should then share those things we learn with others.

Much informal learning can be done as a family. Families can make things together. They can turn picnics, camping trips, vacations, and even short walks into family learning experiences.

26-a, Education is important for young people.

Learning by Doing

Heavenly Father placed us on the earth to learn and gain experience. Many of the things we should learn can be learned only by doing; it is not enough just to study about them. For example, we cannot learn how to swim simply by reading about swimming; we must get in the water and practice if we are to develop this skill.

The Lord has provided many opportunities for us to serve and lead in His Church and thereby learn. As we perform the tasks assigned to us in an office or calling, we are often presented with challenges. As we overcome these challenges by doing our tasks, we increase our abilities, and tasks that were once difficult become easier to do. We are then able to help others overcome similar challenges.

Learning by doing is something we all can do, no matter how much formal education we have. One woman, for example, once complained to Dr. Louis Agassiz, a distinguished scientist, that she had never really had a chance to learn. She told him that she and her sister ran a boardinghouse and that she did not have time for anything else. He asked what type of work she did, and she replied:

" 'I skin potatoes and chop onions.'

"He asked, 'Madam, where do you sit during these interesting but homely duties?'

" 'On the bottom step of the kitchen stairs.'

" 'Where do your feet rest?'

" 'On the glazed brick.'

" 'What is glazed brick?'

" 'I don't know, sir.'

"He said, 'How long have you been sitting there?'

" 'Fifteen years.'

" 'Madam, here is my personal card,' said Dr. Agassiz. 'Would you kindly write me a letter concerning the nature of a glazed brick?' "

She took him seriously. She looked up "brick" in the dictionary but felt that the definition was too simple to send to a famous scientist. So she looked in the encyclopedia. As she read about bricks, she came to words that she did not understand. So she looked them up. And then, because she really became interested in what she was learning, she visited a brickyard. When she finished her studies, she sat down and wrote Dr. Agassiz a 36-page letter on the subject of glazed brick.

Back came a letter from Dr. Agassiz informing her that with just a few minor changes he had published her letter and was sending her $250. At the bottom of the letter he asked, "What was under those bricks?"

She found ants under the bricks, so she began to study ants. She found there were between 800 and 2,500 different kinds. She became fascinated by the many varieties of ants and how and where they lived. After wide reading and careful study, she wrote 360 pages on the subject to Dr. Agassiz. He published it as a book and sent her more money.

With the money she had received she went to visit all the lands of her dreams. (Adapted from Marion D. Hanks, *The Gift of Self* [1974], 151–53.)

▪ Besides the money she received, how was this woman's life enriched? (By increased knowledge and new interest in the world around her)

Elder Richard L. Evans taught: "There are some things you can give another person, and some things you cannot give him, except as he is willing to reach out and take them, and pay the price of making them a part of himself. This principle applies to studying, to developing talents, to absorbing knowledge, to acquiring skills, and to the learning of all the lessons of life" (*Richard Evans' Quote Book* [1971], 74).

▪ Discuss the opportunities that are available in your area for increasing knowledge and experience.

Conclusion

The Lord has instructed us to gain knowledge about the gospel and the world. We can do this by studying the scriptures and words of the prophets, praying, living righteously, attending school or taking other courses, taking interest in the things around us, and seeking to understand our experiences. As we gain knowledge, we will learn to appreciate all that the Lord has provided for us. Increased knowledge and training will also help us support our families, build the kingdom of God, be better citizens, and become more like our Father in Heaven.

Challenge

Fathers: Encourage your children to gain an education. Set an example of learning for them to follow. Plan family activities that will help everyone learn together.

Young priesthood holders: Make the plans necessary to obtain a good education.

26-b, Education should continue throughout one's life.

Teacher Preparation

Before presenting this lesson:

1. Become familiar with the educational opportunities in your community and the surrounding areas.

2. Assign class members to present any stories, scriptures, or quotations you wish.

GOSPEL PRINCIPLES AND DOCTRINES

JESUS CHRIST, OUR SURE FOUNDATION

Lesson 27

The purpose of this lesson is to help us make Jesus Christ the sure foundation of our lives.

Introduction

▪ Display visual 27-a, "The Lord Jesus Christ." Ask the class members to look at the picture and then close their eyes. Have them imagine they are in the presence of the Savior. Explain that the following account will help us better understand our Savior, Jesus Christ.

Elder Melvin J. Ballard once served as a missionary among the North American Indians. While on his mission he desired a witness that he was doing the Lord's will. Upon asking the Lord for this confirmation, he said he had a dream in which he found himself in the temple, entering one of its rooms.

"As I entered the door," Elder Ballard said, "I saw, seated on a raised platform, the most glorious Being my eyes have ever beheld or that I ever conceived existed in all the eternal worlds. As I approached to be introduced, he arose and stepped towards me with extended arms, and he smiled as he softly spoke my name. If I shall live to be a million years old, I shall never forget that smile. He took me into his arms and kissed me, pressed me to his bosom, and blessed me, until the marrow of my bones seemed to melt! When he had finished, I fell at his feet, and, as I bathed them with my tears and kisses, I saw the prints of the nails in the feet of the Redeemer of the world. The feeling that I had in the presence of him who hath all things in his hands, to have his love, his affection, and his blessing was such that if I ever can receive that of which I had but a foretaste, I would give all that I am, all that I ever hope to be, to feel what I then felt!" (quoted by Bryant S. Hinckley, in *Sermons and Missionary Service of Melvin J. Ballard* [1949], 156).

27-a, The Lord Jesus Christ

Our Need for a Savior

Before we came to earth, we lived with Heavenly Father. While we lived with Him, the plan of salvation was presented to us. We were so happy about this plan that we accepted it and shouted for joy. (See Job 38:1–7.)

The plan of salvation required us to leave Heavenly Father's presence and come to earth as mortals. Here we would be separated physically from God and be given the freedom to choose for ourselves to obey or disobey His commandments. If we chose to commit sin, we would become unclean. This would mean that someone free of sin would have to pay the penalty for our sins and cleanse us, because no unclean person can enter into the kingdom of God (see 1 Nephi 15:34).

To help us return to His presence, Heavenly Father appointed a Savior to redeem us. This Redeemer is our eldest spirit brother, Jesus Christ, who volunteered to come to earth and be our Savior. In volunteering He said that the glory for our salvation would belong to our Father in Heaven. (See Abraham 3:27; Moses 4:2.) Lucifer, another spirit brother of ours, also desired to be our Savior. But he wanted to force us to be saved and wanted to retain the honor for himself. (See Moses 4:1.) Heavenly Father rejected his offer and foreordained Jesus to be our Savior (see 1 Peter 1:18–20). In doing so, our Father in Heaven preserved our agency.

Jesus Christ Is Our Sure Foundation

▪ What is a sure foundation? (A strong, solid base that cannot be moved or destroyed)

A sure foundation will support whatever rests upon it. When we construct a building, for example, we are careful to make the foundation as strong as possible so the building will endure. In the same way, we must build our lives upon a sure foundation so that we can endure the trials in this life.

▪ Display visual 27-b, "Jesus Christ is our sure foundation."

Our Savior, Jesus Christ, is the only sure foundation upon whom we can build our lives. The prophet Helaman said, "It is upon the rock of our Redeemer, who is Christ, the Son of God, that ye must build your foundation; that when the devil shall send forth his mighty winds, . . . yea, when all his hail and his mighty storm shall beat upon you, it shall have no power over you . . . , because of the rock upon which ye are built, which is a sure foundation, a foundation whereon if men build they cannot fall" (Helaman 5:12).

Jesus is the sure foundation because He was foreordained by our Heavenly Father to be our Redeemer. Nephi said, "There is none other name given under heaven save it be this Jesus Christ, . . . whereby man can be saved" (2 Nephi 25:20). It is only through the Atonement of Jesus Christ that we can be forgiven of our sins and receive eternal life. We cannot do these things for ourselves. Only Jesus has this power.

Building upon Christ

We can build our lives upon the Sure Foundation, Jesus Christ, in the following ways:

- Display a poster of the following list, or refer to the information on the chalkboard:

**How to Build upon Christ,
the Sure Foundation**

1. Seek the companionship of the Holy Ghost.
2. Partake of the sacrament.
3. Pray and fast.
4. Keep the commandments.
5. Study the scriptures.
6. Follow the living prophet.
7. Love and serve the Lord.

Seek the Companionship of the Holy Ghost

The Holy Ghost, or the Spirit of the Lord, gives us insight into the life and character of our Savior, for one of the purposes of the Holy Ghost is to testify of Christ (see John 15:26). In fact, it is only through the Holy Ghost that we can learn the deeper meaning of the Lord's sacrifice for us. The Holy Ghost also blesses us to know and understand the truth of the scriptures and the inspired teachings of the living prophets.

Partake of the Sacrament

We help keep the Holy Ghost with us following our baptism and confirmation by worthily partaking of the sacrament (see D&C 20:77, 79).

- What should we think about as we partake of the sacrament?

Pray and Fast

Praying and fasting can help us draw close to the Lord, feel His love through the power of the Holy Ghost, and find comfort and peace of mind.

One woman related how she came to know Heavenly Father and the Savior better through prayer. One day she was called home from work and told that her son had drowned. The shock was overpowering. In

27-b, Jesus Christ is our sure foundation.

her agony she cried, "My Lord, my God, why?" Clear, immediate, and kind, the answer came as an impression to her mind: "I need him."

In the days that followed, she received wonderful comfort. "As I poured my heart out in prayer to my Father," she said, "he heard me and in his own way and in his own time answered those prayers. . . .

"This trial could have driven me far from my Father in heaven. . . . Instead, I am nearer to my Creator now than I have ever been, and he has blessed me with knowledge and a testimony" (Anita L. Hughes, "Why Did You Take My Son?" *Ensign,* July 1978, 66).

Keep the Commandments

The scriptures say that only those who keep Christ's commandments truly know Him (see 1 John 2:3). As we keep His commandments, we gradually become more like Him, until we are admitted fully into His presence (see Joseph Fielding Smith, *Doctrines of Salvation,* comp. Bruce R. McConkie, 3 vols. [1954–56], 2:7).

- Have the assigned class member give his three- to five-minute report on Mosiah 4 and 5. Make sure these points are discussed: Because of King Benjamin's words, his people felt the Holy Ghost, or the Spirit of God, and promised to keep God's commandments. Among the commandments King Benjamin counseled them to keep were to remember God's greatness; to humble themselves; to pray daily; not to injure one another; to teach their children to love each other; to give their goods to the poor; and to be pure in thought, word, and deed. As the people did these things, they became more like the Savior. We can become more like the Savior by doing these same things.

Alma tells us that when we live more like the Savior, we receive "his image in [our] countenances" (Alma 5:14; see also verse 19). This means, in part, that we are filled with the love of God and feel compassion for others. It means that we want to keep our covenants with the Lord and be worthy to bear His name.

Study the Scriptures

The scriptures tell us of the Savior's life, doctrines, and teachings. "Search the scriptures," the Lord commanded; "they are they which testify of me" (John 5:39). In them we see how the Savior dealt with those on earth and how we should deal with each other.

The scriptures teach us the gospel. The Lord said that if we build our lives upon the gospel, He will hold us guiltless before the Father at the Judgment Day (see 3 Nephi 27:13–16), the gates of hell shall not prevail against us (see 3 Nephi 11:39), and we can eventually be sanctified and lifted up at the last day (see 3 Nephi 27:17–22). Building our lives on the gospel of Christ means having faith in the Lord, repenting of our sins, being baptized, receiving the gift of the Holy Ghost, and enduring to the end.

- Invite a few class members to share how studying the scriptures has helped them know the Savior.

Follow the Living Prophet

- How will following the living prophet help us build upon Christ?

The President of the Church is the mouthpiece of God on earth. As such, he reveals the will of God for us today. Therefore, when we follow the inspired counsel of the prophet, we are following God and obeying His will. As we obey and gain experience, we develop faith in the Lord. This faith acts as an "anchor" to our souls and motivates us to do good works (see Ether 12:4). By it we find goodness and become worthy sons of God (see Moroni 7:25–26).

Love and Serve the Lord

King Benjamin told his people, "When ye are in the service of your fellow beings ye are only in the service of your God" (Mosiah 2:17). To love and serve others is to love and serve the Lord. And when we love and serve the Savior, we learn to feel as He feels and think as He thinks: "For how knoweth a man the master whom he has not served, and who is a stranger unto him, and is far from the thoughts and intents of his heart?" (Mosiah 5:13).

The Blessings of Making Jesus Christ Our Sure Foundation

We are promised that when our lives are founded upon the rock of Christ, the sure foundation, we will be able to live forever with Him and Heavenly Father again, receiving all they have for us. The Savior has promised us:

"He that receiveth me receiveth my Father;

"And he that receiveth my Father receiveth my Father's kingdom; therefore all that my Father hath shall be given unto him" (D&C 84:37–38).

- What other blessings might we receive when we make Jesus Christ our sure foundation?

Conclusion

- Share your testimony of Jesus as your Redeemer and Savior. If time permits, invite other class members to share their testimonies.

Challenge

Commit yourself as a priesthood holder to know the Savior and become more like Him. Choose a quality of the Lord you would like to perfect in your own life. Begin now to perfect this quality.

Teacher Preparation

Before presenting this lesson:

1. Review *Gospel Principles* chapters 3, "Jesus Christ, Our Chosen Leader and Savior," and 11, "The Life of Christ."

2. Prepare the poster suggested in the lesson, or write the information on the chalkboard.

3. Be prepared to bear your testimony of Jesus as your Redeemer and Savior.

4. Assign a class member in advance to give a three- to five-minute report on Mosiah 4 and 5. Make sure he discusses what King Benjamin asked his people to do and how his people reacted to his message.

5. Assign class members to present any stories, scriptures, or quotations you wish.

AGENCY: A GIFT FROM GOD

Lesson 2 8

The purpose of this lesson is to help us better understand the principle of agency and to teach us the importance of making wise choices.

Introduction

Jacob, the brother of Nephi, declared in the Book of Mormon, "Therefore, cheer up your hearts, and remember that ye are free to act for yourselves—to choose the way of everlasting death or the way of eternal life" (2 Nephi 10:23).

What gives us the power to make decisions? Why, for example, did we decide to be baptized? Or why are we able to decide what clothes to wear, what school to attend, or what job to pursue?

The answer is that we have been given a gift from God called agency. This gift is the power to make choices. The most important choice we have to make, a choice made possible by the Savior's Atonement, concerns eternal life. If we choose to follow the Lord, He will bless us and teach us how to use our agency to become like God and gain eternal salvation.

Lehi explained agency to his son Jacob: "Wherefore, men are free . . . to choose liberty and eternal life, through the great Mediator of all men, or to choose captivity and death, according to the captivity and power of the devil" (2 Nephi 2:27).

Agency: An Eternal Law

Agency is an eternal law. President Brigham Young, speaking of our agency, taught: "This is a law which has always existed from all eternity, and will continue to exist throughout all the eternities to come. Every intelligent being must have the power of choice" (*Discourses of Brigham Young,* sel. John A. Widtsoe [1954], 62).

▪ Have a class member read Abraham 3:22–28 and Moses 4:1–4.

Before we came to earth we met in a heavenly council. One of the great issues before us there concerned the eternal principle of agency.

Lucifer, or Satan, wanted to take away our agency. Jesus Christ, however, wanted to do the will of the Father, which was to allow us to choose for ourselves.

"This agency," said President Wilford Woodruff, "has always been the heritage of man under the rule and government of God. He possessed it in the heaven of heavens before the world was, and the Lord maintained and defended it there against the aggression of Lucifer and those that took sides with him. . . . By virtue of this agency you and I and all mankind are made responsible beings, responsible for the course we pursue, the lives we live, and deeds we do" (*Discourses of Wilford Woodruff,* sel. G. Homer Durham [1946], 8–9).

Using Our Agency

Certain things are necessary in order for us to use our agency. First, we must have a knowledge of good and evil; second, we must have the freedom to make choices; and third, after we exercise our agency, there must be consequences that follow our choices.

- As each is discussed, write on the chalkboard *Knowledge of Good and Evil, Freedom to Make Choices,* and *Consequences of Making Choices.*

Knowledge of Good and Evil

To be judged fairly when we meet our Savior, we must be able to think and reason. We must understand what we are doing, recognizing the difference between good and evil and the consequences of our actions. For this reason the Lord does not hold us responsible for our choices until we are eight years old, the age of accountability (see D&C 68:25–27; 29:46–47). Those who are younger than this cannot be responsible for their actions. Mormon explained:

"Little children are whole, for they are not capable of committing sin. . . .

"Little children cannot repent; wherefore, it is awful wickedness to deny the pure mercies of God unto them, for they are all alive in him because of his mercy" (Moroni 8:8, 19).

Mormon also explained that people who "are without the law" are "alive in Christ" (Moroni 8:22). This means that people who have not been taught the gospel or who are incapable of understanding it, such as those with certain developmental disabilities, are not expected to live by it. They will not be held accountable until the gospel is taught to them or until they can understand it.

Freedom to Make Choices

The greatest use of our agency is choosing between good and evil. The Lord knows that we can be influenced by both good and evil in making choices. Without the conflict between these two forces, we would

237

28-a, "Danger—No Swimming"

not have choices to make—we would not have agency. Therefore, the Lord gives us principles, laws, and commandments to follow, and Satan tempts us to disobey them.

The Lord says, "Thou shalt love the Lord thy God with all thy heart, and with all thy soul, and with all thy mind, and with all thy strength" (Mark 12:30). Satan essentially suggests: "Why love God? Why not disregard Him?" He might even imply there is no God!

The Lord says, "Remember the sabbath day, to keep it holy" (Exodus 20:8). Satan says: "Use the Sabbath as a recreation day. What value is there in attending church and in not working on this day?"

The Lord says, "Honour thy father and thy mother" (Exodus 20:12). Satan puts into our minds the idea of disobeying our parents: "Your life is your own to choose as you wish. Take all your parents will give you. They will soon be old, and someone else can take care of them." (Adapted from Carl W. Buehner, "Who's on the Lord's Side?" *Improvement Era*, June 1961, 402.)

- Show visual 28-a, "Danger—No Swimming." Have the assigned class member relate the story about the sign "Danger—No Swimming" (see "Teacher Preparation").

As the story about the "Danger—No Swimming" sign shows us, following the temptations of Satan limits our choices. Each time we choose evil we lose some freedom. Freedom is increased only when we choose the right.

President Spencer W. Kimball once wrote a letter to a young man who was struggling with a decision concerning religion. President Kimball wanted to make sure that this young man understood his choices. He wrote:

"Dear John:

"Your resistance and argument against the truths of the gospel have given me grave concern.

"I realize I cannot convince you against your will. . . . I would not, even if I could, force your thinking, for free agency is the basic law of God and each one must assume the responsibility for his own response; but certainly each of us must do his part in influencing for good those who might need some assistance" ("Absolute Truth," *Ensign*, Sept. 1978, 3).

Consequences of Making Choices

The natural result of using our agency is experiencing the consequences of our choices. However, we must understand that while we are free to choose, we are not free to choose the consequences of our choices. Good consequences follow right choices; bad consequences follow wrong choices. The Book of Mormon prophet Samuel declared: "[God] hath given unto you that ye might know good from evil, and he hath given unto you that ye might choose life or death; and ye can do good and be restored unto that which is good, or have that which is good restored unto you; or ye can do evil, and have that which is evil restored unto you" (Helaman 14:31).

- Show visual 28-b, "The principle of agency is like the law of the harvest: whatever we sow, we shall also reap."

The law of the harvest is that we reap what we sow (see Galatians 6:7–8). A farmer lives by this law. The kind of seed he plants determines what he will harvest. If he plants wheat seed, he will harvest wheat, not corn. Nor can he choose to neglect his crop once he has planted the seed and have a good harvest.

The principle of agency is like the law of the harvest: when we make a choice, we must accept the results of that choice. Sometimes we will not realize the total consequences of our choices until we are judged by God. But many times our choices affect us immediately. For example, we are given the gift of the Holy Ghost following our baptism. The full benefit of having the Holy Ghost as a companion cannot be realized until after our resurrection, but if we choose to disobey the Holy Ghost and commit sin, we lose His influence in our lives. The immediate consequence of choosing to do wrong is that we no longer experience the comfort, understanding, love, and guidance the Holy Ghost provides when we do what is right.

- When a young man breaks the Word of Wisdom, what are the consequences of his actions? (He is unworthy to be advanced in the priesthood. The Spirit withdraws. He is unworthy to serve a mission. He may become addicted to substances that harm his body.)

- When a father fails to teach the gospel to his children, what are the consequences? (There may be less love in the family. Children may not know good from evil. He may lose his children in the eternities if as adults they fail to become and remain temple worthy. The children's spiritual progress may be delayed.)

Whether consequences come immediately or in the future, our lives will reflect how we use our agency. The blessings that come from making right choices include "development, growth, and progress" (Elder James E. Faust, in Conference Report, Oct. 1984, 73; or *Ensign*, Nov. 1984, 59). In addition, we do not need to fear either immediate consequences or those that will follow in the future.

28-b, The principle of agency is like the law of the harvest: whatever we sow, we shall also reap.

- Sing "Do What Is Right" (*Hymns,* no. 237; or *Gospel Principles,* 342–43).

We Are Accountable for Our Choices

We are free to act, but we will be held accountable for our actions. One day each of us will stand before God and give an accounting of how we used our agency. Then God will judge us. His judgments will be both just and merciful, based on His love and the laws of heaven.

President Joseph F. Smith said: "God has given to all men an agency and has granted to us the privilege to serve him or serve him not. . . . But he will hold us strictly to an account for the use that we make of this agency, and as it was said of Cain, so it will be said of us; 'If thou doest well, shalt thou not be accepted? and if thou doest not well, sin lieth at the door' (Gen. 4:7)" (*Gospel Doctrine,* 5th ed. [1939], 49). Alma said:

"It is requisite with the justice of God that men should be judged according to their works; and if their works were good in this life, and the desires of their hearts were good, that they should also, at the last day, be restored unto that which is good.

"And if their works are evil they shall be restored unto them for evil" (Alma 41:3–4).

Because our actions are a result of our choices, it is important that we make correct choices. Joseph in the Old Testament is a good example of one who made correct choices and received great blessings because of his righteous actions.

After Joseph was brought to Egypt he became a servant of Potiphar, an officer of Pharaoh and captain of the guard. Joseph was blessed because he had chosen to follow the Lord. Potiphar saw that everything Joseph did was good, so he gave Joseph responsibility over all he had. For Joseph's sake the Lord blessed and prospered the house and fields of Potiphar.

During this time, however, Potiphar's wife began to lust after Joseph. Her feelings grew until one day she tried to tempt Joseph to commit adultery with her.

- Show the color visual of Joseph resisting Potiphar's wife, found in the "Picture Section" of this manual. Have a class member read Genesis 39:7–12. Did Joseph know the laws of God concerning adultery? What choices did Joseph have? What did he choose to do?

In facing this temptation, Joseph thought about the great trust Potiphar had placed in him; but more importantly, he thought about the Lord and his promise to obey Him. Joseph knew he was ultimately accountable to God. This knowledge gave him strength to resist Potiphar's wife. He chose to obey God.

The efforts of Potiphar's wife to tempt Joseph did not cease because he refused her once. She tempted him day after day, and he continued to resist her. Finally, in her anger and frustration, she accused Joseph of the very sin of which she was guilty. As a result, Joseph was put in prison.

"But the Lord was with Joseph" because he chose to obey. Eventually, Joseph was released from prison and became a ruler over all of Egypt. (See Genesis 39–41.)

- How can Joseph's example help us use our agency correctly?

Conclusion

President David O. McKay stated: "Next to the bestowal of life itself, the right to direct our lives is God's greatest gift to man. Freedom of choice is more to be treasured than any possession earth can give. It is inherent in the spirit of man. It is a divine gift to every normal being. . . . To man is given a special endowment, not bestowed upon any other living thing. God gave to him the power of choice. Only to the human being did the Creator say, '. . . thou mayest choose for thyself, for it is given unto thee; . . ." (Moses 3:17). Without this divine power to choose, humanity cannot progress" ("Man's Free Agency—An Eternal Principle of Progress," *Improvement Era*, Dec. 1965, 1073).

We must have agency to progress. But we must use our agency correctly because God will hold us responsible for our choices. We should seek to obey Heavenly Father, pray, listen to His prophets, and be worthy of the guidance of the Holy Ghost so we can one day gain eternal life.

Challenge

Select an area of your life you want to improve, and make and carry out decisions that will bring the desired result.

Additional Scriptures

- 2 Nephi 2:11 (opposition in all things)

- Doctrine and Covenants 58:26–29 (the Lord does not command in all things)

- Doctrine and Covenants 101:78 (accountability for sins)

Teacher Preparation

Before presenting this lesson:

1. Review *Gospel Principles* chapter 4, "Freedom to Choose."

2. Ask a class member in advance to prepare to give the following analogy: "When we follow the temptations of Satan, we limit our

choices. The following example suggests how this works. Imagine seeing a sign on the seashore that reads: ['Danger—No Swimming.'] We might think that is a restriction. But is it? We still have many choices. We are free to swim somewhere else. We are free to walk along the beach and pick up seashells. We are free to watch the sunset. We are free to go home. We are also free to ignore the sign and swim in the dangerous place. But once the [danger the sign warned us of] has us in its grasp and we are pulled under, we have very few choices. We can try to escape, or we can call for help, but we may drown" (*Gospel Principles* [1997], 23).

3. Prepare to have the class sing "Do What Is Right" (*Hymns,* no. 237; or *Gospel Principles,* 342–43).

4. Assign class members to present any stories, scriptures, or quotations you wish.

KEEPING THE SABBATH DAY HOLY

Lesson 29

The purpose of this lesson is to teach us to keep the Sabbath day holy.

Introduction

In the United States during the 1930s many people could not find work. It was a time of great hardship. One priesthood bearer in Salt Lake City, Utah, got a job with the government. It paid well and promised security. There was only one problem: the new job required him to work on Sunday. But he needed the money to support his family.

He knew that the Lord is not always displeased when people have to work on Sunday, so he prayed that the Lord would approve of his work on the Sabbath. But the Lord gave him the feeling that, in his case, he should not work on Sunday. The man discussed the matter with his wife. They both felt he should tell his boss he would not come to work on Sunday. When he did this, the boss warned him that he would lose his job.

- What would you do if you were this man?

When this priesthood holder refused to work on Sunday, he lost his job. A short time later, however, he was blessed to find another job that did not require him to work on the Sabbath.

The Sacredness of the Sabbath

In the beginning the Lord spent six days creating this earth, but on the seventh day He rested (see Genesis 2:2–3). He called this day the Sabbath. He set the example, showing us that we should honor the Sabbath by resting from all our work. God has always expected His children to devote one day in seven to Him.

Before the time of Christ, the Sabbath was observed on the seventh day of the week. But following Christ's Resurrection most Christians have observed the Sabbath on the first day of the week (see Acts 20:7). It was called the Lord's Day (see Revelation 1:10) in honor of His Resurrection on that day (see John 20:1).

29-a, On the Sabbath day we are to "offer up . . . sacraments."

Christ is Lord of the Sabbath (see Mark 2:27–28). As such, He has commanded us to keep "[His] holy day" (see D&C 59:9–13).

During Moses' time the Lord emphasized the importance of keeping the Sabbath when He included it among the Ten Commandments.

- Read Exodus 20:8–11.

The Lord told the people of Israel that the Sabbath was very important —that their obedience in honoring it was a sign of their faithfulness to Him (see Exodus 31:12–17).

The Sabbath was observed as directed by the Lord in these and other scriptures until the time of Jesus Christ. During these centuries, many uninspired religious leaders placed many restrictions on what a person could do on the Sabbath. For example, they taught that a fire could not be started or put out on the Sabbath. A person could untie a knot only if it could be done with one hand. One mile was the limit anyone could walk. Broken bones could not be reset until after the Sabbath.

It became so difficult for the people to obey all the rules that they forgot the true purpose of the Sabbath day. Rather than being a blessing and a joy, the Sabbath became a burden.

President George Albert Smith explained what our attitude toward the Sabbath should be: "[The Lord] has set apart one day in seven, not to make it a burden, but to bring joy into our lives and cause that our homes may be the gathering place of the family, . . . increasing our love for one another" ("Obey the Commandments," *Improvement Era*, Jan. 1949, 9).

- How can the Sabbath be a joy in our lives?

Keeping the Sabbath Day Holy

The Lord has not given us many rules about the Sabbath; He has simply given us some directions to guide us in keeping it holy.

- Read Doctrine and Covenants 59:9–13. Why has the Lord asked us to keep the Sabbath day holy? (To keep ourselves unspotted from the world.) What does it mean to "keep thyself unspotted from the world"?

- Display visual 29-a, "On the Sabbath day we are to 'offer up . . . sacraments.' "

- According to these verses, what should we do to keep the Sabbath day holy? (We should go to the house of prayer, rest from our labors, pay our devotions, offer up oblations and sacraments, confess our sins, prepare our meals with singleness of heart, fast, and pray.) What are oblations? (Gifts to the Lord. They include tithes and offerings.) What is meant by letting "thy food be prepared with singleness of heart"? (Prepare only simple meals on that day.)

The First Presidency of the Church said: "The Sabbath is not just another day on which we merely rest from our work, free to spend it as our light-mindedness may suggest. It is a holy day, the Lord's Day, to be spent as a day of worship and reverence" ("The Sabbath," *Church News*, 11 July 1959, 3).

- What other kinds of things may we do on the Sabbath to keep it holy?

In addition to the instructions given to us in the scriptures and by our living prophets, we can learn how to keep the Sabbath day holy by studying the Savior's life. One Sabbath day, for example, as Jesus was going into a synagogue to teach, He met a man with a withered hand. The scribes and the Pharisees, convinced that healing the man would break the Sabbath, gathered around the Savior to see what He would do.

Knowing what they were thinking, the Lord asked them, "Is it lawful on the sabbath days to do good, or to do evil? to save life, or to destroy it?" Then, looking around at all of them, He said to the man, "Stretch forth thy hand." The man did so, and his hand was completely healed. (See Luke 6:6–10.)

On another Sabbath day Jesus asked, "Which of you shall have an ass or an ox fallen into a pit, and will not straightway pull him out on the sabbath day?" (Luke 14:5–6).

- According to the Savior's example, what kind of work is appropriate on the Sabbath?

President Spencer W. Kimball said:

"It is true that some people must work on the Sabbath. And, in fact, some of the work that is truly necessary—caring for the sick, for example—may actually serve to hallow the Sabbath. However, in such activities our motives are an important consideration.

"When men and women are willing to work on the Sabbath to increase their wealth, they are breaking the commandments; for money taken in on the Sabbath, if the work is unnecessary, is unclean money" ("The Sabbath—A Delight," *Ensign*, Jan. 1978, 5).

When we are faced with the decision to engage in an activity that may or may not be appropriate for the Sabbath, we might ask ourselves three questions:

Is it doing good?

Is it spiritually uplifting?

Would Jesus do it?

When we cannot avoid working on Sunday, we should keep the spirit of the Sabbath in our hearts.

Blessings for Observing the Sabbath

The Lord has promised us great temporal and spiritual blessings if we keep the Sabbath day holy. If we honor it "with thanksgiving, with cheerful hearts and countenances, . . . the fulness of the earth is yours, . . . whether for food or for raiment, or for houses, or for barns, or for orchards, or for gardens, or for vineyards" (D&C 59:15–17).

- What other blessings might we receive by keeping the Sabbath day holy?

Conclusion

The Lord has told us not to trifle with sacred things. One of the most sacred things the Lord has given us is His holy day. Elder Ezra Taft Benson said: "The purpose of the Sabbath is for spiritual uplift, for a renewal of our covenants, for worship, for rest, for prayer. It is for the purpose of feeding the spirit, that we may keep ourselves unspotted from the world by obeying God's command" ("Keeping the Sabbath Day Holy," *Ensign,* May 1971, 6). Keeping the Sabbath day holy expresses our love for the Lord and shows our gratitude for His goodness. When we follow this commandment, we receive great blessings from Him.

Challenge

Seek to make the Sabbath more spiritual. Gather together your family and discuss your family's conduct on the Sabbath. Discuss ways to keep the Sabbath day holy. Remind family members to ask themselves three questions to determine if their activities are appropriate:

Is it doing good?

Is it spiritually uplifting?

Would Jesus do it?

Additional Scriptures

- Leviticus 19:30 (we are commanded to keep the Sabbath)

- Nehemiah 13:15–21 (we should not sell on the Sabbath)

- Isaiah 58:13–14 (we are not to seek worldly pleasure on the Sabbath)

Teacher Preparation

Before presenting this lesson:

1. Review *Gospel Principles* chapter 24, "The Sabbath Day."

2. Assign class members to present any stories, scriptures, or quotations you wish.

TITHES AND OFFERINGS

L e s s o n   3 0

The purpose of this lesson is to help us live the law of tithing and be generous in our offerings.

Introduction

▪ Write on the chalkboard *Will a man rob God?*

When Christ visited the American continent after His Resurrection, He asked the Nephites a question previously asked by Malachi, an Old Testament prophet: "Will a man rob God?" (Malachi 3:8; 3 Nephi 24:8).

▪ How is it possible to rob God? Read Malachi 3:8.

The Law of Tithing

The law of tithing is more than a commandment from the Lord. Through it we have an opportunity to return to Him a part of all He has given us. Through it we can also help build His kingdom and show our faith in Him.

The question is often asked, "What is a full, honest tithe?" A tithe is one-tenth of our increase (see D&C 119). This means that we give one-tenth of our income; or, if our increase is in flocks, herds, or crops rather than money, we give one-tenth of those things. (See Leviticus 27:30, 32.)

We pay tithing by giving it to the Lord's representative: a member of the bishopric or branch presidency. He then sends these funds to Church headquarters, where a record is kept of our tithing and other contributions.

Once a year each member is asked to make a special appointment with the bishop or branch president. At this time he privately reviews our tithing record with us and asks us if we have paid a full tithing for the year. This meeting is called tithing settlement.

The Lord considers the paying of tithing so important that we cannot receive a temple recommend unless we pay a full tithe. Furthermore, men and young men should be full-tithe payers before they are advanced in the priesthood.

Elder Matthew Cowley of the Quorum of the Twelve told of a good Maori sister living in a remote village of New Zealand who had the true spirit of paying tithing:

"Now, on one occasion I called in as I always did when I visited that vicinity, to see this grand little woman, then in her eighties, and blind. She did not live in an organized branch, had no contact with the priesthood except as the missionaries visited there. . . .

". . . She was out in her back yard by her little fire. I reached forth my hand to shake hands with her, and I was going to rub noses with her [in the Maori fashion] and she said, 'Do not shake hands with me.' . . .

". . . Then she got on her hands and knees and crawled over to her little house. At the corner of the house there was a spade. She lifted up that spade and crawled off in another direction, measuring the distance she went. She finally arrived at a spot and started digging. . . . [Her spade] finally struck something hard. She took out . . . a fruit jar. She opened that fruit jar and reached down in it, took something out and handed it to me, and it turned out to be New Zealand money. In American money it would have been equivalent to one hundred dollars.

"She said: 'There is my tithing. Now I can shake hands with the priesthood of God.'

"I said: 'You do not owe that much tithing.'

"She said: 'I know it. I do not owe it now, but I am paying some in advance, for I do not know when the priesthood of God will get around this way again.'

"And then I leaned over and pressed my nose and forehead against hers, and the tears from my eyes ran down her cheeks" (in Conference Report, Oct. 1948, 159–60).

- How does paying tithing show our love for the Lord? How does it show our faith?

Offerings

We may contribute other money besides tithing to help build the Lord's kingdom. These contributions are called offerings.

On fast Sunday each month, members should contribute fast offerings that are at least equal to the value of the two meals not eaten during the fast. Other offerings members may make include contributions to the Church missionary fund, the LDS Foundation, or Church humanitarian aid. Members may use the Tithing and Other Offerings form when making these and other contributions.

The following story, told by Elder Boyd K. Packer, helps us understand the importance of paying tithes and offerings:

Several years ago two missionaries reported to their branch president that a family they were teaching had suddenly decided against baptism. The father had learned about tithing and canceled all further meetings with the missionaries.

"A few days later," Elder Packer explains, "the branch president persuaded the elders to join him in another visit to the family.

" 'I understand,' he told the father, 'that you have decided not to join the Church.'

" 'That is correct,' he answered.

" 'The elders tell me that you are disturbed about tithing.'

" 'Yes,' said the father. 'They had not told us about it; and when I learned of it, I said, "Now that's too much to ask. Our church has never asked anything like that." We think that's just too much, and we will not join.'

" 'Did they tell you about fast offering?' he asked.

" 'No,' said the man. 'What is that?'

" 'In the Church we fast for two meals each month and give the value of the meals for the help of the poor.'

" 'They did not tell us that,' the man said. . . .

" 'Did they explain the welfare program to you?'

" 'No,' said that father, 'What is that?'

" 'Well, we believe in helping one another. If someone is in need or ill or out of work or in trouble, we are organized to assist, and you would be expected to help.'

" 'Did they also tell you that we have no professional clergy? All of us contribute our time, our talents, our means, and travel—all to help the work. And we're not paid for it in money.'

" 'They didn't tell us any of that,' said the father.

" 'Well,' said the branch president, 'if you are turned away by a little thing like tithing, it is obvious you're not ready for this Church. Perhaps you have made the right decision and you should not join.'

"As they departed, almost as an afterthought, he turned and said, 'Have you ever wondered why people will do all of these things willingly? I have never received a bill for tithing. No one has ever called to collect it. But we pay it—and all of the rest—and count it a great privilege.

" 'If you could discover *why,* you would be within reach of the pearl of great price. . . .

" 'But,' said the branch president, 'it is *your* decision. I only hope you will pray about it.'

"A few days later the man appeared at the branch president's home. . . . He wanted to schedule the baptism of his family" (in Conference Report, Oct. 1974, 126–27; or *Ensign,* Nov. 1974, 88).

▪ What influenced this man to join the Church?

Use of Tithes and Offerings

The tithes and offerings we give to the Church are used for the Lord's work. This money is spent by our priesthood leaders in ways the Lord has appointed. These contributions help bring our brothers and sisters back to our Father in Heaven.

▪ Why does it take money to accomplish the Lord's work?

Some of the ways our tithes and offerings are used are to help:

1. Operate the missionary program.
2. Build and maintain chapels, temples, and other buildings.
3. Educate people in Church schools, seminaries, and institutes.
4. Create, print, and distribute the scriptures, lesson manuals, and other Church materials.
5. Further family history work.
6. Provide for those in need.
7. Meet the expenses of general conferences.

Paying Tithes and Offerings Willingly

▪ Why is it a privilege to give tithes and offerings to the Lord?

We should pay our tithes and offerings willingly. The scriptures tell us to give "not grudgingly, or of necessity: for God loveth a cheerful giver" (2 Corinthians 9:7). The scriptures also say that if a man "doeth it grudgingly . . . it is counted unto him the same as if he had retained the gift" (Moroni 7:8).

Elder Marion G. Romney had an experience that helps us understand this scripture. The experience occurred during a time when Church members were asked to contribute money specifically for the building of new meetinghouses.

"About a quarter of a century ago Sister Romney and I moved into a ward in which they were just beginning to build a meetinghouse. The size of the contribution the bishop thought I ought to contribute rather staggered me. I thought it was at least twice as much as he should have asked. However, . . . I said, 'Well, I will pay it, Bishop, but I will have to pay it [a little at a time] because I don't have the money.' And so I began to pay. And I paid and paid until I was down to about the last three payments, when, as is my habit, I was reading The Book of Mormon, and came to the scripture which said:

" '. . . if a man . . . giveth a gift . . . grudgingly; wherefore it is counted unto him the same as if he had retained the gift; wherefore he is counted evil before God' (Moroni 7:8.)

"This shocked me because I was out about a thousand dollars. Well, I went on and paid the [rest of what] I had promised to pay, and then I paid . . . more . . . to convince the Lord that I had done it with the right attitude" ("Mother Eve, A Worthy Exemplar," *Relief Society Magazine,* Feb. 1968, 84–85).

Blessings of Paying Tithes and Offerings

The Lord has promised that when we willingly contribute tithes and offerings, He will bless us.

- Read 3 Nephi 24:10–12. What does the Lord promise when we pay our tithes?

President Joseph F. Smith told the following story about the blessings that come from paying tithing: "I recollect most vividly a circumstance that occurred in the days of my childhood. My mother was a widow, with a large family to provide for. One spring when we opened our potato pits, she had her boys get a load of the best potatoes and she took them to the tithing office; potatoes were scarce that season. I was a little boy at the time, and drove the team. When we drove up to the steps of the tithing office, ready to unload the potatoes, one of the clerks came out and said to my mother, 'Widow Smith, it's a shame that you should have to pay tithing.' . . . He chided my mother for paying her tithing, called her anything but wise or prudent; and said there were others who were strong and able to work that were supported from the tithing office. My mother turned upon him and said: '. . . You ought to be ashamed of yourself. Would you deny me a blessing? If I did not pay my tithing, I should expect the Lord to withhold his blessing from me. I pay my tithing, not only because it is a law of God, but because I expect a blessing by doing it. By keeping this and other laws, I expect to prosper, and to be able to provide for my family.' . . . She prospered because she obeyed the laws of God. She had abundance to sustain her family. We never lacked as much as many others did. . . . That widow was entitled to the privileges of the house of God. No ordinance of the gospel could be denied her, for she was obedient to the laws of God" (*Gospel Doctrine,* 5th ed. [1939], 228–29).

- Why did Sister Smith have her boys take the best potatoes for tithing? How did this experience help the boys understand the importance of tithing? What blessings did Sister Smith receive for paying tithing?

Elder Henry D. Taylor said this about the blessings we receive from paying tithes and offerings: "The Lord does keep his promises. He truly opens the windows of heaven and pours out his blessings upon those who are faithful and who obey his commandments. . . . These blessings may come in a financial or temporal way or may be realized by a spiritual outpouring, bringing strength, peace, and comfort" (in Conference Report, Apr. 1974, 158; or *Ensign,* May 1974, 108).

Conclusion

The Lord has commanded us to pay tithes and offerings. As we do this, we build up the kingdom of God. We help bring happiness to many people, both living and deceased. When we obey these laws, we show our love for our Father in Heaven, Jesus Christ, and our brothers and sisters. We also demonstrate our faith in God. In return, we receive both temporal and spiritual blessings worth far more than what we give.

Challenge

If you are not already doing so, commit yourself to paying an honest tithing and attending tithing settlement. Carefully consider your offerings to the Church. If you feel that you should be contributing more, do so. Teach your family members the blessings of paying tithes and offerings, and help them obey these laws.

Additional Scriptures

- Genesis 14:19–20 (Abraham paid tithes)

- 2 Chronicles 31:5–6 (Israelites paid tithing)

- Nehemiah 10:37–38 (children of Israel paid tithing)

- Alma 13:13–16 (Abraham paid tithes)

- Doctrine and Covenants 64:23 (those who are tithed will not be burned)

Teacher Preparation

Before presenting this lesson:

1. Review *Gospel Principles* chapter 32, "Tithes and Offerings."

2. Assign class members to present any stories, scriptures, or quotations you wish.

BEING HONEST

Lesson 31

The purpose of this lesson is to teach us the importance of being honest.

Introduction

Elder Howard W. Hunter wrote about a young man who learned a very important lesson:

"I recall a young man who . . . traveled around with a crowd that thought it was smart to do things that were not right. On a few occasions he was caught in some minor violations. One day I got a call from the police station and was told he was being held because of a traffic violation. He had been caught speeding. . . . Knowing the things he was doing might prevent him from going on a mission, he straightened up, and when he was 19 years of age, he received his call.

"I shall never forget the talk we had when he returned. He told me that while he was in the mission field he had often thought of the trouble he had caused by the mistaken belief that the violation of little things was not important. But a great change had come into his life. He had come to the realization that there is no happiness or pleasure in violation of the law, whether it be God's law or the laws that society imposes upon us. . . .

"I was impressed by the great change that had come over this young man while he served on his mission and studied moral principles. How unfortunate it is that he had to learn his lesson the hard way, but what a great blessing comes when there is the realization that one cannot be in violation and feel good about that conduct" ("Basic Concepts of Honesty," *New Era*, Feb. 1978, 4–5).

- Are we being dishonest when we break the laws of the land? Why?

- Write on the chalkboard *We believe in being honest.*

The thirteenth article of faith, written by the Prophet Joseph Smith, states, "We believe in being honest, true, . . . virtuous, and in doing good to all men." In this and many other scriptures the Lord has commanded us to be honest in our personal lives and in our dealings with others.

- What does it mean to be honest? (It is doing what we know is right. If we make promises, we keep them. If we have a debt, we pay it. Honesty is to speak the truth and act truthfully. It means that we do not lie, steal, or break the laws of the land. It means that we do not deceive in any way.)

The Importance of Honesty

Being honest is necessary if we are to live the gospel of Jesus Christ. If we know the truth but do not live it, we are dishonest with ourselves and with God. To be honest with ourselves and the Lord, we must keep the covenants we have made. We must be honest to have the Holy Ghost as our companion.

Being honest with ourselves and God means that we must also be honest with those around us. If we are, the Lord will bless us with His Spirit, and we will earn the trust, honor, and loyalty of those with whom we associate. Our honesty with others will enable us to serve them and magnify our callings.

- Read the following situations. Discuss as a class what you would do in each situation.

Example 1

Elder O. Leslie Stone recalled this experience: "Recently, our grandson, Adam, was traveling with Sister Stone and me on a trip to California. About noontime we stopped for lunch. When the waitress brought the bill I didn't pay very close attention, and after she gave me my change, I realized that she had charged me for only two sandwiches instead of three."

- What was the honest thing to do? If this happened to you, how could you teach your children about being honest?

Elder Stone continued:

"I knew that the girl would be short [of money] at the end of the day, and there suddenly flashed into my mind the thought of how my father had taught me to be honest. I felt this was a good time to talk to Adam about honesty, and so we sat down and I explained what had happened. I told him we had a problem.

"I said we could leave now and keep the extra change and no one would ever know the difference, or we could tell the girl that we still owed her for a sandwich. Our decision wasn't at all difficult to make when we decided that if we kept money that did not belong to us that we would be breaking the commandment, 'Thou shalt not steal.' We agreed that our Heavenly Father would be displeased with us and we would be unhappy too because we would know in our hearts that we had not been honest.

"Adam and I approached the girl at the counter, and I explained to her that she had undercharged us and that we owed almost a dollar more. Her face flushed in embarrassment for a moment, and then she thanked us for telling her of the mistake. We continued on our way with a good feeling, and I am sure our Heavenly Father approved of what we had done" ("Be Honest," *Friend,* Jan. 1975, 7).

Example 2

Elder Gordon B. Hinckley recalled: "Recently we rode a train from Osaka to Nagoya, Japan. At the station were friends to greet us, and in the excitement my wife left her purse on the train."

- If you had found Sister Hinckley's purse, what could you do?

Since Elder Hinckley believes that most people are honest, he "called the Tokyo station to report it. When the train arrived at its destination some three hours later, the railroad telephoned to say the purse was there. We were not returning via Tokyo, and more than a month passed before it was delivered to us in Salt Lake City. Everything left in the purse was there when it was returned" ("An Honest Man—God's Noblest Work," *New Era,* Oct. 1976, 47).

- What does the Lord expect of us when we find someone else's property?

The Lord has said, "If thou shalt find that which thy neighbor has lost, thou shalt make diligent search till thou shalt deliver it to him again" (D&C 136:26). The Lord expects us to be completely honest. To Him, anything that is not completely honest is dishonest; there is no such thing as partial honesty.

- How can we recognize what is honest and what is not? Have a class member read Moroni 7:16–17.

- Who is the source of good? What are the results of honest acts? (Good, belief in Christ, service to God) Who is the source of evil? What are the results of dishonest acts? (Evil, unbelief in Christ, denial of Him, disservice to God)

- Have class members discuss the following situations. They should decide if the person involved is being completely honest.

1. Dad has never had a traffic ticket. He is a good driver. He always watches carefully and tries to obey all traffic laws.

2. While at work, John uses company stamps to mail letters to his sick mother (see D&C 42:54).

3. Jack and Leo are the best of friends. They are willing to let each other borrow anything. After one borrows something from his neighbor, he promptly returns it. (See Mosiah 4:28; D&C 136:25.)

Honesty in the Family

Priesthood holders should not only strive to be honest themselves but should also teach their children to be honest. President N. Eldon Tanner said: "This training in honesty begins in the home. Each of us has personal possessions which . . . should not be taken without the consent of the owner. A child who respects such honesty in the home is not apt to violate the principle outside the home. On the other hand, lack of such training fosters disrespect for the rights and property of others" (in Conference Report, Apr. 1978, 64; or *Ensign,* May 1978, 44).

▪ What can we do in our families to teach and encourage honesty?

President Brigham Young said:

"Be honest. Woe to those who profess to be Saints and are not honest.

"Honest hearts produce honest actions" (as quoted by Spencer W. Kimball, in *Faith Precedes the Miracle* [1972], 234).

When we are interviewed to receive a temple recommend, we are asked if we deal honestly with others. An experience of one member of the Church, President Ruben Dario Pacheo of Caracas, Venezuela, illustrates the kind of honesty expected of us:

President Pacheo and his family wanted to go to the temple. After much sacrifice and spiritual preparation, he and his family raised the money for the long trip. President Pacheo sent his daughter to the bank to get 500 U.S. dollars. He said:

"My wife took the envelope and put it away without counting the money. The night before leaving, I asked for the money and noticed that the envelope was unusually heavy. We counted the money. They had given us $4,065. I was astonished. . . . The bank receipts indicated a purchase of only $500—that meant that the bank had erred some $3,500 in our favor!

"Some nonmember friends at our home that night tried to persuade us to use the money to enjoy our trip to the United States. To be honest, I myself had never seen so much money in my life. However, I energetically said, 'We cannot keep this money because it is not ours. The purpose of our trip to the temple is to make covenants with the Lord. What good will they do if we are dishonest?'

"We returned the money to the bank; they had noticed that they had lost funds but had no records indicating to whom it had been paid. Some bank clerks asked me that day, 'Why did you do it? Nobody knew that you had that money.' My only answer was: 'Because I am a Mormon' " (as quoted by Mario G. Echeverri, in "Venezuela," *Ensign,* Feb. 1977, 30).

- How did the Pacheo family show honesty? How do you suppose the family felt as they were sealed in the temple?

- Invite class members to share some recent examples of honesty they have experienced or observed.

The Blessings of Honesty

We receive blessings when we are honest with others, ourselves, and the Lord. Some of these blessings include the following:

We Develop Trust

Other people will trust us when we are honest. They will know that they can come to us for help and guidance. Elder Spencer W. Kimball told of such a man:

"On one of the trips to Mexico City I was asked by one of the stake presidents to ordain a bishop who had been called. I was glad to do so. The President and the newly called bishop came to our room and we visited and got acquainted. As I remember it, this small but impressive man was introduced as a full-blooded Aztec Indian. This itself pleased me greatly since I have always had such a special interest in the Indians.

"I was told about him and his family and his occupation. It seems that he was employed by a man with a rather large business, and our new bishop was entrusted with the keeping of the accounts. The employer had decided to take his wife to Europe on a rather extended vacation, and he called in this dear brother and turned over the total responsibility to him and admitted that this was the only one of his employees in whom he had confidence sufficient to turn over his bank accounts.

"As we laid our hands on the head of this young man, my heart swelled with pride and I thanked the Lord for men who could be trusted, for men who could inspire confidence and affection" (in Conference Report, Mexico City Area Conference 1972, 32).

- What is the value of being trusted by friends, associates, and employers? by the Lord?

The following story, told by the son of an early pioneer, illustrates the confidence and trust others have for us when we are honest with them: "One day my father sent me to trade a horse with an old Navajo Indian Chief. I was a little fellow and I went on horseback, leading the horse

261

to be traded. The old chief came out and lifted me down from my horse. I told him my father wanted me to trade the horse for some blankets. He brought out a number of handsome blankets, but, as my father had told me to be sure and make a good trade, I shook my head and said I would have to have more. He then brought two buffalo robes and quite a number of other blankets and finally, when I thought I had done very well, I took the roll on my horse and started for home. When I gave the blankets to my father, he unrolled them, looked at them, and then began to separate them. He put blanket after blanket into a roll and did them up and told me to get on my horse and take them back and tell the chief he had sent too many. When I got back, the old chief took them and smiled. He said, 'I knew you would come back; I knew Jacob would not keep so many; you know Jacob is our father as well as your father' " (told by Le Roi C. Snow, "Honesty Means Character," in Preston Nibley, comp., *Inspirational Talks for Youth* [1941], 101).

We Please God

We please God when we are honest. Elder Howard W. Hunter told how honesty pleases God and blesses us: "There is a joy that comes to one from being honest. Let me tell you how. By this means you can have the companionship of the Master and you can have the Spirit of the Holy Ghost. Violations of the code of honesty will deprive you of these two great blessings. Could you believe that one who would lie or cheat . . . could have the companionship of the Master or have the Spirit of the Holy Ghost?" (*New Era*, Feb. 1978, 5).

Priesthood holders displease God when they are dishonest. A dishonest man or boy cannot represent an honest, truth-loving God.

We Feel Good about Ourselves

When we are honest, we feel good about ourselves.

- How does being honest increase our self-respect?

An honest man has self-respect. He has nothing to hide and can look anyone straight in the eye. A dishonest man, however, feels cheap, ashamed, and often afraid. And he should, because dishonesty never goes unrecognized. Elder Howard W. Hunter asked: "Do you think you can be alone when you commit a dishonest act? Do you think you can be unobserved when you cheat in an examination, even though you are the only person in the room?" (*New Era*, Feb. 1978, 5).

We Influence Others for Good

Our honesty has a positive influence on others. President Spencer W. Kimball told of an instance when a member's good example influenced a nonmember:

"On the train from New York to Baltimore we sat in the dining car with a businessman whom we engaged in conversation.

" 'Have you been to Salt Lake [City, Utah]? Do you hear the Tabernacle Choir?' And these questions led us naturally into the golden ones. 'How much do you know about the Church and its doctrine, practices, and people?'

" 'I know little about the Church,' he said, 'but I know one of its people.' He was [building houses] in New York. 'There is a subcontractor working for me,' he continued. 'He is so honest and full of integrity I never asked him to bid on a job. He is the soul of honor. If the Mormon people are like this man, I'd like to know about a Church which produces such honorable men.' We left him literature and sent the missionaries in New York to proselyte him" (in Conference Report, Mexico City Area Conference 1972, 30).

Conclusion

The Lord has commanded us to be honest. We must therefore distinguish between honest and dishonest acts. We must practice honest thoughts, words, and actions in our homes, our neighborhoods, and the Church. We must also teach our children honesty. If we do these things we will have a clear conscience, peace of mind, a feeling of self-worth, and the companionship of the Holy Ghost.

- Read Mosiah 4:30. What does King Benjamin warn us to do?

- If you feel inspired to do so, bear your testimony of the principle of honesty.

Challenge

During the coming week, evaluate your thoughts, words, and actions to test your honesty. Seek the Lord's help to speak the truth and act truthfully.

Fathers: Counsel with your wife to find ways to teach your children honesty.

Young men: Determine now to be honest with your parents and Church leaders and to obey the laws of God and of the land.

Additional Scriptures

- Exodus 20:15–16 (commandment not to steal or bear false witness)

- Alma 27:27 (people of Ammon perfectly honest and upright)

- 3 Nephi 1:22 (Satan sent lyings to destroy faith but largely failed)

- Doctrine and Covenants 42:20–21 (punishment for thieves and liars)

- Doctrine and Covenants 51:9 (every man to deal honestly)

- Doctrine and Covenants 97:8 (the Lord accepts those who are honest, contrite, and obedient)

- Doctrine and Covenants 98:10 (seek and uphold honest and wise men)

Teacher Preparation

Before presenting this lesson:

1. Review *Gospel Principles* chapter 31, "Honesty."

2. Assign class members to present any stories, scriptures, or quotations you wish.

PURITY OF THOUGHT

Lesson 32

The purpose of this lesson is to help us strengthen our commitment to have pure thoughts.

Introduction

President Spencer W. Kimball told the following fable to illustrate how pure thoughts and righteous living affect us:

"Lord George had led an evil life. He had been a drunkard, a gambler, and a cheat in business, and his face reflected the life he had led. It was a very evil face.

"One day he fell in love with a simple country girl to whom he proposed marriage. Jenny Mere told him that she could never marry a man whose face was so repulsive and so evil-looking; and also that when she did marry, she wanted a man with a saint-like face, which was the mirror of true love.

"Following a custom of the day, Lord George went down to Mr. Aeneas. . . . Aeneas made waxen masks for people, and his skill was so art-perfect that the person's identity was completely hidden. . . . Aeneas went to his storeroom, selected a mask, heated it over a lamp, fixed it to Lord George's face; and when Lord George looked in the glass, he had the face of a saint who loved dearly. So altered was his appearance that Jenny Mere was soon wooed and won.

"He bought a little cottage in the country, almost hidden in an arbor of roses, with a tiny garden spot. From then on his entire life changed. He became interested in nature; he found 'sermons in stones, books in brooks, and good in everything.' Formerly he was blasé and life had no interest for him; now, he was engrossed in kindliness, and the world around him.

"He was not content with starting life anew, but tried to make amends for the past. Through a confidential solicitor he restored his ill-gotten gains to those whom he had cheated. Each day brought new refinements to his character, more beautiful thoughts to his soul.

"By accident, his former companions discovered his identity. They visited him in his garden, and urged him to return to his old evil life. When he refused, he was attacked, and the mask was torn from his face.

"He hung his head. Here was the end of all; here was the end of his new-found life and his love dream. As he stood with bowed head, with the mask at his feet on the grass, his wife rushed across the garden and threw herself on her knees in front of him. When she looked up at him, what do you suppose she found? Line for line, feature for feature, the face was the same as that of the mask. Lines of beauty—regular features."

President Kimball concluded the story, saying, "There is no doubt that the life one leads, and the thoughts one thinks are registered plainly in his face" (as quoted in Conference Report, Apr. 1975, 119–20; or *Ensign,* May 1975, 80–81).

Our Thoughts Lead to Actions

- How do our thoughts affect our actions?

Our thoughts greatly influence our actions. If we think righteous thoughts, we will perform righteous acts. If we think evil thoughts, we will eventually commit the sins we have been thinking about.

President David O. McKay often spoke of the effect that thoughts have on actions. On one occasion he said: "Thoughts are the seeds of acts, and precede them. . . . The Savior's constant desire and effort were to implant in the mind right thoughts, pure motives, noble ideals, knowing full well that right words and actions would inevitably follow" (*Stepping Stones to an Abundant Life,* comp. Llewelyn R. McKay [1971], 206).

The son of a great prophet, Nephi sought to receive revelation, just like his father. His righteousness was rewarded, and he himself became the prophet for his people.

- What did Nephi do that helped him be righteous?

Nephi gave us a clue to how he was able to live righteously when he wrote:

"For my soul delighteth in the scriptures, and my heart pondereth them, and writeth them for the learning and the profit of my children.

"Behold, my soul delighteth in the things of the Lord; and my heart pondereth continually upon the things which I have seen and heard" (2 Nephi 4:15–16).

President David O. McKay told the following story:

"Many years ago a young man came to me while I was president of the European Mission and made a confession of a wrong and sinful act. He justified himself by saying that he happened to be in a bookstore at the closing hour, and when the door was locked he yielded to temptation. He rather blamed the *circumstances* for his fall.

"But I said, 'It wasn't the circumstances; it wasn't the locked door, nor the enticement. You had thought of that before you went to that bookstore. If you had never thought of that act, there would have been no circumstance strong enough to entice or to tempt you, a missionary, to fall. The thought always precedes the act' " ("Cleanliness Is Next to Godliness," *Instructor,* Mar. 1965, 86).

James Allen once wrote:

"A man's mind may be likened to a garden, which may be intelligently cultivated or allowed to run wild; but whether cultivated or neglected, it must, and will, *bring forth*. If no useful seeds are *put* into it, then an abundance of useless weed-seeds will *fall* therein, and will continue to produce their kind.

"Just as a gardener cultivates his plot, keeping it free from weeds, and growing the flowers and fruits which he requires, so may a man tend the garden of his mind, weeding out all the wrong, useless, and impure thoughts, and cultivating toward perfection the flowers and fruits of right, useful, and pure thoughts. By pursuing this process, a man sooner or later discovers that he is the master-gardener of his soul, the director of his life. He also . . . understands, with ever-increasing accuracy, how the thought-forces and mind-elements operate in the shaping of his character, circumstances, and destiny" (*As a Man Thinketh* [1983], 15).

- What must we do to have a garden that produces good foods and flowers? What have we done if our garden produces weeds?

- What must we do to have a mind that leads us to good actions? What have we done if our mind leads us to evil or worthless actions?

Elder Bruce R. McConkie said, "If we are pondering in our hearts the things of righteousness, we shall become righteous" (in Conference Report, Oct. 1973, 56; or *Ensign,* Jan. 1974, 48). Said another way, "The Lord hath said he dwelleth not in unholy temples, but in the hearts of the righteous doth he dwell" (Alma 34:36). When we have pure thoughts, the Spirit of the Lord will be with us; and if we have the Holy Ghost with us, our lives will eventually be purified.

Keeping Thoughts Pure

It is not enough to keep our minds free from evil if we are to become like Christ. We have to keep our minds filled with righteous thoughts.

▪ Have a class member read Philippians 4:8. What does Paul tell us to think about? (List the answers on the chalkboard. Answers could include whatever is true, honest, just, pure, lovely, of good report, virtuous, or praiseworthy.)

Whenever we can, we should think about the truths of the gospel. One of the best ways to do this is to keep the promise we make when we partake of the sacrament: to always remember the Savior.

When President Spencer W. Kimball was a member of the Quorum of the Twelve, he said: "When you look in the dictionary for the most important word, do you know what it is? It could be 'remember.' Because all of you have made covenants—you know what to do and you know how to do it—our greatest need is to remember. That is why everyone goes to sacrament meeting every Sabbath day—to take the sacrament and listen to the priests pray that they '. . . may always remember him and keep his commandments which he has given them' " (*Circles of Exaltation* [address delivered at seminary and institute summer school, Brigham Young University, 28 June 1968], 8).

▪ How can we always remember the Savior?

The great prophet Alma gave wise counsel to his son Helaman that could help us always remember the Savior.

▪ Have a class member read Alma 37:35–37. How can directing our thoughts always to the Lord help us? (We can resist temptation and develop greater faith, obedience, hope, and love.) How can prayer help us keep our thoughts and actions pure?

Evil influences surround us in the world, and Satan uses them to try to influence us. However, we can do much to defeat him if we avoid listening to and reading or watching things that are evil. Elder J. Thomas Fyans clarified this principle by using the rivers of South America to illustrate how our thoughts are affected by what we read or see:

"One interesting feature about [the rivers of South America] is their different colors. The Madeira, for example, is called a white river because its waters carry fine clay particles along its course. The black color of the Rio Negro comes from decaying organic materials picked up in the forests through which it passes. Still other rivers flow over white sands and often appear emerald green or turquoise blue.

"Just as these rivers are colored by the substances picked up as they flow along, so the streams of our thoughts are colored by the material through which they are channeled" (in Conference Report, Buenos Aires Area Conference 1975, 28).

- How is a mind like a river? (Just as a river is colored by what it touches, our minds are affected by what we read, see, or hear.)

- What evil things does Satan use to try to influence our thoughts? (Pornography; immoral or immodest people; vulgar language; and certain types of music, dance, and entertainment)

We should avoid all things that will cause evil thoughts and destroy our spirituality. This is difficult because we live in a world filled with evil. When an immoral or wicked thought does enter our minds, we must banish it immediately.

Elder Boyd K. Packer explained one way we can fight against evil thoughts:

"The mind *is like* a stage—the curtain is always up except when we are asleep. There is always some act being performed on that stage. It may be a comedy, a tragedy, interesting or dull, good or bad; but always there is some act playing on the stage of the mind.

"Have you noticed that without any real intent on your part, in the middle of almost any performance, a shady little thought may creep in from the wings and attract your attention? . . .

"If you permit them to go on, all thoughts of any virtue will leave the stage. You will be left, because you consented to it, to the influence of unrighteous thoughts. If you yield to them, they will enact for you on the stage of your mind anything to the limits of your toleration. They may enact a theme of bitterness, jealousy, or hatred. They may be vulgar, immoral, or even depraved. . . .

"What do you do at a time like that? . . .

"I would teach you this. Choose from among the sacred music of the Church a favorite hymn, one with words that are uplifting and music that is reverent, one that makes you feel something akin to inspiration. Go over it carefully in your mind. Memorize it. Even though you have had no musical training, you can think through a hymn.

"Now, use this hymn as the place for your thoughts to go. Make it your emergency channel. Whenever you find that these shady actors have slipped from the sidelines of your thinking onto the stage of your mind, put on this record, as it were.

"As the music begins and as the words form in your mind, the unworthy thoughts will slip shamefully away. The hymn will change the whole mood on the stage of your mind. Because it is uplifting and clean, the baser thoughts will disappear, for while virtue, by choice, *will not* associate with filth, evil *cannot* tolerate the presence of light. . . .

"Once you learn to clear the stage of your mind from unworthy thoughts, keep it busy with learning worthwhile things. Change your environment so that you have things about you that will inspire good and uplifting thoughts. Keep busy with things that are righteous" (*Teach Ye Diligently* [1975], 46–47).

- What else can we do to channel our thoughts? (Pray; recite an uplifting poem, scripture, or thought; or think about a sacred experience or place)

- Why is it important to banish evil thoughts the moment they enter our minds?

We must cultivate clean, righteous thoughts if we are to experience true happiness. "Real happiness is not dependent on external things. . . . The kind of happiness that stays with you is the happiness that springs from inward thoughts and emotions. . . . You must cultivate your mind if you wish to achieve enduring happiness. You must furnish your mind with interesting thoughts and ideas. For an empty mind grows bored and cannot endure itself. An empty mind seeks pleasure as a substitute for happiness" (William Lyon Phelps, quoted by Harvey Fletcher, *The Good Life* [1961], 137).

- Read Psalm 1:1–3.

Conclusion

Our thoughts influence our actions. Pure thoughts and desires lead to righteous living. Evil thoughts cause us to lose the Spirit of the Lord and can lead us to do evil.

To keep our minds clean, we should always strive to think about the things of God. We should ponder the truths of the gospel and pray constantly. As we do these things, we are promised great blessings. The Lord has promised: "Let virtue garnish thy thoughts unceasingly; then shall thy confidence wax strong in the presence of God. . . . The Holy Ghost shall be thy constant companion" (D&C 121:45–46).

We can keep our thoughts pure by avoiding evil. When a bad thought enters our minds, we should immediately think about something inspiring such as a hymn, poem, or scripture. We can also pray for the Lord's help to resist unclean thoughts.

Challenge

Several times a day think about the things of the Lord. Do your best to "always remember him." Decide on a way to channel your thoughts. You could memorize one of your favorite hymns, scriptures, or poems. Whenever you are faced with an unclean thought, immediately think through the words you have memorized to force the evil thought away.

Teacher Preparation

Before presenting this lesson:

Assign class members to present any stories, scriptures, or quotations you wish.

EXTENDING AND RECEIVING FORGIVENESS

Lesson 33

The purpose of this lesson is to motivate us to forgive others and receive forgiveness.

Introduction

In the following parable the Savior taught us about Heavenly Father's love for us:

A certain man had two sons. The younger son asked his father for his share of the family's possessions. He then took what his father gave him and went to another country, where he quickly wasted all his money and broke the commandments of God.

When the wayward son had spent all he had, a great famine occurred. He soon became hungry, so he found a job feeding pigs. But he was still so poor and hungry that he wanted to eat the food given to the pigs.

In his misery the young man realized his mistakes. He remembered that even his father's servants had enough to eat. He decided to return home and ask to live as a servant. When he approached his home, his father saw him coming and ran out to meet him. As they embraced, the son said, "Father, I have sinned against heaven, and in thy sight, and am no more worthy to be called thy son." But the father was so happy to have his son home again that he took his best robe and put it on him. He gave him shoes to wear and placed a ring on his finger. Then he commanded his servants to prepare a great feast.

When the older brother, who had remained faithful, saw what was happening, he was hurt. The father had not given *him* such a feast. The father comforted him by telling him that everything the family owned was to be his. His brother had squandered his inheritance, but his return home was a reason to rejoice. He said, "This thy brother was dead, and is alive again; and was lost, and is found." (See Luke 15:11–32.)

Each of us has sinned in some way, but the Lord's Atonement makes it possible for us to be forgiven of our sins. In speaking of His sacrifice,

He said, "For behold, I, God, have suffered these things for all, that they might not suffer if they would repent" (D&C 19:16).

▪ Show visual 33-a, "Christ suffered for our sins in the Garden of Gethsemane."

In another scripture the Lord says, "Behold, he who has repented of his sins, the same is forgiven, and I, the Lord, remember them no more" (D&C 58:42). Each of us must repent to receive forgiveness from the Lord.

▪ What did the younger son in the parable need to do to change his life? (Realize his mistakes, return home, confess his sins, and forsake them.) What feelings do you think the son had while approaching home? (He may have felt fear of being rejected. He may have felt happy to be going home. He may have felt he was doing the right thing.)

Forgiveness Brings Joy

▪ How do you think the son felt after his father welcomed him?

▪ How do you feel toward the Savior, knowing that His suffering made it possible for you to repent of your sins?

When we repent, Heavenly Father rejoices and forgives us—just like the father in the parable. Think about your own life and the joy you feel from repenting and being forgiven.

Alma the Younger was the son of a prophet of God, but he had committed some serious sins. One of his worst sins was his attempt to destroy the Church of God by leading people away from the truth. As the leader of the Church, Alma's father felt much grief over his son's wickedness and prayed often to the Lord that his son might come to know the truth.

Because of the faith and prayers of his father and other servants of the Lord, the younger Alma was visited one day by an angel. The angel spoke with such force that Alma fell to the earth. He became convinced of God's great power. The angel commanded Alma to stop trying to destroy the Church. When the angel left, Alma was so astonished he could not speak. He fell again to the ground and had no strength for two days. When he could speak again, he told the people that he had experienced a great change in his life, repented of his sins, and been redeemed by the Lord. Alma decided to keep the commandments of God and do all he could to make up for his past sins. His efforts were so great that he became a great missionary and later became the prophet of the Church. (See Mosiah 27; 29:42.)

33-a, Christ suffered for our sins in the Garden of Gethsemane.

In describing his experience, Alma said:

"And now, for three days and for three nights was I racked, even with the pains of a damned soul.

"And it came to pass that as I was thus racked with torment, while I was harrowed up by the memory of my many sins, behold, I remembered also to have heard my father prophesy unto the people concerning the coming of one Jesus Christ, a Son of God, to atone for the sins of the world.

"Now, as my mind caught hold upon this thought, I cried within my heart: O Jesus, thou Son of God, have mercy on me, who am in the gall of bitterness, and am encircled about by the everlasting chains of death.

"And now, behold, when I thought this, I could remember my pains no more; yea, I was harrowed up by the memory of my many sins no more.

"And oh, what joy, and what marvelous light I did behold; yea, my soul was filled with joy as exceeding as was my pain!

"Yea, . . . there could be nothing so exquisite and so bitter as were my pains. Yea, and . . . on the other hand, there can be nothing so exquisite and sweet as was my joy" (Alma 36:16–21).

- What did Alma do to be forgiven? (He repented and called upon God for forgiveness.) How did Alma know he had been forgiven? (His soul was filled with joy.)

King Benjamin's people also knew the joy of receiving forgiveness. Upon hearing King Benjamin's last great sermon, they repented and asked to be forgiven of their sins. The scripture explains that "the Spirit of the Lord came upon them, and they were filled with joy, having received a remission of their sins, and having peace of conscience, because of the exceeding faith which they had in Jesus Christ" (Mosiah 4:3).

We Are Required to Forgive Everyone

Because of the Savior's perfect love for us, He willingly forgives us if we truly repent. In return, He has asked us to be like Him and forgive one another.

- Have a class member read Doctrine and Covenants 64:8. Why did Christ chasten His disciples? (They did not forgive each other.)

- Have a class member read Doctrine and Covenants 64:9–11. Write on the chalkboard *Of you it is required to forgive all men.*

275

- What does the Lord mean when He says that the greater sin remains in us when we do not forgive?

Jesus illustrated the principle of forgiveness through the parable of the unmerciful servant:

A certain servant owed his master 10,000 talents—a great sum of money. When it was time to repay the debt, the servant begged his master to have patience; he did not have the money, but with time he would repay it. The master felt compassion for the servant and forgave him the debt. This same servant, however, went out and demanded payment from a fellow servant who owed him a very small amount of money. When the man could not pay, the servant had him imprisoned. When the master learned what had happened, he was very angry with the unmerciful servant and made him pay all that he owed. (See Matthew 18:21–34.)

Jesus finished the parable by teaching the people, "So likewise shall my heavenly Father do also unto you, if ye from your hearts forgive not every one his brother their trespasses" (Matthew 18:35).

- How are we like the servant who had been forgiven his great debt? If we do not forgive others, how are we like the unmerciful servant?

The greatest example of forgiveness comes from the life of the Savior. As He hung in agony upon the cross, He prayed that the Father would forgive the soldiers who crucified Him. "Father," He said, "forgive them; for they know not what they do" (Luke 23:34).

President Spencer W. Kimball said: "To be in the right we must forgive, and we must do so *without regard to whether or not our antagonist repents,* or how sincere is his [change], or whether or not he asks our forgiveness. We must follow the example and the teaching of the Master" (*The Miracle of Forgiveness* [1969], 283).

Forgiving Others Brings Us Peace

Many times when someone has sinned against us, we become bitter and angry. These feelings can make us miserable, even if we did not commit the sin. If we allow these feelings to stay in our souls, we will drive the Spirit of the Lord away. This is one reason the Lord has commanded us to forgive those who hurt us.

President John Taylor said, "To have in your heart the spirit of forgiveness and to eliminate from your hearts the spirit of hatred and bitterness, brings peace and joy" (quoted by Heber J. Grant, in Conference Report, Oct. 1920, 7).

President Spencer W. Kimball told the following story to illustrate the peace that comes from forgiving others:

In 1918, three officers of the law were murdered when they attempted to arrest several criminals. Glenn Kempton's father was one of the officers killed. Sometime later the murderers were captured, tried, and sent to prison for life.

- How would you feel toward someone who had taken the life of your father? Why would it be hard to forgive such a man?

Brother Kempton described his experience this way:

"As a young boy in my early teens, there grew in my heart a bitterness and a hatred toward the confessed slayer of my Father, for Tom Powers had admitted killing my Dad.

"The years swept by, I grew up, but still that heavy feeling stayed inside me. High school ended, and then I received a call to go to the Eastern States Mission. There my knowledge and testimony of the gospel grew rapidly, as all of my time was spent studying and preaching it. One day while reading the New Testament, I came to Matthew, fifth chapter, verses 43 to 45."

- Read Matthew 5:43–45.

Brother Kempton continued: "Here it was, the words of the Savior saying we should forgive. This applied to me. I read those verses again and again and it still meant forgiveness. Not very long after this, I found in the 64th section of the Doctrine and Covenants, verses 9 and 10, more of the Savior's words. . . ."

- Reread Doctrine and Covenants 64:9–10.

"I didn't know whether or not Tom Powers had repented but I did know now that I had an appointment to make after I returned home, and I resolved before I left the mission field to do just that.

"After returning home, I met and married a fine Latter-day Saint girl, and the Lord blessed our home with five lovely children. The years were passing rapidly and the Lord had been good to us, yet guilt arose within me every time I thought of the appointment I had not kept.

"A few years ago, just shortly before Christmas, a season when the love of Christ abounds and the spirit of giving and forgiving gets inside of us, my wife and I were in Phoenix on a short trip. Having concluded our business in the middle of the second afternoon, we started home. As we rode along, I expressed the desire to detour and return home via Florence, for that is where the state prison is located. My wife readily assented.

"It was after visiting hours when we arrived but I went on inside and asked for the warden. I was directed to his office.

"After I had introduced myself and expressed a desire to meet and talk to Tom Powers, a puzzled expression came over the warden's face, but after only a slight hesitation, he said, 'I'm sure that can be arranged.' Whereupon he dispatched a guard down into the compound who soon returned with Tom. We were introduced, and led into the parole room where we had a long talk. We went back to that cold, gray February morning thirty years before, re-enacting that whole terrible tragedy. We talked for perhaps an hour and a half. Finally, I said, 'Tom, you made a mistake for which you owe a debt to society for which I feel you must continue to pay, just the same as I must continue to pay the price for having been reared without a father.' "

▪ Show visual 33-b, "Tom Powers and Glenn Kempton."

"Then I stood and extended my hand. He stood and took it. I continued, 'With all my heart, I forgive you for this awful thing that has come into our lives.'

"He bowed his head and I left him there. I don't know how he felt then, and I don't know how he feels now, but my witness to you is that it is a glorious thing when bitterness and hatred go out of your heart and forgiveness comes in.

"I thanked the warden for his kindness, and as I walked out the door and down that long flight of steps I knew that forgiveness was better than revenge, for I had experienced it.

"As we drove toward home in the gathering twilight, a sweet and peaceful calm came over me. Out of pure gratitude I placed my arm around my wife, who understood, for I know that we had now found a broader, richer and more abundant life" (quoted in *The Miracle of Forgiveness*, 291–93).

Conclusion

The Savior forgives us of our sins if we repent and then follow Him, doing all He asks of us. One of the things He expects us to do is to forgive others. As we do so, He has promised us joy and peace, teaching us that both forgiving and being forgiven are essential to our eternal salvation.

Challenge

Repent of any wrongdoings you have committed. If anyone has hurt you in any way, cleanse your soul of any bitterness by forgiving that person.

Additional Scriptures

▪ Matthew 6:14–15 (what happens when we forgive others and when we do not)

33-b, Tom Powers and Glenn Kempton

- Matthew 7:1–5 (we should not judge others)

- Matthew 18:21–22 (forgive seventy times seven)

- Ephesians 4:32 (forgive one another)

- Doctrine and Covenants 42:88 (be reconciled with those who offend us)

Teacher Preparation

Before presenting this lesson:

1. Review *Gospel Principles* chapter 19, "Repentance."

2. Prepare yourself spiritually for giving the lesson by taking care of any problem in your own life related to forgiveness.

3. Assign class members to present any stories, scriptures, or quotations you wish.

SPIRITUAL GIFTS

Lesson 34

The purpose of this lesson is to help us understand and seek the gifts of the Spirit.

Introduction

In March 1961 a terrible storm swept through the Tongan Islands in the South Pacific. Buildings were blown over. Large trees were uprooted. Houses were torn apart and thrown through the air. A man was even killed.

In one village, members of a Latter-day Saint family huddled together in their small home, fearing for their lives. In describing this experience, the father of the family said that he could feel their home shaking as if it was ready to fall. He knew that if his family stayed in the house they would die, and if he went outside for help he would die. As he struggled with the decision of what to do, he felt prompted to use his priesthood to protect his family.

Climbing on a chair, he placed his hand on the part of the roof he thought would go off first. Then he said, "By the power of the priesthood which I hold, and in the name of Jesus Christ, I command you to stand solidly and completely throughout this storm." After he had said these words, the house quit shaking and the roof quit rattling.

After the storm, his home was the only one nearby that remained standing. (Adapted from Eric Shumway, "Faith in the Tongan Islands," in Margie Calhoun Jensen, comp., *Stories of Insight and Inspiration* [1976], 71–73.)

- Have the class members ponder this question: If an emergency occurred right now, would I be prepared to exercise my faith and priesthood?

If we are faithful and worthy, the Lord will give us spiritual blessings. The Book of Mormon prophet Jacob described just such a condition among his people: "We search the prophets, and we have many revela-

34-a, We should ask the Lord for the gifts we desire to receive.

tions and the spirit of prophecy; and having all these witnesses we obtain a hope, and our faith becometh unshaken, insomuch that we truly can command in the name of Jesus and the very trees obey us, or the mountains, or the waves of the sea" (Jacob 4:6).

The Gifts of the Spirit

Gifts of the Spirit are special blessings of spiritual knowledge and power that the Lord gives to us. Many gifts of the Spirit are listed in 1 Corinthians 12, Moroni 10, and Doctrine and Covenants 46.

- Invite a class member to read Doctrine and Covenants 46:13–26. What spiritual gifts are listed in this scripture? (List the answers on the chalkboard. Answers could include revelation, testimony, judgment, knowledge, wisdom, teaching, faith to heal, faith to be healed, miracles, prophecy, discernment of spirits, speaking with tongues, and interpretation of tongues.)

While we can receive many of these spiritual gifts, no one enjoys all of them:

"For all have not every gift given unto them; for there are many gifts, and to every man is given a gift by the Spirit of God.

"To some is given one, and to some is given another, that all may be profited thereby" (D&C 46:11–12).

- Have the class members ponder for a moment their own spiritual gifts.

Obtaining Spiritual Gifts

The Lord has many spiritual gifts that He desires to bestow on us. In order to receive them, we must discover these gifts, or talents, and then develop and use them. We must also live worthy to receive these gifts. President Joseph Fielding Smith explained why some members never receive the gift of the Holy Ghost: "It is my judgment that there are many members of this Church who have been baptized for the remission of their sins, and who have had hands laid upon their heads for the gift of the Holy Ghost, but who have never received that gift—that is, the manifestations of it. Why? Because they have never put themselves in order to receive these manifestations. They have never humbled themselves. They have never taken the steps that would prepare them for the companionship of the Holy Ghost. Therefore, they go through life without that knowledge" (" 'Seek Ye Earnestly the Best Gifts,' " *Ensign*, June 1972, 3).

The Lord has commanded us to seek the best gifts (see D&C 46:8). Often we are told which gifts we have or are to seek when we are set apart to an office or calling or when we receive a patriarchal blessing. A missionary called to a foreign country, for example, may be promised the gift of tongues to help him or her learn a new language, or a newly called teacher may be told to seek the gift of teaching.

To receive gifts of the Spirit, we must do the following:

Purify Our Lives

Before we can receive spiritual gifts, we must purify our lives by continually repenting of our sins.

Obey the Commandments

We must obey the Lord's commandments to be worthy of spiritual gifts. Obedience is one of the most important requirements for receiving gifts of the Spirit.

Fast

Fasting can help us overcome pride and gain the humility necessary to receive spiritual gifts. It helps us put our spiritual needs before our physical needs.

Pray

- Show visual 34-a, "We should ask the Lord for the gifts we desire to receive."

The Lord has commanded us to ask Him for the gifts we desire to receive (see Matthew 7:7–11). Such prayers require faith—faith that we will receive the gifts and faith in the Giver of the gifts.

Elder James A. Cullimore gave us some questions to consider as we seek for spiritual gifts: "As members of the Church, is our faith sufficiently strong? Are we in tune with the Spirit that we might be blessed by these great gifts? Do we believe a miracle can be performed or a blessing given? Do we call upon the priesthood as often as we should to administer to the sick? Do we believe we can be healed? Do we have faith to heal? Is the priesthood always prepared to give a blessing? How strong is your faith?" (in Conference Report, Oct. 1974, 34; or *Ensign,* Nov. 1974, 27).

- Have the class members ponder for a moment what they must do to prepare themselves for spiritual gifts and to keep the gifts they already have.

As we receive our gifts, we must be careful not to boast about our experiences or speak to the world about them (see D&C 84:65–73). We may share our spiritual experiences with family members and close friends, but we should remember that our gifts are sacred and must be spoken of with care (see D&C 63:64).

The Purposes of Spiritual Gifts

The Lord has revealed that the best spiritual gifts are given to help those who love Him and keep His commandments and those who try to do so (see D&C 46:9). Through the proper use of these gifts, the sick are healed, devils are cast out, revelations are received, knowledge is gained, and missionaries are able to communicate in different languages. Through the gifts of the Spirit, the Holy Ghost can guide, comfort, encourage, and teach us. These gifts help us to walk uprightly before the Lord and prevent us from being deceived by false doctrines. As we live worthy to feel the promptings of the Spirit, we will know when to use our gifts and when not to use them (see Alma 14:10–11).

The Lord has commanded us to remember always that spiritual gifts are given to those who humbly ask in faith (see D&C 46:8–9). Paul compared the Church to a body to show the importance of each member's gift or gifts to the rest of the Church (see 1 Corinthians 12:12–31). Just as a body needs arms, legs, eyes, and ears, so also does the Church need each member's gifts. Therefore, each of us should exercise our gifts. As we do so, everyone can be blessed. (See D&C 46:11–12.) Heavenly Father emphasizes that these gifts should not be sought as signs or for selfish reasons (see D&C 46:9).

Elder Franklin D. Richards told of certain blessings that come from the Spirit in time of need:

"The Savior has promised that to worthy members the Holy Ghost would be a comforter in times of sickness and death.

"Many have borne witness of the comforting spirit that has attended them in times of sorrow, helping them to find peace and understanding.

"A few weeks ago it was my privilege to meet two wonderful women, close friends, who had lost their husbands in a tragic airplane accident. Did I find them in despair and deep mourning? No, indeed. I have never witnessed greater courage and strength. They both bore witness to the fact that they had truly felt the comfort of the Spirit, that they knew there was a purpose in the call that had been given to their husbands, and that they had an assurance that all would be well with them and their families as they lived close to the Church and kept the commandments of the Lord" (in Conference Report, Apr. 1973, 171; or *Ensign*, July 1973, 117).

- Show visual 34-b, "Joseph Smith taught by the power of the Spirit."

On one occasion the Prophet Joseph Smith was invited to preach the gospel to a group of native Americans. They could not understand English, and he could not speak their language, so he paid a special government agent to interpret his words. The Prophet spoke for a few

34-b, Joseph Smith taught by the power of the Spirit.

minutes, and the agent then interpreted. When the people showed resentment and anger at the Prophet's message, the Spirit revealed to him that the agent was telling lies in order to turn them against him. Joseph pushed the interpreter aside and then preached a sermon to them. They understood every word. (Adapted from E. Cecil McGavin, in *The Historical Background of the Doctrine and Covenants* [1949], 156.)

- What spiritual gifts did the Prophet Joseph Smith use during this incident? (Discernment, revelation, gift of tongues, and teaching)

- If time permits, allow a few class members to bear their testimonies about blessings they have received through spiritual gifts.

Conclusion

Doctrine and Covenants 46 reads:

"Seek ye earnestly the best gifts, always remembering for what they are given;

"For verily I say unto you, they are given for the benefit of those who love me and keep all my commandments, and him that seeketh so to do; that all may be benefited that seek or that ask of me, that ask and not for a sign that they may consume it upon their lusts.

"And again, verily I say unto you, I would that ye should always remember, and always retain in your minds what those gifts are, that are given unto the church.

"For all have not every gift given unto them; for there are many gifts, and to every man is given a gift by the Spirit of God.

"To some is given one, and to some is given another, that all may be profited thereby" (verses 8–12).

Challenge

Seek to discover your spiritual gifts. Continue to repent, obey the commandments, fast, and pray to purify your life and prepare yourself to receive spiritual gifts.

Fathers: Help your children recognize and develop their gifts.

Young men: Seek the counsel of your parents and leaders to help you develop spiritual gifts.

Additional Scriptures

- John 11:22 (ask God for gifts)

- Acts 2:17–18 (many to receive spiritual gifts)

- 1 Corinthians 7:7 (all people have their proper gift)

- 1 Timothy 4:12–16 (neglect not your gift)

- James 1:17 (every good gift comes from God)

- Alma 9:21 (Nephites received many gifts)

Teacher Preparation

Before presenting this lesson:

1. Review *Gospel Principles* chapter 22, "The Gifts of the Spirit."

2. Assign class members to present any stories, scriptures, or quotations you wish.

BUILDING
THE KINGDOM
OF GOD

L e s s o n   3 5

The purpose of this lesson is to motivate us to help build the kingdom of God.

Introduction

Elder Gordon B. Hinckley once told about a brilliant young naval officer from Asia who had come to the United States for advanced training. While training with the United States Navy, this young man had met some members of the Church. At his request they taught him about the gospel. The Spirit touched his heart, and he was baptized.

Elder Hinckley said:

"He was introduced to me just before he was to return to his native land. We spoke of these things, and then I said, 'Your people are not Christians. You come from a land where Christians have had a difficult time. What will happen when you return home a Christian and, more particularly, a Mormon Christian?'

"His face clouded, and he replied, 'My family will be disappointed. I suppose they will cast me out. They will regard me as dead. As for my future and my career, I assume that all opportunity will be foreclosed against me.'

"I asked, 'Are you willing to pay so great a price for the gospel?'

"His dark eyes, moistened by tears, shone from his handsome brown face as he answered, 'It's true, isn't it?'

"Ashamed at having asked the question, I responded, 'Yes, it's true.'

"To which he replied, 'Then what else matters?' " (in Conference Report, Apr. 1973, 72; or *Ensign*, July 1973, 48).

- Why did this young man give up his family and career for the kingdom of God? (He knew the gospel is of greater value than anything else.)

Our Responsibility to Build the Kingdom

- Display a poster of the following quote, or refer to it on the chalk-board: *The Kingdom of God is all that is [of] real worth. All else is not worth possessing, either here or hereafter* (Brigham Young, *Discourses of Brigham Young*, sel. John A. Widtsoe [1954], 444).

- What is the kingdom of God?

President Joseph F. Smith said, "The kingdom of God is the organization of The Church of Jesus Christ of Latter-day Saints, over which the Son of God presides, and not man" (*Gospel Doctrine*, 5th ed. [1939], 72).

Ever since the Lord's kingdom was restored to earth, every member of the Church has had a responsibility to see that it continues to grow. Each of us is obligated to share the gospel with nonmembers and to strengthen other members. Our work is God's work, which is "to bring to pass the immortality and eternal life of man" (Moses 1:39). As we help build the kingdom of God, we are not only preparing the world for the Second Coming of the Savior, but we are also helping our brothers and sisters gain eternal life. Nothing is more important than this work.

In building the kingdom of God we must remember that the family is the basic unit of that kingdom. The very purpose of the kingdom of God, in fact, is to exalt families in the kingdom of heaven (see 1 Corinthians 11:11; D&C 93:40; 131:1–4). We must always make sure, therefore, not to neglect our families as we serve in the Church. The Lord's counsel is clear: "Every man who is obliged to provide for his own family, let him provide, and he shall in nowise lose his crown; and let him labor in the church" (D&C 75:28).

The Law of Consecration

One of the covenants we make with the Lord when we receive our temple endowments is to live the law of consecration. The Lord has called this law a celestial law, under which we give our time, talents, and possessions to build the Lord's kingdom.

- Read Doctrine and Covenants 88:22 and 105:1–5. Why must we understand the law of consecration and be willing to live it?

Concerning this law the Prophet Joseph Smith said, "A religion that does not require the sacrifice of all things never has power sufficient to produce the faith necessary unto life and salvation" (*Lectures on Faith* [1985], 69).

As the Prophet explained, we must develop the kind of faith that will lead us to eternal life. Such faith comes as we put the things of God's kingdom first in our lives.

Living the Law of Consecration Today

Although the law of consecration requires us to be willing to give all we have to the Lord to build up His kingdom, "we are not always called upon to live the whole law of consecration" (Bruce R. McConkie, in Conference Report, Apr. 1975, 74; or *Ensign,* May 1975, 50). This is the situation in the Church today.

- Although we do not live the law of consecration fully at this time, what can we do to show our willingness to live it? (List the responses on the chalkboard. Responses could include giving our time, talents, and possessions to help build the Lord's kingdom. Specific answers might include caring for our family; assisting others in need; being missionaries to our neighbors, friends, relatives, and others; doing family history research and temple work; faithfully serving in our Church callings; paying an honest tithe and contributing other offerings; and praying to know what the Lord expects of us.)

Consecrating Our Time, Talents, and Possessions

It is a privilege to consecrate our time, talents, and possessions to help build up the Lord's kingdom. Elder Bruce R. McConkie said: "It is [Christ's] voice which invites us to consecrate of our time, our talents, and our means to carry on his work. It is his voice that calls for service and sacrifice. This is his work. He is . . . guiding and directing the destiny of his kingdom" (in Conference Report, Apr. 1975, 77; or *Ensign,* May 1975, 52).

Time

- How might we use our time to help build up the kingdom of God?

Each of us has 24 hours in every day, but we each use them differently. Some of us waste time or are too disorganized to do all we want to do for our families, the Church, our jobs, and our community. President Spencer W. Kimball said, however, that if we plan and organize our time wisely, "there will be time for service in the Church organizations and quorums; time for missionary work; time to be a quorum president, auxiliary leader, bishop, Relief Society president, [or] teacher" (*The Miracle of Forgiveness* [1969], 253).

Talents

- How might we use our talents to help build up the kingdom of God?

The Lord has given each of us talents (see D&C 46:11). President Brigham Young said: "What is the best thing you have to devote to the Kingdom of God? It is the talents God has given you. How many? Every one of them" (*Discourses of Brigham Young,* 445).

Sister JoAnn Ottley, wife of Jerold D. Ottley, related an experience that shows how she and her husband used their talents for music to serve the Lord. They had spent their entire lifetimes studying and developing these gifts and have had to make many decisions regarding their use. When they were in Europe studying, Brother and Sister Ottley realized that they had an especially important and difficult decision to make. Both of them knew that if they remained in Europe, they would have many opportunities for success. They wanted above all, however, to do what the Lord wanted them to do. The Ottleys desired to be obedient, but beyond that they yearned to be used by the Lord in the building of His kingdom here on the earth.

Brother and Sister Ottley repeatedly fasted and prayed for the direction of the Spirit and to know the will of the Lord. Their answer came during a sacrament meeting at the close of a fasting period. They had both received the same instructions by the Spirit—that their work was at home. The Ottleys were to return to the United States.

There followed more months of study, preparation, and testing. Then the Lord made it possible for them to return to Salt Lake City. Sister Ottley became a member of the Tabernacle Choir, and Brother Ottley joined the Music Department at the University of Utah.

A short time later, Brother Ottley was called by the First Presidency of the Church to be the conductor of the Tabernacle Choir. The Lord had indeed been preparing them for special service.

The Ottleys understood that our time, talents, and possessions are really not ours at all, but the Lord's. The greatest joy we can reap on this earth is to use them in building up the kingdom of God. (See "The Apples in a Seed," in *Turning Points* [1981], 23–29.)

- What attitude did Brother and Sister Ottley have that made them want to use their talents to build the kingdom? (They believed that their talents came from the Lord and are His.)

- Have the class members suggest several talents, and list them on the board. Discuss how each could be used to build the kingdom of God. Then have the class members ponder for a moment their own talents and how they can use them to further the Lord's work.

Possessions

- How might we use our possessions to help build up the kingdom of God?

Joseph Smith wrote, "For a man to consecrate his property . . . to the Lord, is nothing more nor less than to feed the hungry, clothe the naked, visit the widow and fatherless, the sick and afflicted, and do all he can to administer to their relief in their afflictions, and for him and his house to serve the Lord" (*Teachings of the Prophet Joseph Smith*, sel. Joseph Fielding Smith [1976], 127).

Even though the Lord has given us all we possess, we sometimes find it difficult to use our possessions to help His work. But when we willingly use our possessions to build the Lord's kingdom, we show love for others, Heavenly Father, and Jesus Christ. An account in the New Testament shows how difficult—but how important—it sometimes is to willingly give up earthly possessions:

A man approached Jesus one day and asked, "What shall I do that I may inherit eternal life?"

Jesus answered that he should keep the commandments: he should not commit adultery, murder, steal, bear false witness, or defraud others. Jesus also told him to honor his father and his mother.

The man answered that he had always done these things. Jesus replied, "One thing thou lackest: go thy way, sell whatsoever thou hast, and give to the poor, and thou shalt have treasure in heaven: and come, take up the cross, and follow me." When the young man heard this, he went away sad because he was very rich. (See Mark 10:17–22.)

Sometimes we, like this rich man, are unwilling to give what we have to the Lord, while others would like to give more than they can. The Lord understands our situations and deals with us accordingly. Of those who cannot give what they would like to give, King Benjamin said:

"And again, I say unto the poor, ye who have not and yet have sufficient, that ye remain from day to day; I mean all you who deny the beggar, because ye have not; I would that ye say in your hearts that: I give not because I have not, but if I had I would give.

"And now, if ye say this in your hearts ye remain guiltless" (Mosiah 4:24–25).

We should be willing to give the Lord all we have—possessions, time, and talents. We will find that this willingness helps us develop faith in the Lord and love for others.

Conclusion

As members of The Church of Jesus Christ of Latter-day Saints, we have a responsibility to build the kingdom of God. We can do this by keeping our promise to serve the Lord with all our heart, might, mind, and strength. This means that we should be willing to give whatever time, talents, and possessions we are asked to give to spread the gospel. As we do this, we develop faith and love and show the Lord that we put His kingdom first. We must live this law if we are to inherit the celestial kingdom.

Challenge

Ponder your willingness to give what the Lord asks of you. Evaluate how well you are consecrating your time, talents, and possessions to the Lord's work. Then resolve to do better.

Additional Scriptures

- Daniel 2:44 (kingdom of God to roll forth)

- Luke 12:16–21 (parable of the foolish rich man)

- Acts 2:44–45 (early Christians had all things in common)

- 1 Nephi 13:37 (blessings to those who help bring forth Zion)

- Jacob 2:18–19 (seek the kingdom of God before riches)

- 4 Nephi 1:3 (Nephites and Lamanites had all things in common after Christ visited them)

- Doctrine and Covenants 42:29–36 (one way to give to the poor is through offerings delivered to the bishop)

Teacher Preparation

Before teaching this lesson:

1. Read *Gospel Principles* chapter 34, "Developing Our Talents."

2. Review lesson 19, "Developing Our Talents," in this manual.

3. Prepare the poster suggested in the lesson, or write the information on the chalkboard.

4. Assign class members to present any stories, scriptures, or quotations you wish.

INDEX

NOTES

PICTURE SECTION

This section contains selected pictures from the Gospel Art Picture Kit (34730). These pictures can be used as an additional resource for gospel study and teaching at church and in the home.

Old Testament

1. Abraham Taking Isaac to Be Sacrificed
   Genesis 21:1–8; 22; Joseph Smith Translation, Genesis 22:2

2. Joseph Resists Potiphar's Wife
   Genesis 39

3. Moses and the Burning Bush
   Exodus 3:1–4:17

4. Three Men in the Fiery Furnace
   Daniel 3

New Testament

5. The Prodigal Son
   Luke 15:10–32

6. Jesus Raising Lazarus from the Dead (by Carl Bloch. Used by permission of the National Historic Museum at Frederiksborg in Hillerød.)
   John 11:1–45

7. Jesus Washing the Apostles' Feet
   John 13:4–15; Joseph Smith Translation, John 13:8–10

8. Go Ye Therefore
   Matthew 28:16–20; Mark 16:14–20

9. The Ascension of Jesus
   Acts 1:3–11

Book of Mormon

10. The Liahona
    1 Nephi 16:6, 9–10, 16, 28–29; Alma 37:38

11. Ammon Defends the Flocks of King Lamoni
    Alma 17:19–39; 18

12. The Brother of Jared Sees the Finger of the Lord
    Genesis 11:3–8; Ether 1:33–43; 2–3; 6:2–3

13. Moroni Hides the Plates in the Hill Cumorah
    Mormon 6:6; 8:1, 3–4; Moroni 1:1; 10:2, 4–5

Church History

14. Translating the Book of Mormon
    Doctrine and Covenants 20:8–11; Joseph Smith—History 1:34–35,
    71 footnote

15. Pioneer Wagons Going West
    Our Heritage: A Brief History of The Church of Jesus Christ of
    Latter-day Saints, 75–80

Temple Pictures

16. México City D.F. México Temple

17. Celestial Room, Billings Montana Temple